Western Dominance
and Political Islam

Western Dominance and Political Islam

Challenge and Response

❧

Khalid Bin Sayeed

State University of New York Press

Published by
State University of New York Press, Albany

© 1995 State University of New York

For information, address State University of New York Press,
State University Plaza, Albany, N.Y. 12246

Production by M. R. Mulholland
Marketing by Nancy Farrell

Library of Congress Cataloging-in-Publication Data

Bin Sayeed, Khalid, 1926-
    Western dominance and political Islam : challenge and response /
  Khalid Bin Sayeed.
        p.   cm.
    Includes bibliographical references and index.
    ISBN 0-7914-2265-8. — ISBN 0-7914-2266-6 (pbk.)
    1. Middle East—Relations—Europe. 2. Europe—Relations—Middle
  East. 3. Islam and politics. 4. Islam—20th century. I. Title.
  DS63.2.E8B56 1995
  303.48′25604—dc20   94-4119
                                                          CIP

10 9 8 7 6 5 4 3 2 1

Contents

Preface   vii

Introduction   1

1. Islamic Resistance to Western Hegemony
   in the Middle East   5

2. The Intellectual Challenge of the West and the
   Faltering Islamic and Arab Response   33

3. American Dominance and Islamic Defiance in Iran   51

4. Pragmatic versus Militant Strategies
   in Post-Khomeini Iran   65

5. Islamic Opposition and the
   Stability of the Saudi State   77

6. The Islamic State of Pakistan:
   Internal Conflicts and External Pressures   103

7. Islamic Political Theory and Human Development   131

8. Epilogue   155

Notes   171

Select Bibliography   189

Index   193

Preface

In the first two chapters we try to show how Western dominance was being resisted by several forms of political Islam. Movements like the Ikhwan al-Muslimun in Egypt as well as Arab nationalism pressured the governments in the Middle East to use the oil weapon against the West. But behind these political pressures and movements, Arab and Muslim societies were undergoing rapid changes. The trends of social changes can very often be predicted. But when these social forces and the long-term Islamic force combined we witnessed a volcanic eruption in the form of the Islamic revolution in Iran.

Given the conflict between Western dominance and Islamic opposition—an opposition that consists of both political Islam and nationalism—the question that scholars have to explore in the case of the three countries we have examined is what similar or varying combinations of the two forces are emerging. In the chapters on Iran, Saudi Arabia, and Pakistan we have examined these forces, but particularly in the case of Saudi Arabia and Pakistan we have brought in a third decisive force; namely, the roles of governments dependent upon Western influence.

We have argued that Western dominance of Muslim countries is of a multidimensional nature, not just military or political hegemony. Economic and intellectual forces are important components of the dominant power that the West wields. Therefore, it is apparent that Muslims will have to organize their response not through the simplistic ways of the fundamentalists.

Our finding is that the response of political Islam is still faltering because Muslims have not yet embarked on a multidimensional and systematic strategy. Such a strategy can be built on a reinterpretation of some of the fundamental Islamic ideas leading to a reconstruction of Islamic thought. All scholars and observers of the Muslim world are aware of the activities of Islamic fundamentalists. But probably few have discerned some of the attempts at reinterpretation of Islamic ideas. We have argued that such attempts were initiated by Muhammad Iqbal in the 1930s. He has been followed by intellectuals like Fazlur Rahman of Pakistan and Ali Shari'ati and Abd al-Karim Surush of Iran. We have also included a Saudi intellectual Abu Sulayman in this category because he strongly believes that the Muslim community has been facing an intellectual crisis for a long time. But his ideas of reconstruction of Islamic thought do not involve the same kind of reinterpretation we have noticed particularly in the case of Fazlur Rahman and Abd al-Karim Surush. The fundamentalists have often seized the headlines but other forces are also working to change the Islamic social landscape from a long-term perspective.

All this may suggest that we have strayed from the familiar path of a social scientist who in works of this kind tends to spend most of the time in explaining things as they are. We have created the impression of being prescriptive and normative. But our prescriptive and normative analysis in many ways is based on the observed fact that certain normative propositions influence Muslim social and political behavior. Propositions that indicate that a large number of Muslims think or desire that certain things should be done are also empirical facts. Therefore, to eliminate all propositions that are couched in terms of "ought" and focus only on those that are stated in terms of "are" is to put beyond the pale of our study a whole range of activities in which human beings are rightly or wrongly engaged or engrossed. It may be recalled that Ibn Khaldun, unlike Machiavelli, recognized the relevance or importance of both realism and idealism. Muslims do not want to oppose the West only as nationalists but would perhaps like to respond to Western challenges in several areas relating to politics, economics, and social relations in such a way that a comprehensive Islamic way of life emerges.

I am grateful to the Social Sciences and Humanities Research Council of Canada (SSHRC) for providing the research funding for this book during 1984-1985 and 1987-1988. I also received a partial grant during 1991-1992 from the Queen's University Advisory Research Committee. The SSHRC grants included both travel and other funds for interviewing scores of individuals drawn from various walks of life in Iran, Saudi Arabia, and Pakistan. Towering above these forms of assistance is the moral, intellectual, and editorial support that I received at every stage of this study from my wife, Janet. I must also mention Clay Morgan of the SUNY Press for the cooperation he has given in the development and completion of this work.

Introduction

We indicate throughout the book that even though Islamic resistance to Western dominance has persisted, the response of socio-political Islam to the Western challenge has been ineffective. We argue that the response could be more effective if there were a systematic effort on the part of Muslim societies to reinterpret their values and traditions and reorganize their political and economic institutions. Therefore, the book is prescriptive in this respect but by no means wishful. We argue that Islamic ideas, if reinterpreted and reorganized, have the capability of promoting human development and strengthening political structures. Our main argument is that a reconstructed Islamic system can perhaps provide more energy for purposes of national and human development than it has so far as a rallying cry for opposing Western dominance. Many of the political leaders do not seem to have used the Islamic appeal as much for creative and developmental purposes as they have used if for somewhat negative purposes.

The fog of misunderstanding and confusion that surrounds the term *Islamic fundamentalism* is endless but understandable. Muslims feel that because of the strategic location of the Middle and Near East, they have been under siege for nearly two centuries. When faced with such a continuing and often overwhelming force, they have taken recourse to what is easily and immediately available. Because adherence to the Islamic Sharia brought so much glory to seventh century Islam, a number of Muslims feel that their present plight can be explained largely because of their failure to practice and follow certain clear and rigid principles and institutions of the Qur'an and the Sunna (Traditions of the Prophet). It should be emphasized that Islamic fundamentalism is not the same as any other fundamentalism for the simple reason that Islam professes to be a political religion in which certain religious principles were formulated with a clear intention of implementing them and even transforming them into institutions. Islamic fundamentalists seem to think that Islam has put forward certain immutable principles that were

already translated into appropriate institutions in the seventh
century during the time of the Prophet and that such principles
and institutions are adequate to tackle the problems that the
modern world poses for Muslims. They seem to grossly underes-
timate both the complexity of the modern world and the nature of
Western dominance of the Muslim world. In this regard an oft-
quoted Tradition of the Prophet is apposite: "Learn from the
world and do not [merely] pass through it."

We argue that even leaders like Khomeini, who give the
impression of being primarily fundamentalist in their thinking,
have made it clear that some of the Islamic principles need to be
reformulated and implemented as an Islamic ideology. This
explains why we argue that socio-political Islam as a program
and a strategy differs from traditional fundamentalism, because
all the advocates of the former believe that Islamic principles
should be reinterpreted and perhaps even given new priorities to
suit modern conditions. Among such advocates of socio-political
Islam, we include the Society of Muslim Brothers (the Ikhwan) of
Egypt and adjacent lands, both conservative and liberal ruling
circles in Iran, and if the new trends in the Jamaat-i-Islami in
Pakistan are an indication, followers of socio-political Islam there
as well. In Saudi Arabia as well the first glimmerings of political
Islam may be discerned. University intellectuals, religious leaders, and liberals with their different perspectives have started
wondering as to why the Saudis under the spell of the royal family should be content in only wallowing in their riches when
these resources fueled by Islamic ideas should be able to create
a better social and economic system and a country that would
follow a more independent foreign policy.

One can understand why people in the West have failed to
see the clear and long-term movement within the world of Islam.
Islamic fundamentalists because of their rage and impatience
often capture the headlines. But the socio-political change that is
taking place in the world of Islam is like a spectrum, with wide
ranges and graduated series of programs and strategies. On the
conservative side stand the Ikhwan and some of the hardliners in
Iran, but even these are not frozen in time and attitude. They are
also moving. Those who beckon the Islamic forces to move faster
are the progressive, liberal, and dynamic thinkers like Iqbal of the
1930s of the Indian subcontinent, Ali Shari'ati of the 1960s and
1970s in Iran, followed by Fazlur Rahman of Pakistan of the
1970s and early 1980s and Abd al-Karim Surush of postrevolu-

tionary Iran. We take the view in this book that it is socio-political Islam in its broader programmatic and intellectual sense and not Islamic fundamentalism that provides the possibility for Muslims to launch a more effective response to Western dominance. But the possibility suggests a potential that is not yet a fact. The dynamic and progressive ideas of socio-political Islam will have to so radically transform the Muslim masses educationally, intellectually, and politically that the opposition to Western dominance will create a new intellectual and civilizational force. This alternative force does not have to follow a confrontational path. The battle will be for winning human minds between Western ideas and Islamic ideas. This represents the future but the hard realities of the present are such that Muslims engaged in their current struggle still seem to be faltering and groping.

It may be noted that three countries were chosen for detailed analysis because they represent the religious, ethnic, and ideological spectrum of the Muslim world. Saudi Arabia fits into the Arab and conservative category. Iran, the center of Shi'ite Muslims, has also become the pioneer of Islamic revolution during this century. Pakistan is Sunni and South Asian and therefore a part of predominantly Sunni South Asia, where there are over 300 million Muslims. In addition, Pakistan was established as an Islamic state but has displayed tendencies of veering toward a secular orientation.

1

Islamic Resistance to Western Hegemony in the Middle East

In this chapter, we explore the central theme of Western hegemony and the kinds of resistance it has provoked in the Middle East basically in terms of two dimensions. The first is to clearly identify the parameters of the struggle between Western hegemony and the forces opposing the West in the form of political Islam and Arab and other forms of nationalism. In the second dimension, which is dialectical, we show what specific characteristics of hegemony have triggered what forms of resistance. This dialectical struggle proceeds along both normative and objective tracks.

By *hegemony* we mean the dominant role that countries like Britain, other European states, and the United States either singly or in partnership with others have tended to exercise in the region of the Middle and Near East. This hegemonic or dominant role is exercised by certain countries because of the ascendant position they occupy in the world market and the community of nation states, often as we shall see, buttressed by military and technological superiority. Another meaning we have attached to the term *hegemony* is that the dominant country or countries of the West have not only penetrated the Islamic or Arab countries of the region in economic and political terms but also in very significant cultural areas. Thus, the overall Islamic resistance or defiance to Western dominance has been articulated not only in political or economic terms but also in major ways in cultural and religious terms. As Leonard Binder has noted, as compared to Latin America, which has largely been concerned about European or American economic exploitation, the focal point of Middle Eastern resistance to Western dominance has been primarily religious and cultural. "I think it correct to say that no other cultural region is as deeply anxious about the threat of cultural penetration and westernization. And the central symbol of this anxiety is Islam, with which authenticity, identity, dignity, and even manhood are associated."[1]

One can trace the history of British dominance of some of the principalities of the Middle East from the early and middle part of the nineteenth century. British penetration of India started as early as 1814 with Clive's victories in Bengal. One also witnessed the British penetration of the United Arab Emirates (1820s), Bahrain (1861), and Kuwait (1899). These were followed by the extension of British control over Oman in 1891 and Qatar in 1916. Thus, between 1913 and 1922, the British were able to extract vital concessions from different rulers "who undertook not to award any oil concession except to a company appointed by the British government."[2]

One could see that in the 1920s, that is, soon after the First World War, in addition to the British, the Italians and French had replaced the Ottoman Empire. Thus, in the Islamic world of the Middle East, the dar al-Islam (zone of Islam) had virtually fallen under either direct colonial control or become a part of European protectorates. The only independent states left were Turkey, Persia, Afghanistan, and central Arabia.

Political Islam in the nineteenth and early twentieth centuries had come to rest on the central principles of the solidarity of the umma (community of believers), which was institutionalized in the form of the caliphate. The Ottoman Caliphate, abolished in 1924, in the eyes of millions of Muslims was the living and institutionalized form of the umma. However, when the Ottoman Empire started disintegrating in the nineteenth century, one could see that the overall resistance on the part of the Muslim community was extremely feeble and, where it was strong, it tended to be febrile and short lived at best. The Iranian Jamal al-Din al-Afghani (1839-1897) emerged as the passionate champion of the unity of the umma against the European and particularly British threat. His attempts to construct a pan-Islamic movement were defeated again and again because of the different and conflicting interests pursued by the various rulers of Muslim states. He became a precursor of reformist and pan-Islamic movements which were to come later.

An even more revealing development was the way the Ottoman Empire was dismantled at the end of the First World War. There was no resistance against its dismantling in the Arab world. In fact, under the influence and leadership of T. E.

Lawrence, Arabs were responsible for dealing devastating blows at its power and prestige in regions like central Arabia and Syria. In India, which was ruled by the British, an intense and emotional movement was launched in support of the Turkish caliphate. This movement demonstrated the enormous hold that Islamic symbols had over the minds of Muslims in India. When the leader of the Khilafat movement, Muhammad Ali, was arrested, thousands of Muslims belonging to elite professional groups like lawyers, physicians, and the ulama courted arrest enthusiastically. Because the British had attacked Turkey, thereby endangering the very existence of the caliphate, Muslims, particularly in the provinces of the North-West Frontier and Sind, were led to believe that India had become a dar al-harb (zone of war) and as many as 18,000 of them migrated to Afghanistan in August 1920. On March 3, 1924, the ruler of Turkey, Mustafa Kemal Pasha, by sending the Caliph, Abdul Majid, into exile and abolishing the caliphate dealt the final and deadly blow to the Khilafat movement in India.

One could also discern certain ironic ingredients in the way the kingdom of Saudi Arabia had evolved. The Saud family had relied heavily on the support of the Wahhabis and their organization, the Ikhwan, in establishing their ascendancy over the tribal structure in Saudi Arabia. In the final stages King Abd al-Aziz used British support and particularly the mechanized weaponry that he received from them in suppressing the Ikhwan and establishing the kingdom of Saudi Arabia in 1932. Thus, it was ironic that in the very heartland of Islam the Saudi state first developed largely with the help of a religious movement and later the same state had to use British assistance to tame the Ikhwan into submissive partnership. The Saudi state followed the same traditions in seeking technical help from the British and the Americans for the establishment of the highly lucrative oil industry in the kingdom.

In the eyes of Muslims and Arabs there was a clear purpose behind the pattern of dominance that the Western powers were crafting in the Middle East. First of all, the Middle East constituted a vital strategic area because it provided a land mass and sea links through the Suez Canal for European powers to penetrate the Asian mainland or the subcontinent of India. Perhaps an even more important consideration in these calculations emerged with the discovery of almost inexhaustible resources of oil in the Persian Gulf and the Arabian peninsula. Those Muslims and Arabs who subscribe to a conspiracy theory of international affairs would argue that the establishment of Israel in 1948 was deliberately designed by the West so that the state might serve as the outpost of Western hegemony.

One can discern several types of responses on the part of Muslims to what they term *Western dominance* and *imperialism.* There is the traditional Islamic response, which one comes across in the sermons given by Muslim preachers either in public meetings or in mosques. The line of argument is that Christians and Jews from the very inception of Islam, and particularly since the Crusades, have implacably opposed any manifestation of Muslim power. Certain verses of the Qur'an are cited. One of the usual citations runs as follows: "Never will the Jews or the Christians be satisfied with thee unless thou follows their form of religion" (2: 120).[3]

Khomeini was one of the most clear-headed and determined leaders who argued that the struggle between the West and political Islam was not just between Western imperialism and Islam as a religion. To him, Islam represented a whole way of life and civilization and he, as a spokesman for the Third World nations, opposed what he termed the oppressors and imperialists.

If you pay no attention to the politics of the imperialists, and consider Islam to be simply the few topics you are always studying and never go beyond them, then the imperialists will leave you alone. Pray as much as you like; it is your oil they are after—why should they worry about your prayers? They are after our minerals, and want to turn our country into a market for their goods. That is the reason the puppet governments they have installed prevent us from industrializing, and instead, establish only assembly plants and industry that is dependent on the outside world.[4]

Western observers refer to Khomeini and the Islamic revolution in Iran or the Islamic Salvation Front of Algeria as manifestations of Islamic fundamentalism. We characterize them as movements led by certain leaders and ideologues who think that Western power can be opposed effectively not by emotional invocations to an Islamic umma but only by mobilization of political and economic power. This explains why we describe the Iranian Islamic revolution and other attempts like the Algerian Islamic Salvation Front as movements that represent a program or a strategy of socio-political Islam. *Socio-political Islam* refers to both the global crisis and the Islamic crisis. It is significant that the introductory statement of the *Political Plan of the Islamic Salvation Front*, while referring to both the global and the internal crises that Algeria is facing, states:

> When the governments that have ruled Algeria have demonstrated their inability to cope with the multidimensional crisis that is shaking the country to its very depths, the Algerian people have initiated a process of resurgence which is moving them in the direction of a democratic and pluralist polity anchored in an authentic Islamic societal foundation. The failures of different ideologies, Western and Eastern, have compelled us to turn to our religion in order to safeguard and protect our history and civilization and our human and natural resources.[5]

Socio-political Islam is not the only form of resistance that the West has encountered in the Middle East. As we emphasize in Chapter 2, President Nasser spearheaded a movement that he characterized as Arab nationalism because he probably felt that a purely Islamic organization like the Ikhwan al-Muslimun (Society of Muslim Brothers) would not be able to mobilize adequate political power through internal and external means to oppose American, Western European, and Israeli domination of the Middle East. Therefore, he sought Soviet economic and military assistance and also constructed the Egyptian state on secular and socialist lines. Nasser's construction of barricades against the West was preceded by an outright suppression of the Ikhwan. As we argue in Chapter 2, this response ended in failure because Nasser's economic organization did not bring economic prosperity or stability to Egypt, and his military organization turned out to be ineffective against a series of Israeli and Western attacks in 1956 and more disastrously in the war of 1967.

The Nature of Dominance versus the Nature of Resistance—1951-1973

This section analyzes in very broad terms three major events: the conflict between the Iranian government and the British Anglo-Iranian Oil Company, 1951-1954; the 1956 Arab-Israeli war; and the oil embargo of 1973. In this analysis of these three episodes, a pattern emerges that indicates the nature of the conflict that took place between certain Western dominant powers and Middle Eastern states. These episodes reveal first the declining role of European powers and particularly the British, the growing importance of the United States as the dominant power, and finally, it is noted that the struggle against Western dominance was being waged largely by nationalist forces with perhaps political Islam very much in the background.

In the 1951-1954 Iranian conflict with the Anglo-Iranian Oil Company (AICO), the Iranian complaint was that British interests monopolized the entire Iranian oil production. In 1950 the net profits of AIOC were over 33 million pounds sterling, which were double what the AIOC paid that year to the Iranian government. The attempts of the Iranian government to renegotiate the concession with the AIOC were turned down even though the United States intervened and suggested to the company officials that they should accept a 50:50 formula for profit sharing. The Americans also pointed out that this was the standard practice that the American companies followed with their host countries. The nationalists led by Muhammad Mussadeq, who became prime minister in May 1950, decided to nationalize the AIOC. The AIOC, being supported by the British government, would not budge from its position. Later, the Americans, becoming increasingly apprehensive of the growing strength and popularity of the communist Tudeh party, followed a plan engineered by the CIA to overthrow Prime Minister Mussadeq and restore the Shah to the throne. Robert O. Keohane, drawing on several sources, observes: "Aided by thugs whose services were secured with CIA funds, the Iranian army deposed Mossadegh and restored the Shah, who fled briefly to Italy during the disturbances, to his throne. As a result of this American-sponsored revolution, the old political institutions of Iran were either destroyed or reduced to only symbolic importance, as the Shah became an absolute monarch."[6]

American intervention in this dispute turned out to be successful because of U.S. links with the Iranian military and the way the government persuaded and pressured the American oil companies to accept the terms proposed under a carefully worked out consortium. The Department of Justice also came out with a ruling in 1954 that the participation of American oil firms in the consortium would not be interpreted as an illegal restraint of trade. Under the terms of the consortium worked out by the

State Department, American firms were accorded a 40 percent share of the Iranian operation with the AIOC retaining 40 percent. The shares of Shell and CPF, the French company, would be 14 percent and 6 percent, respectively. Commenting on the terms of the consortium, one observer remarked that "even after the compensation payable to Anglo-Iranian any stake in that venture was like getting a 'license to print money'."[7] Referring to the enormous advantages that the American government and American firms had extracted from this episode, Keohane points out: "The remarkable part of the trick was that the American government, and American firms, profited immensely while appearing reluctant to become involved and only to be doing so to aid in reconciliation, economic development, and the provision of public order. Hegemonic leadership was never more rewarding than this!"[8]

When we turn our attention to the emerging political situation in the Arab world, we find that most of the Arab states, despite public declarations that they were opposed to the presence of Israel as a Western bastion and intensely suspicious of its expansionist policies, did not have much capability to pursue an effective anti-Israeli strategy because of their internal divisions. One great exception was Nasser's Egypt where he had nationalized the Suez Canal in 1956. In doing this, he had demonstrated that he could overcome British opposition to his policies and thereby improved his image as a dominant leader of Arab nationalism. He had often defined Arab nationalism as an outcome of Arab solidarity. This solidarity could grow only out of Arab independence, which could assert itself if the Arab countries were to defeat Western designs to interfere in the internal politics of their countries. "Arab nationalism means Arab solidarity, that is Arab independent countries cooperating together."[9]

Nasser's success in emerging as a leader of Arab nationalism and unity aroused Israeli and Western fears. Another factor that reinforced Nasser's leadership and that, in its turn, was a thorn in Western and Israeli sides, was his success in attracting Soviet support to his cause and strategy. In addition, Nasser felt sufficiently strong after nationalizing the Suez Canal to deny to Israeli ships passage through the Suez Canal and particularly the Straits of Tiran. However, the justification that Israel used for invading Egypt on October 30, 1956, was the growing number of raids on Israel being launched from Egyptian territory.

It was significant that within a short period of four days of the Israel invasion, Israel had occupied the Sinai and the Gaza Strip. European powers like the British and the French were so opposed to Nasser emerging as the dominant leader of the Arab world that they joined hands with Israel in mounting an invasion to seize the Suez Canal. The Soviet Union took a stand against this invasion and hinted that it would have to intervene. The United States not only opposed the Israeli, British, and French concerted action against Egypt, but supported the Canadian-inspired resolution of the United Nations which called for the removal of the invading forces from Egyptian soil and the placement of United Nations troops along the Egyptian-Israeli borders.

One could see in both the Iranian-British oil dispute of 1951-1954 and the 1956 Arab-Israeli war that European powers like Britain and France were being steadily eliminated from the Middle East, with the United States emerging as the most influential power. Even though Israeli forces had triumphed so speedily over Egyptian forces in 1956, Nasser's position as a hero and leader of the pan-Arab movement was considerably strengthened. He could claim that he had been successful in rolling back a powerful invasion launched by Israel, France, and Britain.

The third episode being examined here is related to the Arab-Israel war of 1973, leading to the oil embargo decision. This episode indicates that the dominant position the United States had acquired in the Middle East ever since the 1950s was being challenged by the Arab desire to use the oil weapon to pressure the United States into changing its policies toward Israel in such a way that the latter country would be effectively induced into returning Arab lands captured by Israel in the 1956 and 1967 wars.

On October 6, 1973, Anwar Sadat unleashed his surprise attack on Israel. As Israel started reeling from the initial attack and as there was growing evidence by October 10 that the Soviet Union was beginning a massive resupply of arms to Syria, American military aid was rushed to Israel. The American administration led by Nixon and Kissinger could not allow an American ally like Israel to be overwhelmed by Soviet arms. The surprise of Sadat's military invasion was perhaps more than matched by the unsheathing of the Arab oil weapon under the leadership of King Faisal. King Faisal had consistently complained of the twin threat that the Middle East faced from Zionism and Communism. But American calculations were that the Saudi ruling family led by Faisal was not likely to turn against the United States by using the oil embargo. Faisal had faced mounting threats to his kingdom from Nasser's Arab nationalism and particularly from his military intervention in Yemen. In 1969, when the monarchy in Libya and the military government in Sudan were overthrown by military cabals, a plot against the Saudi monarchy on the part of some air force officers was uncovered in Saudi Arabia. Therefore, Faisal knew that Saudi prosperity and security could be guaranteed only by the continuing economic and strategic support that the United States gave to Saudi Arabia. The question arises as to why Faisal changed his mind in October 1973. A clue to Faisal's thinking rested not only on his concern for security and prosperity but also on the fact that he was at heart both an Islamicist and an Arab nationalist.

Faisal had formerly believed that the oil weapon against the United States would not work because the United States was a swing producer of oil in the sense that American sources like Texas, Louisiana, and Oklahoma could produce additional oil to make up for any deficit created by an Arab curtailment of oil supplies. It was apparent, however, that the United States could no longer fulfill the function of the producer of last resort and that any reduction of oil supplies brought about by Arab action could create havoc on the Western economy. Joseph Sisco, the American assistant secretary of state, emphasized in an interview on Israeli television in September 1973 that American interests could not be regarded as "synonymous with the state of Israel. . . . I'm in no position to be clairvoyant and predict it. . . . But there are obvious voices in the Arab world who are pressing for the linking of oil and politics."[10]

In September 1973, the Agency for Resources and Energy in the Ministry of International Trade and Industry in Japan released a White Paper that disclosed: "The oil-supply management system, until now run by the international oil companies, has crumbled" and that the Japanese could discern that the oil supply would be controlled not so much by the companies but by the oil exporting countries.[11] In other words, it had become clear to the Japanese as early as 1973 that some of the major producing states from whom they purchased their oil were nationalizing the production of oil even though the great multinational oil companies were still controlling the transport and selling of oil. This shows that Arab nationalism had infected even conservative states and that bureaucrats in these states were trying to assert state control over a major industry like oil.

It should also be noted that the bureaucrats were a part of the nationalist trend that could be seen in the 1970s and 1980s in the Arab world. Presumably this nationalist trend was also the outcome of the spread of education in countries like Egypt, Saudi Arabia, and Iraq, where the proportion of children going to school was increasing rapidly. Arab national consciousness was also a product of several hundred thousand television sets and other forms of media creating the feeling in these countries that Arabs were united by bonds of common language and culture. It may be recalled that the initial impetus for Arab nationalism came from Nasser's leadership during the 1950s and 1960s.

An equally important factor that influenced a man like King Faisal was his considerable commitment to Islam. He held the view that the Saudis were not only protectors of the holy cities of Mecca and Medina but were also responsible for protecting "the third most holy spot in Islam—Al Aqsa, the Dome of the Rock mosque in Jerusalem."[12] During our visits to Saudi Arabia in 1984-1985, one could see how some of the Egyptians occupying important positions in universities in Mecca, Jeddah, and Riyadh venerated Faisal, because he had provided refuge to them when they fled from Nasser's persecution of the Ikhwan in Egypt. Thus, Faisal's decision to impose the oil embargo in 1973 was also motivated considerably by the Islamic factor.

Faisal's oil minster, Zaki Yamani, refers to a meeting that took place on May 23, 1973, when Faisal addressed executives of the oil companies of ARAMCO, Texaco, Exxon, Mobil, and Socal. According to the transcribed notes of this meeting, Faisal said: "Time is running out with respect to US interest in Middle East, as well as Saudi position in the Arab world. Saudi Arabia is in danger of being isolated among its Arab friends because of the failure of the US Government to give Saudi Arabia positive support, and that HM [His Majesty] is not going to let this happen. You will lose everything."[13] When, a week later, some of the oil representatives informed American government departments like the State, Defense, and CIA about what Faisal had said in his meeting with the oil executives, they were told that Faisal should be able to cope with such pressures because he had faced much greater pressures from Nasser and that Faisal needed America. The ARAMCO conclusion was, "Some believe his Majesty is calling wolf when no wolf exists except in his imagination. Also, there is little or nothing the U.S. government can do or will do on an urgent basis to affect the Arab/Israel issue."[14]

The book on Yamani reveals that in August 1973 the king had started asking Yamani to provide him with detailed and periodic reports on the production and expansion plans of ARAMCO and how adversely American consumers would be affected as a result of curtailed production of oil. Yamani thought that this was a new development as the king never bothered him with such details. The book on Yamani points out: "The Aramco official also reported that there were elements in Saudi Arabia which, 'for their own reasons', were trying to tell the United States that Saudi Arabia would not follow up on its threats. 'Reference here to Fahd's group.' There were also elements in the US which were misleading Nixon as to the seriousness of Saudi Arabia's intention. Yamani mentioned Kissinger. For that reason, the king has been giving interviews and making public statements designed to eliminate any doubt that might exist."[15]

Faisal and his minister, Yamani, thought that there was a possibility to influence the decision making in the White House in favor of the Arabs directly or indirectly by mobilizing public opinion in favor of the Arab cause through interviews with newspapers and television. The Saudis used all these methods. Three of the oil companies—Texaco, Chevron, and Mobil—came out publicly in support of a change in the American Middle East policy. Mobil, through a large advertisement in the *New York Times*, clearly suggested that since the United States depended on Saudi Arabian oil, it should do everything to bring about a settlement in the Middle East otherwise U.S.-Saudi relations would deteriorate and the Saudis would have to base their decisions on political considerations.

James Akins, who was the American ambassador to Saudi Arabia and was close to King Faisal, is quoted by Yamani. Akins's account reveals the way Faisal was wrestling with the problem as to at what point could the Saudis justifiably impose the oil embargo. Faisal is reported to have told Akins.

> We cannot rationally absorb the income we have from this oil production. We're only doing this because you've asked us to. And we will not continue unless there is some progress in restoring Arab lands. He made that point over and over again. They were sorry to have had to impose the embargo but we were sending arms to Israel during the

war. We were flying planes from Germany straight into the occupied Sinai with military equipment. This was considered a hostile act against the Arabs. Then Congress voted for a massive increase of aid to Israel and that was the last straw. It made the embargo inevitable.[16]

The decision to impose the embargo was the third stage, preceded by two earlier decisions. The first was the decision of OPEC to raise the price of oil to $5.12 a barrel. This action was later followed by the reduction of oil production immediately by 10 percent and then by 5 percent on a monthly basis thereafter. On October 20 King Faisal announced the oil embargo and said: "In view of the increase of American military aid to Israel, the Kingdom of Saudi Arabia has decided to halt all oil exports to the United States of America." Thus, the Saudis could argue that they had explored and exhausted every possible means to impress upon the Americans that, because they were a major supplier of oil to the free world and thus a sustainer of its economy, their pleas for certain changes in Middle East policy should be heeded.

The conclusion that flows from the analysis leading up to the embargo is that the Saudis through their close association with the United States, both in terms of oil production and foreign policy, had learned how to play the game according to the rules of the American political process. In playing this game, they became aware of the norms of American political culture. Those who play this game automatically get captured by a pragmatic approach in which the luxury of ideological purity and simplicity is no longer a possibility. This probably explains why the Saudis, particularly with their enormous financial resources, have become more closely entangled in the American political process than any other Muslim or Arab power. How this process has led to the Saudi regime pursuing an accommodational strategy that excludes confrontational or radical methods is a theme of our chapter on Saudi Arabia.

The dominant imperial systems of Pax Brittanica and Pax Americana that we have seen in the Middle East were created to enforce the rules of an international economic order the main purpose of which was to promote the interests of the respective dominant power. The problem with such regimes was that by their very nature they sowed the seeds of strife and instability. There was not only competition from rival powers but also resistance from those who felt that their territories and resources were being used to ensure their subordination.

Keohane analyzes the foundations on which the structure of hegemonic stability was constructed: "The theory of hegemonic stability, as applied to the world political economy, defines hegemony as preponderance of material resources. Four sets of resources are especially important. Hegemonic powers must have control over raw materials, control over sources of capital, control over markets, and competitive advantages in the production of highly valued goods."[17] As we have seen, in 1973 this regime of hegemonic stability that was functioning under U.S. domination was challenged by the Middle Eastern oil producing countries who organized their cartel known as OPEC. American dominance resulted in Middle Eastern countries using their oil resources to establish a counterdominant regime; namely, OPEC. There was not only an oil embargo but from the point of view of Western interests a skyrocketing of prices by almost 400 percent between October 1973, when the price of oil was raised from $5.12 a barrel, to $11.65 in December 1973. One could see how these prices had undergone steady increases from $1.80 in 1970 to $2.18 in 1971 to $2.90 in mid-1973 to $5.12 in October 1973 and to $11.65 in December 1973.

The United States reacted by proposing the establishment of an international energy agency in 1974. It should be noted that during the postwar period, largely under American leadership, certain international arrangements had been set up, such as a stable international monetary system to facilitate international trade and payments and also to ensure the free flow of oil from the Middle East to Europe and Japan "at prices well below the opportunity costs of substitutes, and even below the protected American price."[18]

It looked as if the oil embargo was imposed by Saudi Arabia to save the Egyptian and Syrian military positions on the battlefront, because it was clear that the American decision to rush military supplies to Israel would actually end in the Arab armies retreating even further from their pre-October 1973 positions in Egypt and Syria. The embargo was lifted in March 1974 because Americans under Kissinger brought about a military disengagement on both fronts. The embargo created a severe economic discomfort for the West, but for the Arabs it did not change the military and political map of the Middle East. As Yamani pointed out, the Americans under Kissinger were not looking for an overall settlement but "simply wanted to water down the fire, to reduce the heat of the situation and keep these pending until some time in the future and there would be no settlement. That way Israel could continue its occupation of the territories taken in 1967 and annex them."[19] Thus, one could argue that the Israelis had actually tightened their hold on the Arab lands taken in 1967. As will be argued in Chapter 2, even after the Israeli agreement to withdraw from the Sinai peninsula and accord some kind of autonomy for the Palestinians in the West Bank and Gaza under the Camp David agreement of 1978, the political situation really did not undergo a sea change. In fact, as a result of the Camp David agreement, any Egyptian threat to Israel was neutralized and the Israelis could expect to so consolidate their position in Gaza and the West Bank that they could settle Russian Jewish immigrants on Arab lands. Thus, all such Arab attempts to change the American policy so that the Arab position vis-à-vis Israel would improve were exercises in futility. To borrow a phrase from Lewis Carroll's *Through the Looking-Glass*, "It takes all the running you can do, to keep in the same place."

Iran's Islamic Revolution: Successes and Setbacks

As will be argued in Chapter 3, the Islamic revolution in Iran refuted a fairly well-accepted maxim of political theory which suggested that rapid urbanization and industrialization very often led to erosion of certain traditional loyalties built around religion or tribe. The Islamic revolution demonstrated that political power could be mobilized through religious solidarity on such a massive scale that it could overwhelm the political support that the Shah thought he enjoyed through economic growth and the enormous military power he commanded. But one could see in the early stages of the revolution that political power mobilized by the clerics for revolutionary purposes could not be translated into support for implementing social reforms like land reforms and nationalization of foreign trade. Land reforms were vetoed by the Council of Guardians, which had twelve members, half of them theologians appointed by Khomeini and the other half Muslim jurists nominated by the Supreme Judicial Council and approved by the parliament. Land reforms provoked opposition from the theologians in the Council of Guardians because they provided for the compulsory purchase and distribution of land owned and cultivated by private individuals. This confirms the impression created by Maxime Rodinson's work that, even though Islamic doctrines could be invoked in favor of a "society without privilege," certain Islamic principles "have up to now most often served to justify societies based upon privilege."[20] However, it should be pointed out that Iran's revolutionary leaders did extend the role of the public sector to include banking, insurance, and major industries as well as the bulk of foreign trade and urban property.

A disturbing factor in the Islamic revolution, particularly for some of the ruling circles in the Gulf states and Lebanon, lay in the fact that for centuries the Shi'ite community had suffered deprivation at the hands of the Sunni ruling classes in these areas. Thus, one of the indications of the way the Iranian revolution was being exported to the Gulf states and Lebanon was the rise of militancy on the part of the Shi'ite masses. The Iranian appeal assumed even more alarming proportions when it was couched in universal Islamic terms emphasizing the solidarity of the umma, which depended upon greater unity and common action between the exploited Sunni and Shi'i classes. The message that was beamed through the Iranian radio and media to the neighboring states spoke of the Muslim mustazafin (the oppressed) who ever since the days of the Prophet had been called upon to rally against monarchies and other forms of oppressive and decadent social and political systems. Joseph Kostiner gives a fairly detailed account of popular demonstrations in countries like Kuwait, Bahrain, and in the al-Ahsa region of Saudi Arabia. According to Kostiner, "subsequent Shi'i assertiveness consisted almost wholly of acts of sabotage and terrorism."[21] He concedes that the "passage to terror" had been conditioned by the outbreak of the Iran-Iraq war and the subsequent attempts of Gulf governments to extend aid to Iraq.

The Iraqi invasion of Iran was launched in September 1980. Throughout the war, Iraq waged a systematic propaganda war against Iran in which the Iranian revolution was condemned as anti-Arab, anti-Islamic, and anti-Sunni. Iraq's military and propaganda campaigns were financed by wealthy Arab states like Saudi Arabia and Kuwait. A constant theme of this propaganda was that the Iranians, who were described as descendants of and similar to the ancient fire-worshippers of Persia, would have to be liberated and Islamicized along the same lines as the Arabs had done to their ancient forebears in the seventh century. The way the war was manipulated through the extension of military aid channelled to Iran by Israeli agents but with U.S. backing created the impression that the United States wanted both sides to bleed each other through this war. Nixon has written: "Our interest demanded that neither side emerge as a clear-cut victor, and the Reagan administration acted correctly in playing both sides."[22]

Nixon's observation was correct except that American officials "in playing both sides" one against the other seemed to have eventually overlooked the fact that the Iraqi conduct of the war in using chemical weapons against Iran was morally reprehensible. George Shultz, the then Secretary of State, in his memoirs writes that in March 1984 there was a debate within the administration circles as to how the United States could overlook the monstrous moral culpability of Iraq in using lethal chemical weapons in the war. Presumably there were groups in the National Security Council who were in favor of developing diplomatic relations with Iraq in spite of its behavior. By November 1984 the negotiations that were going on between the United States and Iraq regarding the American willingness to resume diplomatic relations with Iraq after a seventeen-year hiatus had reached such a crucial and concluding stage that Secretary Shultz had started speaking from both sides of his mouth. According to his memoirs, on November 26, 1984 he told Tariq Aziz, the Iraqi foreign minister, that the United States was "unalterably opposed to the use of chemical weapons and that we would be watching Iraq carefully." But on the same day the United States resumed diplomatic relations with Iraq. "There were no stars in my eyes or in Ronald Reagan's. I simply thought we were better off with diplomatic relations with Iraq . . . Iraq's ambitions and activities were not of a kind to breed confidence in Saddam Hussein. But the fact remained that a radical Iran now posed an immediate threat to the strategic Gulf area, and Iraq was the only military machine that could block the path of Khomeini's forces."[23]

Thus it was quite clear that Americans were interested in the Iraqis turning back the Iranian forces and imposing a strategic and ideological defeat on the Iranians. For American and international consumption the American administration adopted a lofty and highminded approach in denying to both sides military weapons. But their calculations and strategic moves confirmed the American fear which Shultz expressed repeatedly in his memoirs: "If Iraq collapsed, that could not only intimidate but inundate our friends in the Gulf and be a strategic disaster for the United States."[24] The American administration preferred an Iranian defeat in the war even if it came about as a result of the monstrous unleashing by Iraq of chemical weapons against the advancing Iranian forces.

The war terminated during July-August 1988 when Khomeini, as he put it, decided to drink the cup of poison in the face of the mounting massacre of Iranian forces and the Iraqi bombing of the Iranian civilian population. The Iranians and Iraqis agreed to a cease-fire on August 20, 1988. The Iranian strategic and ideological setback turned out to be a major turning point in the sense that Iranians realized that their pursuit of certain pure ideological policies had to be drastically altered to suit the emerging grim realities. Externally they had to make radical alterations in the strategy of exporting the Islamic revolution to Middle East countries. Internally, as will be seen in Chapter 4, Iran had to progressively substitute a pragmatic economic and social strategy for the traditional ideological policies that it had embarked upon during the Khomeini era. It was significant that only a year before the cease-fire Khomeini was exhorting the haj pilgrims in Mecca to be both devout and militant and think of the pilgrimage as a religious act and a political opportunity to denounce the common enemy of the Muslim umma; namely, the United States and its supporter, Saudi Arabia. In October 1988 Rafsanjani admitted that the umma was deeply divided both along political and religious lines and that the ideal of a united umma could be only a distant goal. Disunity existed between Sunnis and Shi'as. "One country's leadership owes allegiance to the United States, for instance, another to the USSR, another one is nonaligned, another is pro-British." Therefore, Rafsanjani ruefully concluded "that the Muslims need highmindedness (se'eh-sadr) and this highmindedness does not exist."[25]

American Strategic Interests versus the Ideological and Political Objectives of Political Islam

It is common knowledge that 65 percent of the world's proven oil reserves are located in the Persian Gulf. As Richard Nixon has pointed out: "Now its oil is the lifeblood of modern industry, the Persian Gulf region is the heart that pumps it, and the sea routes around the Gulf are the jugular through which that lifeblood passes."[26] In another book, Nixon argued that, because the Persian Gulf is likely to continue as "the only source of significant exportable oil in the world for the next twenty-five years—we have no choice but to remain engaged in the area."[27] The regimes, particularly those friendly to the United States, are not very strong politically and very often the United States has to prop them up, knowing full well that they are autocratic. Such regimes have been designated in a recent work as *Friendly Tyrants.* "The most important of all Friendly Tyrants for the United States is Mexico. . . . Washington would undoubtedly be prepared to do much more to keep a Friendly Power in power there than elsewhere if the alternative were viewed as being much worse from the perspective of U.S. interests. Certainly it would be more willing to keep an unfriendly tyrant from taking power there than anywhere else in the world."[28] When one considers that the Persian Gulf supplies nearly 60 to 70 percent of Japan's oil needs, over 50 percent of Europe's, and above all, that ,the mounting debts of the United States are financed by the credit from Japan and Germany, one can see that perhaps the Gulf region and particularly Saudi Arabia is a close second, if not as vital, to the security of the United States as Mexico.

As against all this, the ideological and political objectives of socio-political Islam run counter to those of the United States. Socio-political Islam should be distinguished from the more popular term *Islamic fundamentalism* because the latter often means a rigid adherence to the original principles and rituals of Islam. In this sense, a conservative state like Saudi Arabia would claim to be an upholder of Islamic fundamentalism. Socio-political Islam defines its goals in terms of Islamic resurgence for the purpose of establishing an alternative social and political system that would challenge Western control over the Muslim lands and resources of the Middle East. Thus, the central purpose of socio-political Islam would be to mobilize the power of the masses to wrest political and economic control from the West. Therefore, socio-political Islam in this sense cannot play an accommodative or subordinate role to Western hegemony as Saudi Arabia and Pakistan do.

As we have indicated, American attempts to dominate Iran were motivated by American strategic interests in the area. Later, the American and Soviet role in the Iraq-Iran war were influenced by the same considerations. It has also been suggested that the American and Allied naval intervention in the Gulf area to protect Kuwaiti and Saudi Arabian oil tankers was an attempt to tilt the balance of forces against Iran (the center of political Islam) in the Iraq-Iran war. The American naval presence could have been one of the factors which influenced Iran's acceptance of U.N. cease-fire resolution 598 on July 18, 1988.

Until the fall of the Shah in 1979, the two pillars on which American hegemony in the Middle East rested were Iran and Saudi Arabia. It was obvious that since the United States lacked a major regional power to act as a surrogate, it had to develop under President Carter "initial agreements to allow prepositioning of U.S. equipment and supplies in regional states and created the Rapid Deployment Force, which later became the U.S. Central Command." Thus, Nixon is correct in pointing out that the United States had already laid the basic infrastructural foundations "needed to support a major U.S. intervention to defend Saudi Arabia and the southern Gulf. Without these facilities, Operation Desert Shield/Storm would have become a modern-day Gallipoli."[29]

In the eyes of Muslim and Arab countries, the United States, ever since the formation of the state of Israel has followed a consistent policy of excessive cordiality and favoritism toward Israel. They would argue that Arab oil has contributed heavily toward the enrichment and growth of the Western economy, but that oil has been used to help Israel in such a way that the legitimate interests of the Arab and Muslim states have not only been disregarded but adversely affected. As noted previously, when President Nixon was in the White House, Arab states under the leadership of King Faisal, by imposing an oil embargo in 1973, tried to influence the United States into pressuring Israel to return Arab lands. President Nixon paid no heed to Arab demands, and the embargo had to be lifted. Now it seems that President Nixon has realized how unjust the Israel position has been in these matters. President Nixon quotes Menachen Begin, former prime minister of Israel, who said in August 1982 that the lands that Israel occupied in June 1967 were taken through certain Israeli offensive actions and not because the Arabs lost them by launching an attack on Israel.[30] According to Nixon: "The Arab-Israeli conflict poisons our relations with the Muslim world. . . . Israel's occupation of Arab lands undercuts our ability to cooperate with countries with modernist, pro-Western leaders. Israel's occupation of Arab lands—and particularly its increasingly harsh treatment of the Palestinians—polarizes and radicalizes the Muslim world. It undermines the moderates, such as President Mubarak of Egypt."[31] Similarly, Nixon charges Israel with having reneged on the solemn agreements that it signed with Egypt under the terms of the Camp David accord negotiated by President Carter in 1978. Israel was supposed to grant autonomy to Palestinians living in the West Bank and Gaza, but in the words of Nixon, "Israel stonewalled the United States and Egypt."[32]

The United States, like any other superpower, follows a pragmatic course of action; that is, a policy that is also in tune with the domestic pressures it faces from time to time. At first American public opinion was inclined to support the pro-Israeli policies of both the Democratic and Republican administrations. Now it seems that American public opinion is becoming increasingly skeptical of the view that Israel should be supported on every issue in its conflict with the Arabs and particularly the Palestinians. This skepticism has also arisen because Americans feel that, in view of the economic problems they face as a result of the recession, they can no longer support a policy designed to provide economic aid to Israel year after year. This change of opinion has emerged over the question of loan guarantees that Israel has been demanding for providing housing on Arab lands to thousands of Jewish refugees from the Soviet Union. A nationwide poll of registered voters in March 1992 disclosed that 49 percent were opposed to loan guarantees being provided to Israel under any circumstances with 13 percent in favor of giving the loan guarantees outright and 32 percent supporting President Bush's position of imposing conditions on the deal.[33]

All this suggests that it is up to a superpower like the United States to follow whatever interests its geo-political calculus dictates. After favoring a friendly democrat like Israel, it may decide that its interests demand that some balance should be restored between the favors it grants to friendly tyrants and those it provides to a friendly democrat. By expressing some concern for the rights of the Palestinians, its policy could be both politically expedient as well as morally defensible. In all such varying situations, what remains constant is the dominance of the United States.

The Gulf crisis of 1990-1991 revealed that it suited the strategic interests of the U.S.-led U.N. coalition to ensure that Israel stayed out of the conflict with Iraq because its participation would have weakened enormously the political position of the United States. It has often been argued that because of the persistent Soviet efforts to establish its own bases of support in the Middle East, the United States needed an ally like Israel, which depended so heavily on American support. The disappearance of the Soviet Union as a threat to American interests in the Middle East and the growing realization that American total alignment with Israel very often stood in the way of Americans being able to develop close ties with Arab states changed the entire geo-political calculus of American interests in the Middle East. All this meant that the United States could pursue its own interests in the Middle East unhindered by any serious external factors. The Americans could have a free hand in developing bilateral military relations with countries like Saudi Arabia, Kuwait, and Bahrain. In the case of Bahrain, the possibilities of moving certain parts of the forward headquarters of the command and control of the Central Command based in Tampa, Florida, to Bahrain were explored.[34]

In the aftermath of the Gulf crisis, there was considerable feeling among policy planners in the Pentagon that the United States should emerge as the single superpower that "will retain the preeminent responsibility for addressing selectively those wrongs which threaten not only our interests, but those of our allies or friends, or which could seriously unsettle international relations." These objectives were disclosed in a draft of a document described in the Pentagon as the *Defense Planning Guidance for the Fiscal Years 1994-1999*. This draft document outlined American objectives in areas like the Middle East and Southwest Asia. It stated that the overall American objective was "to remain the predominant outside power in the region and preserve U.S. and Western access to the region's oil." The United States would also "prevent a hegemony or alignment of powers from dominating the region. This pertains especially to the Arabian peninsula." As for South Asia, the draft document stated: "We should discourage Indian hegemonic aspirations over the other states in South Asia and on the Indian Ocean. With regard to Pakistan, a constructive U.S.-Pakistan military relationship will be an important element in our strategy to promote stable security conditions in Southwest Asia and Central Asia. We should therefore endeavor to rebuild our military relationship given acceptable resolution of our nuclear concerns."[35]

The West is dominating the Islamic and Arab Middle East not only through political and military means. Its dominance through ideas and political, economic, and cultural systems has

turned out to be more penetrating. If this comprehensive dominance continues to be effective, the resistance of socio-political
Islam will become increasingly ineffective. Some Islamic scholars
have already expressed the fear that Islam, like Christianity, will
be secularized and become a personal or private religion. The
chapter on Saudi Arabia shows how the economic and industrial
growth of that country is being predominantly influenced through
the market system in such a way that Islamic ideas relating to
interest are being modified and adapted. In the case of Pakistan,
the regimes there have tried to model their political and economic
systems on Western concepts of the parliamentary and party system and the capitalist free enterprise system respectively. The
dominant regimes in Saudi Arabia and Pakistan, supported by the
middle class and other institutional groups like the military and
civilian bureaucracies, have been trying to insulate their cultural,
industrial and banking systems from some of the traditional
Islamic ideas relating to interest and the role of the public sector
in Muslim societies. Like Egypt, they are following the strategies of
infitah, opening the doors of their economies to Western penetration and above all to the invigorating influence of a predominantly
consumption-oriented economy.

In Iran, where the influence of socio-political Islam is
stronger, Westernization has been viewed, particularly by the
dominant clerical circles, as "the degradation of Islamic and oriental identity, the negation of all previous values and the acceptance of a new personality according to the prevailing values in
Western civilization." Such ideas were expressed in a dialogue
that took place between German and Iranian scholars in March
28-30, 1988, in the Oriental Institute in Hamburg. One of the
Iranian scholars taking part in the dialogue emphasized that "in
respect to all forms of exchange, be it science, philosophy or
technology, Iran wants to be critical, evaluating and choos-
ing. . . . For the Islamic value system this means that everything
that fits into the value system of Islam is useful and positive. . . .
The Islamic Republic accepts parliamentarianism even though it
is not part of or mentioned in the Qur'an or elsewhere. But it fits
into the value system of Islam."[36] One of the scholars pointed
out that the Islamic civilization as a living entity should accept
certain positive elements of Western civilization and digest and
develop them. "It would be a mistake if the Muslims would
behave like non-living beings towards Western civilization and
accept everything without digesting it."[37]

When one examines the political and intellectual interactions between the West and Muslim countries like Saudi Arabia and Pakistan, one finds that both on the part of a number of Western scholars and commentators and local political leaders there is unawareness of how the historical process works. These groups have been so swept off their feet by the success of the Western political and economic models and the disintegration of the Soviet system that they seem to assume that developing countries should follow the Western models in a mimetic fashion. The historical process involving the development of societies does not work in such a way that societies can adopt ideas and institutions from abroad in their totality and discard a number of their own traditions and values that they have inherited from their past. Karl Marx pointed out: "Men make their own history, but they do not make it just as they please; they do not make it under circumstances chosen by themselves, but under circumstances directly found, given, and transmitted from the past."[38] Similarly, Michael Oakeshott, the British conservative philosopher, viewed historical processes as those that involved sameness as well as difference. The same sun that rose yesterday would rise today to set in a different environment.

This historical perspective does not seem to sway the thinking of American policy makers and, what is more surprising, even the writings of some of the scholars on international politics. Adam Garfinkle, one of the editors of *Friendly Tyrants: An American Dilemma*, claims:

> From its creation to the present day, no other great power in modern history has had as large a moral dimension to its foreign policy as has the United States, and none has contended with the collision of moral scruples and raison d'etat to the extent that the United States has in its (so far) brief tenure as a great power. . . . In the end, it is American political culture that furnishes the essential precondition of the Friendly Tyrants dilemma and the demands of being a great power in a dangerous world furnish the occasions. Together they form a smith's workshop; strategic prudence is the anvil, moral compulsion is the hammer, and the shape beaten into pained existence is policy.[39]

Joseph S. Nye, in reviewing this work, asserts: "American policy makers have twisted and turned on the horns of the dilemma, searching for democratic 'third forces' where none existed, yielding to reformist impulses at one moment, embracing dictators at another."[40] The result is that both American policy makers and their academic advisors seem to think that the United States, functioning as "a great power in a dangerous world," can pursue the conflicting objectives of promoting its interests by supporting certain friendly tyrants and in course of time converting the friendly tyrants into democratic regimes. There are two problems here. First, how can friendly tyrants, whose main function is to promote American interests, agree to be converted into democracies when their people are not likely to support their policies of pursuing American interests? Second, friendly tyrants in Middle East countries are ruling societies with long histories of their distinct cultures and religious and political values. How can the simple American recipe of democracy based on competitive political parties and the market system be applied straightaway to such societies? The British, on the other hand, with their longer tradition of empire building in distant societies were more modest and did not think that non-Western societies were more or less clean slates on which Western values and political traditions could be inscribed in haste. Therefore, they suggested that democracy should at best be built through stages and this idea was captured in the famous phrase, "progressive realization of responsible government." Lewis H. Lapham was one of the very few observers who questioned the wisdom of President Bush's decision to rush headlong into the war with Iraq. "Careless of the costs, knowing little or nothing of the languages, history, or cultural traditions of the Middle East, confident that the war with Iraq would be won in a matter of weeks if not within hours or days, the makers of American policy assumed (as did Saddam Hussein) that their own moral equations somehow were synonymous with the laws of nature and the will of God."[41]

This analysis demonstrates how overwhelming is the nature of American dominance and how ineffective or effete is the kind of resistance that political Islam and Muslim countries have been able to organize. The book discusses the nature of this relatively ineffective resistance countered by three of the Muslim states: Saudi Arabia, Iran, and Pakistan. The details are discussed in their respective chapters. In this section we are only delineating the political and ideological contours of resistance, as well as lack of it, that have surfaced.

In the case of Saudi Arabia what becomes clear is that the Saudi regime has never expressed any intention of resisting American domination. Saudi Arabia and the United Arab Emirates possess almost 40 percent of the world's oil reserves and often exercise a decisive influence on the policies of OPEC. Because the Saudi rulers have often functioned as an American protectorate, their political debts to the United States have been mounting. The reciprocal relationship epitomized by the term *friendly tyrants* moved to a higher plateau of debt and gratitude when the United States played the role of saving Saudi Arabia from the fate of Kuwait, which the Saudis thought was a distinct possibility given the nature of Saddam Hussein's strategies and ambition. A perceptive observer like James E. Akins, a former U.S. ambassador to Saudi Arabia, has noted: "America's hand on the oil valves of Arabia may be light but the United States will surely take control. Washington has no real choice, having shown no intention of exerting enough self-discipline to free itself from dependence on oil. America will not cut its consumption; it will not even consider a modest increase in gasoline prices. So the United States is constrained to look to the Persian Gulf for its oil and perhaps solutions to its energy problems."[42] Akins is aware that the situation is not frozen in time. There are possibilities of Islamic fundamentalists organizing their opposition to the Saudi regime. But he is confident enough to believe that "Any opposition to the American presence from religious fundamentalists and the few who still entertain broader Arab nationalist views can be bought off. Everyone has his price."[43]

Other observers have commented on how ineffective Arab solidarity has become and that in American eyes the Arab landscape is filled not so much by united Arabs but by Egyptians, Saudis, Libyans, and Algerians, often at odds with each other. Youssef M. Ibrahim thinks that "the West's one big interest in the region, oil, is more secure than ever in the absence of Soviet competition and the relative feebleness of opposition to the West, even from Islamic fundamentalists."[44]

There has been increasing pressure from both the conservatives and liberals in Saudi Arabia in favor of reforms: basic changes in foreign policy, redistribution of wealth and power, and the granting of certain basic rights to women. King Fahd has responded by putting forward certain proposals under which a sixty-member consultative council will be set up to initiate legislation and undertake a review of foreign and domestic policies.

But members of this council will be appointed by the king. The king has ruled out free elections because he thinks that "Western democratic practices are not suited to traditional Arab societies of the Persian Gulf."[45] What has surfaced from this dialogue in Saudi Arabia is that the flame of socio-political Islam continues to flicker. A Saudi religious leader like Shaikh-Haffan al-Safar has put forward the Islamic position by pointing out that "despite the king's claim of Islamic backing for his proposal, neither the limiting of the right to govern the country to the sons of the country's founder, King Ibn Saud, nor indeed the institution of monarchy itself reflect the Islamic concept of government."[46] It is significant that the king thinks that democracy does not suit the traditional Arab societies, but one may ask, Is increasing dependence on Western military and security protection in conformity with traditions of Islam and Arab culture?

The chapter dealing with the emergence of pragmatic politics in Iran tries to show how the government under President Rafsanjani has been trying to maximize economic growth through means like expansion of the private sector and privatization of certain public industries. In its strategic retreat from what it calls excessive ideological fervor, the regime has brought in measures like the opening of Tehran's stock exchange. Some Western observers have noted how Iran is seeking to draw maximum gains from the disappearance of Iraqi dominance in the Middle East. On the political front, Iran does not wish to be seen only as a patron of radical Shi'ite Muslims. Therefore, it has tried to extend its influence to Sunni Muslims in Sudan, North Africa, and the Palestinian movement. On the military front, Iran is expanding its military budget and acquiring hundreds of T-72 tanks from Russia and Eastern Europe and is similarly making purchases of missile and rocket-related technology from China.[47] To ensure the rapid development of a national security state based on military and economic development, President Rafsanjani pressured the Council of Guardians to screen several thousand applicants for the 270-seat parliament with the result that in the April 1992 parliamentary elections the seats won by the hardline fundamentalists were very few.

All this suggests that the government is interested primarily in resisting the military and economic dominance of the West by developing what we have called a national security state. What socio-political Islam has to realize is that it faces as much danger from the West through its cultural penetration. To create a political and social infrastructure to resist cultural penetration, a Muslim state needs to develop its Islamic ideology in such a way that a strong sense of community spirit and participatory democracy emerges. To achieve these goals, a new Islamic program is needed. Such a program, through means like more sophisticated political parties and a new educational system, is likely to win support not only from the hardcore fundamentalists but from middle class groups and particularly from female citizens who tend to be apprehensive that their interests will be jeopardized by a highly rigid fundamentalist system.

Of the three states included in the book's comparative analysis, Pakistan has the most fragile polity. Some of its social indicators are quite discouraging. It is high on social and regional tension. Similarly, it scores high in terms of class cleavage and conflicts. Its Islamic ideological cement is the weakest of the three states. It is obvious that, when its internal social fabric is so weak, it can offer hardly any resistance to Western domination. In fact, its ruling elites like the military and the civilian bureaucracy have often taken pride in maximizing their economic and military dependence on the West. Their argument is that, given the external threats to its security from India and until recently the Soviet Union, they had no other option.

The state broke away from India to establish itself as a model Islamic state. But no systematic effort was made to move the country toward a vibrant social democracy because the ruling circles failed to convert Islamic ideology from its unimaginative and ritualist form toward social and regional justice. One can see this failure manifesting itself again and again. During the October 1990 elections, Nawaz Sharif offered to the voters the promise of converting the existing political and legal system into one based on the Sharia (Islamic law). When in 1991 the country's highest Islamic court declared that all forms of interest or riba on bank loans, deposits, and international borrowing and lending should be abolished because they were repugnant to Islam, the ruling party, the Islamic Democratic Alliance, had obviously not done any systematic thinking on the issue of interest and were taken totally aback by the ruling of the court. They were fearful that such a ruling, if enforced, would jeopardize the country's public works projects, financed by foreign lending. The other reason for their nervousness stemmed from the fear that some of the orthodox Islamic parties might organize street demonstrations against the government. Thus, on several counts Pakistan typifies what Gunnar Myrdal calls a *soft state*—lack of social discipline, high on promise and low on delivery.[48]

In the case of Pakistan, the Islamic challenge is greater than the Western challenge. The contours of Western hegemony and Pakistani dependence are clear. But Pakistan faces the problem of how to construct that kind of Islamic polity that will convert excessive dependence into relative independence, transform a regime of gross economic inequalities and low social productivity into a regime of social and regional justice. This challenge probably awaits the entire Muslim world, but in no other country has the challenge reached such crisis proportions as in Pakistan.

2

The Intellectual Challenge of the West and the Faltering Islamic and Arab Response

There is a pronounced tendency among many Islamic thinkers to assume that every single Islamic idea holds true for all times to come. First, there is a clear need for identifying which Islamic ideas have been presented in the Qur'an as prescriptions and regulations in response to certain specific problems of a given period. These prescriptions and regulations should be distinguished from general values and principles. Because of this inability to draw such distinctions, there is the other tendency among these Islamic thinkers to divorce ideas from their social context. Almost invariably, such Islamic thinkers do not explore links between ideas and certain economic and class structures. Marxists seem to think that class structures or vested interests are the determining variable. Many of the Islamic thinkers, on the other extreme, seem to think that certain immutable ideas, without again making any distinction between ideas and prescriptions or regulations, are independent of changing social or class structures.

Some Islamic intellectuals would assert that these observations do not do justice to thinkers like Maudoodi, Sayyid Qutb, or Khomeini, who have formulated their ideas or concepts in response to Western challenges. This is true, but the point that needs to be made is that these three major thinkers have tended to dismiss the Western challenge as jahiliyya (pre-Islamic ignorance or paganism) and capitalism and Marxism as being animated by materialism and therefore almost indistinguishable. Khomeini did see the greater danger of Western capitalism. But he and his followers did not seem to have made it clear how capitalism had the continuing capacity to penetrate Islamic ideological frontiers and even corrode the very core of Islamic society.

Albert Hourani has offered a new interpretation of modern Middle East history in terms of the interaction that emerged between Western ideas and Islamic or Middle Eastern responses. Hourani refers to two interlocking rhythms of change: (1) "that which reforming governments and thinkers and external forces tried to impose upon society" and (2) "that which a great stable society with a long and continuous tradition of thought and of life in common was producing from within itself, partly by its own internal movement, and partly in reaction to forces coming from outside."[1] One could infer from this argument that at first in the nineteenth and early twentieth centuries there was a convergence or even fundamental agreement between external forces like the colonial governments and reformers and thinkers in the Middle East and Muslim world. The two such thinkers that come to one's mind are Sayyid Ahmad Khan from India (1817-1898) and Muhammad Abduh (1849-1905) from Egypt. Both thinkers recommended reformation of Islamic society along similar lines though from slightly different perspectives. Sayyid Ahmad Khan, coming from an aristocratic family of Mughal origin, had become a civil service official under the British. He was in favor of showing that modern science and technology were "in conformity with the articles of Islamic faith."[2] Muhammad Abduh had risen from the ranks of the legal service to become a Mufti (expert who can give rulings on questions of the Sharia or the sacred law). His rulings were influenced by the principle of maslaha (public interest). He observed: "If a ruling has become the cause of harm which it did not cause before, then we must change it according to the prevailing conditions."[3]

It was significant that these thinkers came from a class of urban notables. The reformist ideas of accommodation that they recommended between Western thought and Islam led to a certain dilution of Islamic ideas that had a pronounced effect upon Muslim behavior. Sayyid Ahmad Khan was the founder of the Muslim university of Aligarh. This university, in spite of its emphasis on Islamic education, had become an integral part of the British educational system in India, the central object of which was to produce a class of persons "Indian in blood and colour but English in taste, in opinions, in morals and in intellect."[4] Muhammad Iqbal, in his presidential address to the All-India Muslim League in December 1930, complained that the community was not producing leaders who "by divine gift or experience, possess a keen perception of the spirit and destiny of

Islam, along with an equally keen perception of the trend of modern history."[5] As for Abduh, Hourani's perceptive comment was that his view of Islam "was itself affected by his view of what the modern mind needs." He further argued: "In this line of thought, *maslaha* gradually turns into utility, *shura* into parliamentary democracy, *ijma'* into public opinion: Islam itself becomes identical with civilization and activity, the norms of nineteenth-century social thought."[6] In his book, *A History of the Arab Peoples*, Hourani observes:

> By the 1930s a large part of the educated elite was no longer living within the bounds of the shari'a. . . . in the new bourgeois quarters the ritual of the five daily prayers, announced by the call from the minaret, was less important as a measure of time and life; perhaps Ramadan was less fully observed than in the past, when life was freed from the social pressures of the madina where everyone watched his neighbours; the use of alcoholic drinks was more widespread. The number of those for whom Islam was an inherited culture rather than a rule of life increased.[7]

One has to see the process of social change not merely, as Hourani has suggested, through the interlocking rhythms in which ideas are imposed on Islamic society, either from the top or from external sources, and how the long-established Islamic society responds to these ideas. Rather, there is an intervening variable; namely, certain classes of elites or nonelites who become progenitors of these ideas and movements. So far, as has been argued, certain Western ideas were being introduced through the prismatic influence of reformers like Sayyid Ahmad Khan in India and Muhammad Abduh in Egypt. These were representatives of the larger class of urban notables. In contrast, the Ikhwan al-Muslimun (Society of Muslim Brothers), which was established in Egypt in 1928 by Hasan al-Banna, was supported largely by certain nonelitist groups. This is a complex historical process in which there is not a straightforward conflict between ideas and the society in which they are being introduced. There is also a conflict between the interests and ideas of certain conflicting classes like the elitist urban notables and the nonelitist supporters of the Ikhwan who were neither very poor nor highly educated—craftsmen, small traders, teachers and professional men—who were outside the dominant elites. They had been educated in Arabic rather than in English and French.

Even though the Ikhwan was established in 1928 and cast a profound influence on Islamic movements in several neighboring Arab countries, its development in the 1940s was influenced profoundly by some of the ideas of Sayyid Abul Ala Maudoodi (1903-1979), the founder of the Jamaat-i-Islami (Islamic Organization) in India. Maudoodi probably contributed two central concepts to the thinking of Islamic movements and particularly the Ikhwan. First was the idea of the jahiliyya, which in its essence meant that the world was faced with the same kind of dichotomous or compartmentalized programs of action that differentiated between man's sacred and secular activities as the society during Prophet Muhammad's time encountered in Mecca. It was Muhammad who had formulated a compact and comprehensive ideology merging the sacred and the secular worlds. Second, Maudoodi also formulated the outlines of an all-encompassing Islamic ideology. It was significant that Karl Marx argued that capitalism through its instrument, the bourgeoisie, had "drowned the most heavenly ecstasies of religious fervour, of chivalrous enthusiasm, of philistine sentimentalism, in the icy water of egoistical calculation."[8] For Maudoodi, capitalism represented jahiliyya (age of ignorance). It was the sacred duty of Muslims to roll back the onward march of capitalism. He argued that an Islamic ideology had one all-embracing point of view that united the mosque, the market and the industrial workplace. Habits of personal hygiene and purification that Islam put forward were all merged with larger notions of economics and international politics. In other words, there was no aspect of human activity which such an ideology and such a way of life did not include and influence.[9]

The subcontinent of India, in addition to being drawn into the capitalist network, had also come under the influence of British education and colonial institutions like the bureaucracy and the military. There had emerged in India during Maudoodi's time, among both Hindus and Muslims, British-trained lawyers, administrators, and military officers. Maudoodi complained bitterly that Muslim politicians were waging a struggle for Pakistan which would be established more or less on secular lines rather than on the firm basis of an Islamic ideology. Another major idea that he put forward was that Muslims should not formulate their political program in terms of Muslim nationalism because Islam did not believe in a territorial nationalism. Its mission was to invite the whole world to its faith and ideology. Therefore, Muslims should not ask for a separate state of Pakistan but should wage a struggle for the conversion of the whole of India to Islam.[10]

It should be noted, and this point will be made again, that Islamicists like Maudoodi were so devoted to ideological purity that they tended to disregard several major realistic considerations. In fact, political realism as a stepping stone to future political idealism had been suggested by the Qur'an itself. The Qur'an states that God has created nations and tribes and it is for Islam to bring them together but perhaps through progressive stages. Even an Islamic thinker like Iqbal had pointed out: "For the present every Mualim nation must sink into her own deeper self, temporarily focus her vision on herself alone, until all are strong and powerful to form a living family of republics."[11] This lack of political realism and a clear appreciation of the political compulsions that Muslim political leaders faced in India turned out to be a major failing of Maudoodi. It was the relatively anglicized Jinnah and not the Islamic Maudoodi who established Pakistan. Maudoodi accepted the existence of Pakistan but also launched a struggle to steer Pakistan along what he considered Islamic lines.

Another weakness that one discerned in Maudoodi and other Islamic thinkers was that they sometimes did not follow rigorously the logic of their own thinking. If Islam is an all-inclusive universal system, one must realize that there exists in it concepts though seemingly inconsistent but, when viewed as parts of the larger system, form logical parts of the system as a whole. Islam advocates private property, but this it does within the parameters of social justice. Thus, the Prophet's injunction that resources "shall be taken from the rich among them and turned over to the poor among them" (through zakat and additional taxes on property and revenue)[12] was consistent with the Islamic doctrine of social justice, but those who would rigidly interpret the doctrine of private property may not agree with the Islamic system of redistributive justice. This explains why the Jamaat in Pakistan and the Ikhwan in Egypt have not been vigorous champions of land reforms, with the result that these Islamic organizations have not been able to establish firm bases in rural areas where the great majority of people live. .

When one compares the organization and activities of the Jamaat-i-Islami with the Ikhwan al-Muslimun, the overall impression one gathers is that perhaps the Ikhwan's organization was more anchored in certain economic activities and also demonstrated its ability through a vigorous militant stance against an occupying power like Britain. The founder of the Ikhwan, Hasan al-Banna (1906-1949), a schoolteacher by training, defined the movement as "a Salafiyya message, a Sunni way, a Sufi truth, a political organization, an athletic group, a cultural-educational union, an economic company, and a social idea."[13] Those followers of Hasan al-Banna who had experienced the humiliations of the British occupation of the Suez Canal area, expressed their feelings as follows: "We are weary of this life of humiliation and restriction. Lo, we see that Arabs and the Muslims have no status [manzila] and no dignity [karama]. They are not more than mere hirelings belonging to the foreigners."[14] Thus, to a number of people drawn from lower middle and poorer classes, the Ikhwan offered a spiritual home and a movement which might restore their national dignity and create a new Arab and Muslim society. From our random sample of interviewees of young and middle-aged members of the Ikhwan, we gathered the distinct impression that for them the main appeal of the Ikhwan lay in the fact that through its activities it showed them how Islam could become a total way of one's life.

It looked as if the organizers of the Ikhwan had done considerable thinking in devising their organization in such a way that it would present to Egyptians and Muslims the possibilities that an Islamic movement could offer in meeting the economic and political challenges of the West. Through certain economic and commercial undertakings that the Ikhwan set up, they tried to impress upon their followers as well as outsiders that an Islamic movement was capable of organizing enterprises where workers could be employed and profits could be made. Thus, they set up the Sharikat al-Mu'amalat al-Islamiyah (The Company for Islamic Dealings), the Brethren Spinning and Weaving Company, the Commercial and Engineering Works Company in Alexandria, and the Islamic Press and Daily Newspaper Company. Such enterprises involved thousands of Egyptian pounds of capital with workers buying shares in these companies in a number of instances. It was significant that some of the goals that the movement was pursuing in setting up such operations were Islamic socialism, liberation of the national economy, and raising the standard of living of the Muslim worker. After analyzing these activities, Ishak Musa Hussaini wrote: "As an example of their trend toward national socialism it is worth mentioning that they first considered that public wealth such as minerals should be subject to legislation to safeguard the national interest, that the state has no right to award concessions to any foreign company which seeks to exploit the national wealth—this, the state should do itself, or, being unable to do so, it should entrust it to companies created with Arab money."[15] Similarly, citing Ikhwan publications, Hussaini referred to certain social and labor welfare aspects of the Ikhwan program, like the guarantee of a livelihood with social security in the form of minimum wages, limitation of work hours, insurance against sickness, prohibition of child labor, and making sure that women worked in occupations "suitable to their nature and social status." The program emphasized that "each peasant should have a minimum amount of property and healthy living conditions, security of health, sufficient food, beneficial education and a spiritual atmosphere."[16] It was significant that the Ikhwan did not demand land reforms of a nature that would break up the large holdings of the Egyptian landowners.

Various estimates suggest that the Ikhwan enjoyed the support of about a million Egyptians in 1948. Half of these were sympathizers and the other half, 500,000, were active members.[17] The organization was very largely urban middle class and was therefore often dubbed as effendi. Its Consultative Assembly of 150 members in 1953 again was predominantly middle class, with 12 coming from religious areas and 10 from a rural background.[18] In spite of this middle class background, the Ikhwan, because of its exposure to the Palestinian war in 1948 and its initiative in organizing the commando raids against the British in the Suez Canal areas, was often dubbed as the most militant organization. Mahmoud Hussein points out:

> The Muslim Brotherhood thus voiced the real aspiration of the masses to cast off the foreign, bourgeois ideological fetters which kept them in a state of repression and national oppression; but it distorted this aspiration by orienting it toward the past and not towards an authentically popular and revolutionary system of values. As a response to the disintegration of all traditional forms of solidarity—under the impact of the market, market relations, and the bourgeois values imported by imperialism—the Brotherhood proposed a return to the life style and practice of solidarity of the earliest Islamic societies, which it represented as a lost paradise.[19]

Even though, as we shall see later, a well-known ideologue of the Ikhwan like Sayyid Qutb claimed that the Islamic system should not be viewed solely as "a replica of the first Islamic society" and many models in response to the needs of modern times could be extracted from the Islamic system,[20] it would be correct to suggest that the Ikhwan often explained problems of poverty in terms of secularism and corruption in high places. It argued that the solution to such problems lay in Muslims reestablishing their community along the lines of the early Muslim community and returning to the moral regime of "austerity, hard work and self-reliance."

Western Challenge and Nasser's Secular Response

Colonel Gamal Abdul Nasser masterminded the July 1952 military coup in Egypt. Soon after Nasser assumed absolute power on behalf of the military revolution in January 1954, the regime dissolved the Ikhwan al-Muslimun. In a speech on July 26, 1956, Nasser announced the nationalization of the Suez Canal Company. Army officers like Nasser and Sadat had worked with the Ikhwan, and they fought together in the Palestinian war. How does one explain that Nasser deliberately chose a secular strategy of Arab nationalism and also opted for strengthening the political and economic structure of the state as the regime's response to Western dominance? Some time after he had organized the seizure of power in July 1952, Nasser wrote a pamphlet entitled *The Philosophy of the Revolution* that encapsulated his views on the revolution, which he described as a "reconnaissance-patrol. . . . a mere patrol in the field in which we are fighting our greatest battle for the liberation of our country from all fetters and shackles." Nasser argued that Arabs and Egyptians had to think of playing a central role in a system of three circles—the Arab circle, the African circle, and the Islamic circle. "There is no doubt," he concluded, "that the Arab circle is the most important and the most closely connected with us."[21]

As a military officer, Nasser regarded the military organization as a chain of command with its monolithic power structure from which orders came from the top to be obeyed and implemented down below. In addition, there was the foreign threat. This threat, Nasser thought, could not be effectively dealt with through a pluralist party system. When asked why a multiparty system had not emerged under his regime, he replied, "If I did that, there would be one party acting as an agent for the American CIA, another upholding British interests, and a third working for the Soviets."[22]

Nasser was aware that no matter how centralized the state power structure was under the regime, he had to make concessions to the diffused power structure that existed in society. One could see how this strategy emerged in the land reforms that he introduced. Under the Agrarian Reform Law of September 1952, a ceiling of 200 feddans for an individual was placed on land ownership, with an additional 100 feddans for his children. This ceiling was further reduced to 100 feddans in 1961 and to 50 feddans in 1969. As a result of these reforms members of the royal family as well as large landowners lost their political power. The reforms introduced some egalitarianism because some redistribution of land did take place in favor of small holders and tenant cultivators. However, it was significant that the intermediate group of medium-sized owners from whom the military officers came was hardly affected, and they continued with their power structure remaining intact at the village level.

The strategy that was pursued in converting private industries into state-owned enterprises was even more methodical. By 1961 the state had nationalized all banks and insurance companies and practically all large industrial enterprises. In spite of so many levers of economic control being available in his hands, Nasser was still fearful that the new state enterprises could develop centrifugal or countervailing power. Therefore, he had to use his power of appointment of managers and state entrepreneurs "to balance through his placements his need for industrial production and his fear of concentrated power in nationalized industries."[23] The result was, as Ali Sabri of the Arab Socialist Union pointed out in 1967, "it appears that in fact that many of those who hold the levers of command in the nationalized enterprises and corporations of the public sector have carried out devious procedures for exploiting that sector while striving to maintain their positions for the longest possible time."[24] All this led to considerable oscillation in decision making on the part of Nasser, because every time he found that excessive centralization of power at the top led to decline in industrial production, he would move toward more decentralization of power in the hands of industrial public sector enterprises.[25]

One wonders why Nasser did not make every effort to create a consensus among the main political forces in Egypt so that the emerging state apparatus would have adequate political support and thus assist him in countering what he regarded as Western designs against Arab and Egyptian interests. One can see why Nasser was both suspicious and apprehensive of the political objectives of the Ikhwan. There is more or less common agreement among scholars and observers that no organization posed as serious and organized a challenge to his regime as the Ikhwan. As we have seen, the Ikhwan had already demonstrated its militancy and organization in its guerrilla activities against the British forces in the Canal and through its participation in the Palestinian war. Mohammed Heikal, who was close to Nasser, although paying tribute to the role of the Ikhwan in the Palestinian war, thought that Nasser and his military colleagues "found much to admire in the Brotherhood and contemplated throwing in their lot with it. If in the end they all drew back this was mainly because they felt that, apart from its generalized religious and ethical principles, the Brotherhood lacked a programme capable of meeting Egypt's needs."[26] It seems that this was not the real reason for the fear and suspicion that might have existed in Nasser's mind toward the Ikhwan. Surely he must have been aware that the Ikhwan would not cooperate with the army officers as their pliable partners because the Ikhwan had its own strategy for capturing power. It has been reported that Nasser as early as 1944 in a meeting with the head of the Ikhwan had received the following advice: "Begin to organize in the army groups which have faith in what we believe so that when the time comes, we will be organized in one rank, making it impossible for one's enemies to crush us."[27]

It was also clear to Nasser that there was a fundamental ideological conflict between the Ikhwan and himself as the leader of the revolution and the socialist program that he had pioneered in Egypt. For Nasser, socialism and Arab nationalism came first with Islam perhaps providing some underpinnings. But for the Ikhwan, it was just the opposite in the sense that the Islamic idea should dominate all political and economic programs. Thus, one of Nasser's observations on socialism ran as follows: "Ours is a scientific socialism based on science not on chaos. It is not at all a material socialism. We have never said that it was, nor have we said that we were opposed to religion. What we have said was that our religion is a socialist one and that in the Middle Ages Islam had successfully applied the first socialist experiment in the world."[28] For Sayyid Qutb, one of the central ideologues of the

Ikhwan, every social form must be "governed by the total Islamic view of life." The Islamic system could accommodate scores of models for meeting "the new needs of the contemporary age as long as the total Islamic idea dominates these models in its expansive external perimeters."[29]

It was obvious that the political struggle between Nasser's state and the Ikhwan could not be conducted along constitutional lines. Nasser was the head of a military, autocratic state and the Ikhwan from its very inception, because of its commitment to the establishment of an Islamic state, had felt justified in nurturing a small terrorist wing in the movement. In October 1954, it was accused of an attempted assassination of Nasser in a public meeting, and this resulted in the suppression of the organization throughout the country. Nasser's suppression of the Ikhwan triggered demonstrations in the streets of Damascus, Amman, Baghdad, Khartoum, and Karachi. Two major consequences followed from these policies of the regime. The Ikhwan adopted the gradualist option of a systematic campaign to produce a select group of leaders to eventually transform the entire Egyptian social system. The leader of such moderates was the head of the Ikhwan, Hasan al-Hudaybi. The militants often prevailed because they argued that Nasser's military state was so ruthless and well organized that the gradualist educational efforts and propaganda would not produce any effective impact. The other consequence of Nasser's policy was that a number of influential Ikhwan leaders fled to countries like Saudi Arabia, where they received political refuge and jobs under King Faisal.

How does one evaluate Nasser's political strategy in terms of its goals and the resources he mobilized in pursuit of those goals? His goal was to forge a grand unity of the Arab nation—a goal that he would pursue first through stages like Egypt and Syria forming a union and then helping other Arab states to liberate themselves from decadent or pro-Western rulers. To do this, he had to first mobilize his political and economic resources within Egypt. We have seen that the results of such mobilization were unsuccessful as measured by nationalization of industries and winning political support at home by enlisting the cooperation of an important group like the Ikhwan. Nasser did achieve certain tangible and diplomatic successes when he obtained military equipment from a Soviet-bloc country like Czechoslovakia in September 1955. Later his successes in turning the tables on powerful countries like Britain, France, and Israel were considered no less spectacular by the Arab masses. In July 1956, loans and grants promised by the United States, Britain, and the World Bank for the construction of the Aswan Dam were withdrawn. In spite of such rebuffs, Nasser announced on July 26 the nationalization of the Suez Canal Company. This action eventually provoked Britain, France, and Israel to launch military action against Egypt in October 1956. However, Egypt scored a moral victory when on November 24, 1956, the U.N. General Assembly approved a resolution in support of an immediate withdrawal of British, French, and Israeli forces from Egypt. Thus, a string of diplomatic successes and the military assistance he had obtained from the Soviet bloc improved Nasser's image among the Arab masses to such an extent that he was hailed as a Saladin, who had the capacity to galvanize the Arabs into a united and dynamic nation. These successes might have aroused in him new dreams of pan-Arabism.[30]

Nasser visualized his role and that of Egypt in grandiose terms. He wrote: "I do not know why I always imagine that in this region in which we live there is a role wandering aimlessly about seeking an actor to play it." And he concluded, "We, and only we, are compelled by environment and are capable of performing this role."[31] In pursuit of performing this role, he forgot that his country was plagued with meager resources, mounting population, and to make matters worse, an economic system he himself had constructed that was not working efficiently. The most formidable problem was the threat of Israel, and he must have known that the Egyptian army was no match to Israel's superior equipment and determination. Of course, he and the Arabs would say that Israel had an unfair advantage because of the enormous American support, both economic and military, that it received. He had tried to counterbalance this Israeli advantage by seeking military and economic aid from the Soviet Union. Thus, instead of taking a hard look at his assets and liabilities, he plunged headlong into creating a united Arab nation by getting himself involved in the Arabian peninsula and particularly in the civil war raging in Yemen. This involvement, starting in 1962, lasted for five years. It soon became apparent that Egyptian troops—at one time as many as 50,000—could not function successfully in mountain guerrilla warfare. Yemen turned out to be Nasser's Vietnam. Egyptians made the painful discovery that the common language and culture of Arab nationalism would not automatically bring about cooperation and concerted action between Egyptians and Yemenis. At the Khartoum conference, which took place in August 1967 after the Egyptian defeat at the hands of the Israelis in June 1967, it was resolved that Libya, Kuwait, and Saudi Arabia would contribute 135 million pounds to compensate Jordan and Egypt for the losses they had suffered during the Arab-Israeli war. This agreement would not have been possible without Nasser agreeing to withdraw his troops from Yemen.

Egypt suffered a humiliating defeat in the June 1967 war that lasted for no more than six days and in which the Egyptian air force was wiped out by the Israeli bombardment while the Egyptian planes were still on the ground. It has been reported that Nasser had diverted all the funds necessary for the construction of bunkers toward financing his military operations in Yemen. Thus, grossly incompetent economic and military planning was a manifestation of a society at war with itself. Nasser had constructed a society in which the government, instead of creating a climate for debate and discussion so that a proper appraisal of the country's resources could be undertaken, was busy watching the activities of its military and political functionaries and keeping the Ikhwan under close surveillance. This destructive process in its turn had created a police state. Thus, the well-known Egyptian poet Nizar Qabbani poured out his anguish as follows:

O Sultan, o my lord,
You have lost the war twice
Because half our people has no tongue—
And what value has the people whose tongue is tied?[32]

Infitah and Its Consequences

Sadat by initiating the 1973 war against Israel was hoping to put pressure upon the superpowers, thereby more or less forcing them to initiate negotiations between Israel and the Arabs for the settlement of some of their outstanding problems. The final outcome was that the Americans emerged even stronger than before because in the ensuing war they first supplied arms to Israel, which not only prevented an Israeli defeat but also strengthened the Israeli position in the emerging balance of power. The United States did bring about an Israel-Syrian agreement which led to the Israelis withdrawing from some of the territory they had conquered in 1967 and 1973. There was a similar agreement between Israel and Egypt. Later, in 1978 President Carter's mediation led to the Camp David agreement, under which there would be a progressive Israeli withdrawal from the entire Sinai peninsula and normal Egyptian-Israeli relations would be established. Under the agreement Israel would accord some kind of autonomy for the Palestinians in the West Bank and Gaza. In later discussions Israel made it clear that its conception of autonomy was quite different from what Egypt or the United States expected. Israeli calculations were that, by reaching the peace accord with Egypt and withdrawing from Sinai, they would be able to neutralize Egypt, which probably offered the greatest threat to their security. They thought their greatest gain would be that such an arrangement would enable them to bring about the final annexation of the West Bank by settling thousands of Jews in that territory.[33] Thus, one could see that their calculations turned out to be correct.

What did Sadat expect to gain from his policy of making peace with Israel through the good offices of the United States? He knew that he would antagonize Arab states but the risk was worth taking because by aligning himself with the United States he would not only eliminate Soviet influence in the Middle East but also, by reaching peace with Israel, become an ally of the United States. In addition, such a policy would result in the United States making some efforts to help the Palestinians in attaining some of their claims.

A major domestic consequence of these policy moves so far as Egypt was concerned was the initiation of a new economic strategy under which, by opening up the economy (infitah) to foreign loans and investment, the Nasserite policy of state control and socialism would be reversed. Sadat expected Egypt to reach a high plateau of prosperity through the new policy of infitah, with its twin advantages of foreign loans and investment and maximum encouragement of the domestic private sector.

Because the Islamic movement, often designated by Western observers as a fundamentalist movement, had posed a major threat to all Egyptian regimes since the 1930s, Sadat and his American supporters did considerable thinking in developing some form of a strategy for containing or coopting a movement like the Ikhwan. Thus, some of the questions examined by academics and strategists were: "What factors caused the rise of Islamic fundamentalism in Egypt and how could the threat it posed to an American-sponsored regime be contained? The question of Islam and politics in Egypt and elsewhere, for academics no less than for the media in the West, presented itself as a security dilemma." A sociological explanation of the Ikhwan was that it was "an indicator or reflex of lower middle class social dislocation and psychological malaise in a society undergoing rapid social change." Others, such as structuralists, put forward the view that the phenomena of the Ikhwan arose "as a reactionary consequence of the blockage by the world market forces of Egypt's development efforts."[34]

How did Sadat grapple with the problem of the Ikhwan? Through his pan-Arab and socialist policies reinforced by considerable coercion, Nasser had been able to keep the Ikhwan bottled up. Sadat, on the other hand, by abandoning Nasser's policies and weakening the Nasserists and the Marxist Left, had facilitated the reentry of the Ikhwan into Egypt's public life. He was able to keep the moderate wings engaged in some kind of a political discourse, but incurred the indignation of the radical elements through his peace initiatives with Israel to such an extent that they assassinated him.

An economist like Galal Amin severely criticized the infitah for opening up the economy to the cult of excessive consumption thereby allowing in its wake gross economic inequalities. The policy of infitah was equally disastrous in the sense that it brought about the erosion of the national culture. As regards the economic havoc it caused, Galal Amin pointed out that infitah not only led to excessive consumption but consumption of goods which were not socially desirable or useful. "Why was a country famed for its wholesome natural fruit juices flooded with expensive 7-Up and colas all of dubious nutritional value?" While referring to the collapse of a ten-story apartment building in a Cairo suburb owned by an unskilled construction worker, he observed that, "An honest construction worker by his own physical and intellectual effort would have to save his entire wage, neither eating nor drinking from it, for at least 500 years to own such a building."[35]

It was significant that the Ikhwan welcomed the abandonment of Nasser's socialist strategy but the Islamic press criticized the Sadat regime for the way the liberal economic strategy was being implemented. The Ikhwan leader, Omar Telmesany, asked, "Couldn't the vast fortunes of the rich have been used to ease the hardships of the needy rather than waste it in ostenta-

tious display?"[36] This is precisely the intellectual problem that a
movement like the Ikhwan faces. It does not seem to realize that
economic liberalism cannot be restrained by any government for
social considerations if it were to function freely and thus bring to
the society economic benefits of unrestrained free enterprise.
The Ikhwan and other Islamic movements need to develop a bal-
anced economic system under which the public sector and social
controls would work harmoniously with relatively free private
enterprise in certain demarcated areas.

A leftist critic of the infitah like Galal Amin has pointed out
that it is true that Egypt is experiencing the growing phenomenon of Islamic fervor. But Amin seems to think that an
Islamic movement and the militancy associated with it do not
come to grips with certain basic social and economic problems
and provide no solutions to the people in terms of getting rid of
backwardness and oppression. He writes: "The religious movement in Egypt has been unable to understand what the socio-
economic situation is. It replaces reality by the vision of a past
that is no longer relevant. It tries to escape from the pains of
this world into a magic world. It uses a toy gun similar to the one
used by children to fire at the world. Such a gun may scratch but
does not kill anyone; may cause noise but does not change anything."[37] It is significant that Galal Amin sees no hope in the
diagnosis of the world situation that the left is offering and therefore thinks that the solutions put forward by the left will not
work either. To say that the capitalists are against workers and
that the solution is socialism with its familiar strategies of public ownership of means of production, central planning, and
redistribution of wealth and incomes will not resolve many of
the problems that the new world faces.[38]

Thus, the world faces three possibilities. First, the Western
system of capitalism with its free market economy will continue
to flounder and become increasingly inapplicable, particularly
in the Third World. Second, does Marxism have any capacity to
rise like a sphinx from its ashes? The third is an Islamic system.
The challenge that the Muslims face is that their intellectuals and
leaders have to develop an understanding of the growing complexity of the world. Gone are the days when they could
denounce capitalism and Marxism as nothing more than
jahiliyya. They have to understand this complex world as dominated by the West and see clearly what challenges it poses and
how some of these challenges can be turned to their advantage.

Second, having done such an analysis, they have to glean from the Islamic world of ideas those principles and values which can tackle the challenges of the present complex world. They have to rethink their priorities of the social order they would like to establish on Islamic lines. They have to broaden a concept like that of shura so that consultation is preceded by mobilization of democratic power. The concept of yas alunika (asking questions) both for information and for redress of their grievances should be treated as an integral part of the shura system.

3

American Dominance and Islamic Defiance in Iran

If resistance is the characteristic of the kind of response to the Western challenge found in Egypt, in Iran the response seems to be stronger and in some respects deeper. Iranian Muslim leaders have interpreted the Western challenge mostly as an attempt to establish Western cultural and ideological hegemony. The empirical evidence is also there in that the Iranian response to the so-called Western challenge has been in the form of the Islamic Revolution. One has to probe still deeper to explain the differences between the two countries in terms of the Islamic response. If one argues that the Iranian response is more fierce because Iranians interpreted the Western challenge as a deliberate attempt to bring about an ideological and structural penetration of the Iranian society, many Islamic scholars would argue that Egypt and other Muslim societies experienced similar kinds of ideological and structural penetration from the West. Many scholars have suggested that the Iranian response to ideological and structural penetration has been qualitatively different because in Iran, which is a Shi'i country, the religious leaders and their institutions were perhaps more autonomous and better organized than their counterparts in Sunni countries. A final difference between the Iranian and other responses arises from the fact that Iran experienced a more systematic attempt on the part of the two Shahs to destroy certain key Islamic institutions in the name of progress and civilization. This explanation may not satisfy some scholars who would argue that a similar attempt toward the destruction or replacement of Islamic institutions was made in Turkey but the result was not an Islamic revolution. Again,the answer we may suggest at this point is the crucial and differentiating variable of leadership exercised by the Shi'i clergy in Iran.

One can argue that few Western political scientists have exercised as great an influence on developmental political scientists as Samuel P. Huntington. He had also stimulated Iranian political scientists who returned to Iran and became advisers to the Shah, who was primarily interested in both stability and development. It has often been said that the Shah promoted economic development and ignored or understressed political institution building.[1] This is not quite accurate. What flows from the ideas of the American-trained social scientists who constituted the Shah's brain trust was that the counterpart of capitalist development in the economic sector was the development of a one-party system in the political sphere. Huntington wrote: "Today, in much of Asia, Africa and Latin America, political systems face simultaneously the needs to centralize authority, to differentiate structure, and to broaden participation. It is not surprising that the system which seems most relevant to the simultaneous achievement of these goals is a one-party system."[2]

Abrahamian argues that the idea of the one-party state in Iran did not come entirely from Huntington but also from ex-communists who had left the Tudeh party in the early 1950s and reentered politics under the patronage of the court minister, Alam. Their contribution was that a Leninist-style organization could modernize a traditional society by removing its barriers and mobilizing the masses. Abrahamian noted: "As the old saying goes, politics makes strange bedfellows."[3] But a careful reading of Huntington will indicate that the strange bedfellows like American pluralism and Leninist single-party state were found in his book, *Political Order in Changing Societies.* Huntington heaped lavish praise on Lenin and Mao who "stressed the primacy of a political organization independent of social forces and yet manipulating them to secure its ends."[4] Abrahamian wrote that the Resurgence party brought about "for the first time in Iranian history, the systematic penetration of the state into the propertied middle class, especially the bazaars and the religious establishment."[5] The coercive power came from the SAVAK (secret police) and the instruments designed to mold the lives of thousands of individuals were the Ministries of Labor, Industry and Mines, Housing and Town Planning, Health and Social Welfare, and Rural Cooperatives and Village Affairs. Behind this totalitarian control lay an elaborate network of communications and mass media provided by the Ministries of Information and Tourism, Art and Culture, Science and Higher Education, and above all, the National Iranian Radio and Television Organization.

Abrahamian has pointed out that the bazaar felt threatened by the new order. The thousands of shopkeepers in the bazaar thought that their main functions of being the retailers and wholesalers of food stuffs and imported goods would be wiped out.

> Furthermore, the government-controlled press began to talk of the need to uproot the bazaars, build highways through the old city centers, eradicate "worm-ridden shops," replace inefficient butchers, grocers, and bakers with efficient supermarkets, and establish a state-run market modeled after London's Covent Gardens. One shopkeeper later told a French journalist that the bazaar was convinced the shah and the "oil bourgeoisie" wanted to "throttle" the small businessman. Another confided to an American journalist that "if we let him, the shah will destroy us. The banks are taking over. The big stores are taking away our livelihoods. And the government will flatten our bazaars to make space for state offices."[6]

The only difference between the totalitarianism of the Left and the totalitarian controls that the Shah was trying to develop was that in the designs of the latter there were a number of traditional or monarchical components. The Resurgence party declared that the Shah was the personification of both spiritual and political leadership. In this totalitarianism as well the people were being forced to be free—free of the ulama, who were dubbed "medieval black reactionaries."[7] The Shah often declared that Iran was already as modern as many of the European states like Sweden and Britain. One could see how confident was the Shah of attaining the goals of his revolution that he would launch an attack against the religious establishment at the same time as he did on the bazaar. The Resurgence party interfered in the management of the religious endowments by requiring that the accounts of the religious endowments be brought under government investigation. It was announced that the College of Theology in Tehran University would set up a special religious corps on the lines of the Literacy Corps, and cadres would be sent to the countryside to propagate true Islam among the peasants. The majlis set aside the Sharia by raising the age of marriage for girls and boys. They brought family disputes under the jurisdiction of secular courts and placed restrictions on the rights of men to divorce their wives or marry more than one wife. To cap it all, the Muslim calendar was replaced by the new royalist calendar which meant that the new calendar had 2,535 years as opposed to the Muslim calendar which at that time had 1,355 years.

Khomeini, who was in exile in Najaf in Iraq, denounced the Shah's festival to celebrate 2,500 years of monarchy. He declared that "more than 150,000 students and scholars of the religious sciences in Iran" should protest collectively against "this scandalous festival" and its extravagances that were destroying the nation. "Let the festival organizers know that they are despised by the Islamic community and by all alert peoples throughout the world, that they are hated by all lovers of freedom, and that Islam and the Muslims are repelled by the very notion of monarchy."[8]

The social and political program of the White Revolution, which was being propagated by the Resurgence party, was viewed by Khomeini and the clerics as a systematic and multidimensional attempt to bring about the social transformation of Iran that would lead to the secularization and de-Islamization of the Iranian society as a whole. This explains the immediate and ferocious reaction of Khomeini to the Shah's program and the Resurgence party. Khomeini pointed out that the party had launched a comprehensive and frontal assault leading to the destruction of Islam, devastation of Iran's agricultural resources, and the wasteful expenditure of the nation's wealth and oil revenue on useless weaponry. He argued that this was all being done at the behest of American imperialism.[9] Soon after Khomeini's denunciation of the Shah and his policies, many of Khomeini's associates and followers were arrested. Thus, one could see that Khomeini on his part was also preparing the ground to resist the Shah's attempts "to firmly anchor the state into the wider society."[10] Khomeini first developed a strategy relying on religious ideas and symbols to defeat the Shah's schemes of social transformation. He argued that Imam Hussain was not only a martyr, but a revolutionary thereby suggesting that resistance to the Shah was like resistance to the hateful Yazid against whom Hussain waged his struggle. In his famous treatise, *Vilayat-i Faqih [Rule of the Supreme Islamic Jurisprudent]*, he pointed out, "It was to prevent the establishment of monarchy and hereditary succession that Husayn revolted and became a martyr. It was for refusing to succumb to Yazid's hereditary succession and to recognise his kingship that Husayn revolted, and called all Muslims to rebellion."[11]

Khomeini's Systematic and Frontal Assault Against the Shah's Regime

As we have indicated earlier, the aim of the Shah's strategy was to transform Iran rapidly into a civilized country along Western lines. His father, Reza Shah, and Mustafa Kemal Pasha of Turkey had similar strategies. The methodology that the Shah pursued to implement the strategy was to attack and eventually eliminate certain pillars of Islamic and Iranian traditionalism. The targets of attack were an Islamic Iranian system which rested on institutions like the clerics and the bazaar and values like segregation of the sexes. The Shah through a series of economic plans tried to transform the relatively backward agricultural economy into an industrialized economy. This created a bourgeoisie and therefore the scene was ready for the next assault on the bazaar, which would be replaced by more modern stores and supermarkets. At first, the counterpart of this economic system was supposed to be a competitive party system. But this was abandoned in favor of a single-party system backed by outright coercion and torture practiced by the SAVAK. The military stood in the background if these means failed.

The resistance to the Shah and his repressive regime came from two sources: the intelligentsia and the clerics. Ali Shari'ati (1933-1977) represented the liberal intelligentsia. He was against some of the members of the intelligentsia whom he accused of "imitating Western ideologies which are being imported to this society like those canned and packaged products to be opened and consumed."[12] Shari'ati was also against making any concessions to tribal and other forms of traditional Islam. He advocated social justice and a war against poverty, but to him poverty was to be a "dialectic factor." Islam had been interpreted by certain mullahs as a system which justified poverty because poverty had been ordained by God as a fate of the poor. Presumably, Ali Shari'ati was suggesting that as long as the poor believed in such a fatalistic system their condition of poverty would not create in them a desire or a demand to end such a system. In other words, when the poor became conscious of the fate that had been imposed on them by a socially unjust system, poverty could become a dialectical factor. "Poverty, therefore, is not by itself a movement causing factor unless it is felt to the extent of being the cause of awakening the poor. . . . So it is not poverty itself to compel the poor to resist, rise, revolt, and change. It is his consciousness of poverty which makes him resist poverty—not poverty alone."[13]

The role of the intellectual was to transfer his perception of the world situation and his country's social situation into "the consciousness of our present generation."[14] In the process of increasing the consciousness of the masses, the intellectual had to make use of certain effective means of communication. Since the mullah was successful in communicating with the crowds, the intellectual must know "whether it is the mulla's own words which are so appealing or whether his words constitute a part of a time-honored heritage and value system for whose sake the people gravitate toward the mulla so obediently. If we can explore these values and communicate them to the mass by means of an intimate understandable and familiar language, we will be capable of replacing the mulla and preparing the mass to grant us a position of confidence and credibility in the heart of the society."[15] Statements like these created an impression not only on conservative clerics but also on Khomeini that Shari'ati wanted "Islam minus the religious scholars."[16]

> Shari'ati thought that only enlightened intellectuals and not the traditional ulama could spearhead an Islamic resurgence. "This can be accomplished through scientific research and logical analysis of political, religious, and philosophical ill-motives and class factors which have been at work throughout our history as well as through diagnoses of religious innovations, deviations and negative justifications that have occurred throughout history plus their negative social effect and ominous ideological and practical consequences in the lives of the Muslims."[17]

Shari'ati was convinced that Islam had been reduced by mullahs and others to a "degenerate and narcotizing religion" and had to be replaced by an Islam which would be progressive and dynamic.[18]

The de-Islamicization process through the world currents of secularism and nationalism was penetrating Muslim societies steadily and sometimes imperceptibly. It was this process which intellectuals like Muhammad Iqbal and Ali Shari'ati felt was more dangerous than the frontal assault of leaders like Mustafa Kemal Pasha of Turkey or the two Shahs of Iran. Shari'ati's lectures on politics and religion had a profound impact on young students and intellectuals. A very perceptive observer of the Iranian scene, John Simpson, pointed out: "Soon cassettes of his lectures were being passed around among those younger generation who had an education and a social conscience. . . . it was Shari'ati who fueled their resentment of Iran's dependence on, and cultural subservience to, the West. He enunciated the sense of alienation which so many better-off, young, Western-educated Iranians instinctively felt. He pointed up the contrast between what they had been taught abroad and what they knew to be happening at home."[19]

Shari'ati was totally opposed to those who emphasized the glories of pre-Islamic Persia like the Shah who referred to 2,500 years of monarchy. There were perhaps many other Iranian nationalists who took pride in the pre-Islamic roots of Iranian civilization. All this was anathema to Shari'ati's way of thinking and his firm commitment to Iran's Islamic past. Thus, he admonished: "Some of you may conclude that we Iranians must return to our racial roots. I categorically reject this conclusion. I oppose racism, fascism and reactionary returns. Moreover, Islamic civilization has worked like scissors and has cut us off completely from our pre-Islamic past. . . . Consequently, for us a return to our roots means not a rediscovery of pre-Islamic Iran, but a return to our Islamic, and specifically our Shi'a, roots."[20]

There is no doubt that Ali Shari'ati was a truly remarkable man to pack so much creative brilliance within a life span of forty-four years. One perhaps associates this intellectual power with Iran. Iqbal referred to the elements which came to constitute the Islamic personality: "Iran's beauty of mind and Arabia's inner fire."[21] Shari'ati had obtained his doctorate from the University of Paris. Therefore, he had probably combined the best of what he had garnered from an Iranian and Western education. Shari'ati, who had steeped himself in Islamic thought and history, had little in common with many of the rigid views of the clerics. The clerics had often been dubbed medieval and out of touch with the social and technological forces of the modern age. On the other hand, one could argue that such strong criticisms of clerics were unwarranted. Those of us who have interviewed the clerics have discounted such prejudiced statements because the clerics at

Qum had received a fairly broad education, which included sociology, economics, and modern history.

However, very few observers and students of modern Iran ever expected that a cleric like Khomeini would emerge as a political strategist and create an unparalleled revolution in this century. The Shah with his tremendous resources had created a political and social environment totally hostile not only to the nationalist forces but perhaps much more so to the clerics and other traditional forces. How did Khomeini convert so many inimical occasions into political opportunities? How did he harness the existing forces and then create new forces? First of all, what was truly extraordinary about this man was that he not only exploited the opportunities created for him by the Shah but he had the historical insight and imagination to change the fundamental modes of thinking of the clerics and his own followers. He knew that the Shi'i clergy by aligning themselves with the mercantile and artisan forces of the bazaar had played a historical role in challenging royal governments in 1890 and again during the constitutional revolution of 1905-1907. During 1923-1924, this formidable coalition posed a threat to Reza Shah. Thus, the foundations of a political Islamic movement had already been laid. From the late 1940s, Khomeini became associated with a group of militant clerics whose activities had been described as even terroristic. "The period of 1962 to 1963 witnessed the birth of a movement led by the militant clerics who remained faithful to Khomeini, continued to protest against his detention and exile, and subsequently kept in contact with him."[22]

As he sat brooding over the nature of the daunting challenge that awaited him as a result of certain deliberate policies of the Shah, Khomeini's first concern must have been to change certain traditional modes of thinking of both the ulama and the masses. The Shi'ite masses had been led to believe that they should wait until the Twelfth Imam reappeared and that Islamic teachings dealt mostly with the rituals and principles of piety and not with the social and political affairs of this world. About waiting until the reappearance of the Hidden Imam, Khomeini said: "Some thousand years have passed since he was hidden, and perhaps a hundred thousand more will pass before he reappears. What would become of the Islamic laws during all that time?"[23] As for the social and political content of the teachings of the Qur'an and the Traditions of the Prophet, he argued: "The ratio of Qur'anic verses concerned with the affairs of society to those concerned with ritual worship is greater than a hundred to one."[24]

Perceptive observers have been struck by the high priority that Khomeini gave to preaching. The mojtaheds (Shi'i religious interpreters of the law) would often leave the activity of preaching to the lower ranks. Khomeini, on the other hand, took great pains to train and influence the preachers so that they would carry his message to the common people. It was ironic that the clerics made use of the opportunities that the Shah had provided them by sending into exile preachers like Ali Khamene'i, Montazeri, and several others to outlying provincial towns with the result that they could spread the message to far-flung areas outside Tehran.[25]

What were the principal support organizations of the clergy? There were the mosques, which were located mainly in large cities; and from these mosques massive demonstrations against the Shah emerged in 1978 and 1979. There were also hoseiniyehs (buildings where recitals commemorating the martyrdom of Hussain were held during the month of Moharram). The hoseiniyehs also became forums for prominent clerical and lay preachers to suggest by clear implication that the Shah represented the tyrant Yazid, who killed the venerated and beloved Imam Hussain. However, the main centers of religious education were the madrasehs (seminaries), where it was estimated there were more than 11,000 students, 60 percent of whom were in the city of Qum with another 25 percent enrolled in the madrasehs of Mashhad and Isfahan. The remaining 15 percent were probably distributed among madrasehs in Tabriz, Yazd, Shiraz, Tehran, Zanjan, and other cities. In addition, there were maktabs (primary schools) run by clergy.[26] When Khomeini claimed that there were "more than 150,000 students and scholars of the religious sciences in Iran, he probably included in his figure all the students at the seminaries as well as the primary schools and possibly the clerical instructors as well. One could see the enormous organized network of the people that the clerical leaders could utilize for spreading the message and developing public opinion against the Shah throughout the country.

As we have indicated earlier, Khomeini's task was not only to harness and convert the existing forces in such a way that his political effectiveness would increase, but also to mobilize and maximize some of the new forces being generated by the Shah's policies of rapid industrialization. *The World Development Report,*

1982 reports that the urban population in Iran increased from 34 percent in 1960 to 50 percent in 1980. When the revolution started, it was estimated that about a third of the population of Tehran and about a quarter of other large cities barely subsisted on the outer fringes of urban society. One could see that such people lived in slums, with poverty, malnutrition, and lack of education for their children and crime staring them in the face day after day.

How did Khomeini create a militant coalition consisting of the mostazafin (the disinherited), the middle class including the bazaar, and the intellectuals? The mostazzafin, the bazaar and some members of the middle class could be swept off their feet through religious symbolism. The middle class and the supporters of the ideas of Shari'ati, who were probably skeptical of clerical domination even in the form of the vilayti-i faqih, that is, the political guardianship of the community of believers by the supreme Islamic jurisprudent, were stirred into supporting an Islamic nationalist movement, for example, on the issue of opposing the Shah for granting extraterritorial jurisdiction to the United States over its military personnel in Iran. The fiery denunciation of Khomeini was, "They have reduced the Iranian people to a level lower than that of an American dog. If someone runs over a dog belonging to an American, he will be prosecuted. Even if the Shah himself were to run over a dog belonging to an American, he would be prosecuted. But if an American cook runs over the Shah, the head of state, no one will have the right to interfere with him."[27]

The organization that the clerics had created was such that in a matter of minutes 500 young men distributed 40,000 leaflets in Tehran and Isfahan of Khomeini's declaration on the granting of capitulatory rights to the United States.[28] One of the most important conclusions that emerges from this analysis is one that challenges conventional political science theory. Rapid industrialization leading to rapid urbanization leads to erosion of traditional loyalties, said Karl Deutsch.[29] But in Iran, rapid urbanization in the 1960s and 1970s was accompanied by increased efficacy of the religious factor.[30] Another conclusion is that the clerical militants had created an organization and a capability to meet two different challenges: the challenge of offering a program and an ideology to attract the intelligentsia and at the same time providing leadership and authority to those thousands of individuals who had recently migrated to the urban from the rural areas.[31]

In view of these developments and perhaps with the knowledge of hindsight, one wonders as to how the American government with such enormous intelligence resources at its disposal would make such strategic mistakes in an area as vital as the oil-rich Persian Gulf. One interpretation would be that all administrations, both Republican and Democratic from Kennedy to Carter, seemed to have crafted their strategy in simplistic terms. Because the Soviet Union as a hostile power was determined to destabilize the Middle East and deny to the West continuous access to the enormous oil supplies of the region, all American administrations were in agreement that perhaps the absolute power that the Shah wanted to exercise would promote American strategic interests.

No American leaders pursued this policy as systematically and relentlessly as Nixon and Kissinger during the 1970s. These leaders took the view that no American weaponry, however advanced or sophisticated, should be denied to the Shah. It has been estimated that, compared to the Iranian purchases of military arms and equipment during the nineteen years (1953-1972) of only $1.2 billion, the Iranian government placed orders of $19.5 billion during the seven years following the Nixon visit in 1972. George W. Ball, who had watched these developments both as an official of the State Department and as a consultant of the president, has observed: "Nixon inadvertently encouraged the megalomania that ultimately contributed to the Shah's downfall. Permitting him free access to the whole range of advanced items in our military arsenal was like giving the keys of the world's largest liquor store to a confirmed alcoholic."[32]

In May 1972, when Nixon and Kissinger visited Tehran, it should have been clear to American officials both in Iran and in Washington in what oppressive and unpopular directions the government of Iran was moving under the Shah's leadership. The SAVAK, which had been trained by MOSSAD, the CIA, and the U.S. Agency for International Development, was the central instrument in the execution of thirty-eight Iranians during 1971-1972. Just prior to Nixon's visit, five young Iranians had been executed as terrorists. In spite of such disturbing developments, it seems that neither in the president's briefing paper prepared by the Department of State nor in the actual discussions that took place between the Shah and Nixon and Kissinger did the American leaders impress upon the Shah how grave and dangerous could be the outcome of the policies he was pursuing. On the contrary, those who have seen the internal memoranda of the conversation suggest that Nixon's advice to the Shah was that he should be relentless in the pursuit of the tough policies that he had already embarked upon.

> The United State depended on him and he embodied the Nixon Doctrine. According to one account, Nixon actually said to the Shah, "Protect Me."
>
> Perhaps more unexpected, from the leader of the world's largest democracy, was that Nixon complimented the Shah on the way he ran Iran itself. He apparently urged him to pay no attention to "our liberals' griping" about human rights. Thus, Nixon must have seemed to the Shah to be endorsing SAVAK. Certainly he made no objections to its methods.[33]

According to Gary Sick, who was an aide on Iran to Carter's National Security adviser Brzezinski and who had reviewed the files relating to Nixon's May 1972 visit, when the opposition were being bludgeoned by the SAVAK during the 1970s, "the Shah had reason to believe that a crackdown on opposition elements would be welcome in Washington and that his methods would be regarded with a considerable measure of tolerance."[34]

It was an extraordinary situation that in a vital strategic area like Iran a superpower like the United States would condone repression by their ally, whose principal role was to protect American interests and keep the region stable. The Shah and his government were so insensitive that, on the one hand, they would continuously oppress their people and, on the other, had become oblivious to the enormous hardships their economic policies of rapid industrialization resting on capital intensive industries and gross economic inequalities had created for thousands of Iranians who had flocked to Tehran from the rural areas. Large numbers of this rootless and unhappy proletariat were spending their days building magnificent villas or palaces for the rich, only to spend their miserable nights in slums and shanty towns. These masses were the combustible material that the religious leaders could ignite in no time. The British ambassador, Anthony Parsons, told the Shah that it was not surprising that large numbers of bitter and angry Iranians had turned to their traditional religious leaders.[35]

When all this had become so transparently clear to foreign observers, Prime Minister Hoveyda confided with the court minister Asadollah Alam in February 1977 "that he senses an atmosphere of unease in the country, though he can't tell exactly what's at the root of it."[36] In July 1977, when Pakistani Prime Minister Bhutto was overthrown and the Shah was expecting a military takeover as the likely outcome to the political deadlock in Turkey, the Shah, according to his court minister Asadollah Alam's diary, told Alam: "You should have told the ambassador (U.S.) that this only goes to show how democracy is unsuited to certain countries. I have even heard that the Turks are casting envious glances at our system here in Iran."[37] Such observations were made barely a year prior to the summer of 1978, when it had become abundantly clear that the Shah's regime was fast disintegrating. Here was a clear instance of absolute power blinding its holder absolutely.

Asadollah Alam wrote in his diary: "This country rests on three basic foundations: Shi'ism, the Persian language, and the monarchy."[38] Of these three foundations, monarchy has been eliminated, perhaps for all time to come. As for the other two manifestations of Iranian nationalism, Shi'ism and the Persian language, we would submit that they constitute major elements in the historical process of Iran and Islam. This historical process, as Oswald Spengler, deriving his insights from Goethe, observed is "the thing—becoming and not the thing—become."[39] Many militant or fundamentalist Muslims tend to regard the Sharia or even Islamic history in rigid terms or as a process which was more or less completed during the time of the Prophet. Our submission is that this is an unfolding and developing process. Iranian Shi'ism under the leadership of Khomeini tried to extend and broaden its Iranian base to an international base to bring within its sweep not only the Shi'ites outside Iran but the Sunnis as well. As a result of this extension, Iranian nationalism became closely aligned with the Islamic revolution, and this alignment could be discerned in the struggle that Iran waged against Iraq during the 1980s. But as we shall see in the succeeding chapter, these processes continue to develop and change. The legacy of militant Islam that Khomeini bequeathed to his successors is undergoing gradual but steady transformation into pragmatic Islam. This is the theme of the next chapter.

Both the Islamic revolution in Iran and the role of Khomeini have often been characterized as clear examples of how Islamic fundamentalism has reasserted itself in this century. For such observers, Islamic fundamentalism represents revivalism or a return to the seventh century Islamic model of the Prophet. Thus Fred Halliday writes that the Iranian revolution "rejects ideas of historical progress: Ayatollah Khomeini explicitly proposes a return to an earlier model of social and political practice and a rejection of almost all that the modern world stands for."[40] Even though the constitution of the Islamic Republic of Iran adopted in 1980 contains numerous references to some of the central Islamic values and ideas derived from the Qur'an, yet it also has chapters and clauses relating to the rights of the people and economy and financial affairs. The rights relate to matters like the formation of political parties, social security, free education up to secondary school, housing, and health. There are also references to the role of the public sector and the utilization of science and technology. In the light of these constitutional provisions and later developments and debates in Iran, how can one infer that the Islamic revolution and the regime associated with it is no more than an exercise of Islamic fundamentalism or revivalism? It would be more accurate to describe both the Khomeini regime and the regime that is in power as examples of how political Islam has tried to convert some of the basic Islamic ideas into a socio-political program and a set of public policies. There were also attempts during the Khomeini regime to introduce land reforms. As for criticisms of the Iranian revolutionary regime on questions like land reforms and its limited success in improving the living conditions in Iran, these are discussed in Chapter 7.

4

Pragmatic versus Militant Strategies
in Post-Khomeini Iran

This chapter examines two themes: (1) Can Islamic ideology exist as a set of monolithic political and economic ideals? When it starts functioning in concrete social reality, it is interpreted and applied by Muslims with certain intellectual predispositions and economic interests. In such interpretations and applications, differences and conflicts arise. (2) How reconcilable are these conflicts depends upon political leadership and particularly the capacity of that leadership in coming to grips with the economic and political challenges that a society faces. In meeting such challenges, Iranian leaders seem to be divided into two camps—pragmatists and radicals. Pragmatists are those who would moderate Iran's revolutionary legacy in the strategies they follow. Radicals are those who are so committed to certain Islamic ideals and what they call *Imam Khomeini's line* that they are not prepared to alter the strategies followed during the Khomeini period. They are also motivated by an uncompromising or implacable hostility toward the West. This attitude seems to influence their strategic thinking.

Islamic Ideal of Unity of Thought and Action
versus the Reality of Factionalism

There is not much discussion in Islamic political theory as to why major conflicts or differences represented by certain factions, groups, or even classes arise in a Muslim society. The traditional view has been that Islam provides such clear political guidelines and enjoins the unity of the umma that Muslims, if they remain loyal to the principles of Islam, cannot divide themselves into groups, factions, political interests, or antagonistic classes. Ayatollah Khomeini declared in 1970 that once an

Islamic government was established, most of the differences, controversies or even problems would cease to exist.

> The entire system of government and administration, together with the necessary laws, lies ready for you. If the administration of the country calls for taxes, Islam has made the necessary provision; and if laws are needed, Islam has established them all. There is no need for you, after establishing a government, to sit down and draw up laws, or, like rulers who worship foreigners and are infatuated with the West, run after others to borrow their laws. Everything is ready, and waiting. All that remains is to draw up ministerial programs, and that can be accomplished with the help and cooperation of consultants and advisers who are experts in different fields gathered together in a consultative assembly.[1]

After the Islamic revolution was successful in Iran leading to the establishment of an Islamic government, major conflicts arose even between the clerics over policy matters like the introduction of agrarian reforms. As Hamid Algar points out, "the debates and controversies that have occurred in Iran since the revolution suggest that the transition from shar'i precept to concretely applicable law is not always easy or straightforward."[2] Two influential ayatollahs denounced the Law for the Reassignment and Revival of Land approved in April 1980 by the Revolutionary Council. The principles of confiscating land from large landowners, and particularly the provision that dealt with the confiscation of large areas of cultivated land, were attacked as contrary to the Jafari fiqh and to the consensus of the ulama of both modern and earlier periods. From the government side Ayatollah Bihishti, one of the authors of land legislation, pointed out that "the understanding of Islam held by certain well known fuqaha does not sufficiently accord with the understanding of Islam that is the basis of our revolution."[3]

The idea that Islam and a revolution carried out in the name of Islam can overcome all conflicts and differences also lay behind Khomeini's decision to close the Islamic Republican party and thus abolish the party system in June 1987. According to one observer, the thinking behind this decision was: "The Imam probably regards all parties as divisive arenas for political conflicts. Such conflicts are often based on clashes of personality and small group ambitions. The Imam probably argued that if a Muslim people as large and diverse as the Iran millat can be united in an Islamic movement, they can also run an Islamic State without parties."[4]

A partyless election, which was held in June 1988, resulted in certain clear-cut factions and groups. The hardcore influential or power group consisted of about thirty clerics who constituted the Society of Combatant Ulama or Ulama-e-Mubariz, all dedicated followers of Ayatollah Khomeini. This group had in it three powerful leaders: Hashemi Rafsanjani, speaker of the majlis; Mousavi Ardabili, chief justice; and Ali Khamene'i, president. It was significant that the larger group around the hardcore group was divided into two factions known as Ruhaniyat and Ruhaniyoon. The Ruhaniyat group adopted a conservative line on economic issues whereas the Ruhaniyoon adopted a more progressive line. These groups also fielded, for example, in Tehran, separate lists of candidates in the elections. It was reported that more of the ulama belonging to the Ruhaniyoon group were elected than those on the Ruhanayat list.[5] All this goes to show that the Islamic ideology of even revolutionary Iran could not eliminate factions and groups. Iran had, after all, a developed economy given its oil wealth and the economic and industrial development that had taken place under the Shah. In addition, it had gone through a revolutionary struggle and the regime had tried to introduce certain fundamental social and economic changes. All these processes as a whole were bound to splinter the social and political system into factions and groups.

To demonstrate how ideological politics gives way to pragmatic politics, one may look at two milestones in the history of revolutionary Iran. The first was Khomeini's message to the Haj pilgrims in July 1987, when he called upon the pilgrims to demonstrate against the United States as the center of world arrogance in the House of Pilgrimage itself. "Which house is more suitable than the Ka'ba, the house of security and piety, where all aggression, injustice, exploitation, slavery, degradation, and inhumanity are practically and verbally condemned, and where allegiance to God is reaffirmed and deities and idols are broken? May the memory of the most important and greatest political movement of the Prophet be revived."[6] Nearly 400 pilgrims, mostly Iranians, died in the clashes that took place as a result of the Saudi action against the demonstrators. In November 1988 Rafsanjani admitted that the true unity of the entire Islamic umma was neither possible at the moment nor for quite some time to come. He also pointed out that a single world-view of a single ideology and a single strategy representing a united Muslim world was "quite difficult as we do not want to be idealists."[7] Thus, it had become apparent that Iran could not in the immediate future expect to arouse international Islamic solidarity against American domination of large parts of the Islamic world.

The second milestone was Iranian willingness to accept a cease-fire and terminate the Iran-Iraq war in July 1988. It was reported that Khomeini was persuaded by his close lieutenants that Iran should accept U.N. Resolution 598 and terminate the war because Iran had temporarily failed in achieving its great objectives and that its role as an inspiring exemplar of a just society had been presented by Iran's enemies as the leader of a Shi'ite revolution. They also pointed out that only a revitalized Iran could provide leadership to Muslim movements in Palestine, Egypt, and North Africa.[8]

Pragmatism in the Post-Khomeini Era

In contrast to the predominantly ideological or revolutionary approach that dominated policy making during the Khomeini era, pragmatism as a mode of solving problems became increasingly influential during the post-Khomeini period. William James defined *pragmatism* as the "attitude of looking away from first things, principles, 'categories,' supposed necessities; and of looking towards last things, fruits, consequences, facts."[9] This pragmatic approach to policy making should be familiar to the clerics in Iran, because in addition to their learning in theology, they were closely aligned both through their relatives and through their work with the merchant class. Ali Akbar Hashemi Rafsanjani, who became president on August 17, 1989, was a cleric who had sprung from a business background, with his family engaged in pistachio farming and exporting as a trade. His brother, who is the managing director of the country's largest and most successful pistachio exporting company, has a work force of 30,000. Rafsanjani has also written a biography of Amir Kabir, the great nineteenth century reformist prime minister of Nasreddin Shah. In this biography Rafsanjani expressed his admiration for a man who advocated Western methods of modernization, including industrialization. Rafsanjani wrote: "Amir Kabir felt that an independent country needed educated individuals and experts in modern sciences and skills and competent specialists in contemporary industries."[10]

As president, Rafsanjani was called upon to reconstruct the war-shattered economy of his country. It was extraordinary with what rapidity and clarity he started expounding a Muslim work ethic that was different from the pronouncements of his predecessor, Ayatollah Khomeini. Ayatollah Khomeini tended to extoll the Islam of the barefooted. Rafsanjani in a Friday sermon emphasized that "the Prophet was very insistent to ensure that the feelings should not gain strength among the people to imagine that an Islamic society should be a poor society." He further added, "When one puts on one's work overall and enters a factory or some other work place, one should feel that one is engaged in the act of worship as in the mosque. If one day such a thing becomes prevalent in our society, then we will be Muslims with true Islamic dimensions."[11] Ali Khamene'i, who on June 4, 1989 became the spiritual leader of the Islamic republic following the death of Ayatollah Khomeini, also seems to belong to the pragmatic school of thought. His argument was that the revolution would not be weakened if the government acted "to solve the people's problems, to increase production, to activate mines and industries and to expand agriculture. We want this world and the next world both, ideals and welfare together—this is attainable."[12] For Rafsanjani , the prudent path may lie in temporizing with some of the principles of ideology or revolution. "We do not always have the power to choose. I believe our principles are obeyed, but in some cases we may be limited and we may have to forego some of these principles."[13]

There are certain clear-cut underlying ideas in the pragmatic strategy of Rafsanjani and his supporters. In fact, Rafsanjani's pragmatism has been evolving over a period of time that goes back to the early 1980s, when the Iran-Iraq war was in its early stages. As early as February 1982, a few of Rafsanjani's close followers in the majlis told the author that the war should be ended and that Iran's interrupted Islamic social transformation should be pursued vigorously and systematically. These supporters were also engineers interested in the application of systems analysis to Iran's social problems. In the thinking of the present supporters of Rafsanjani, and particularly some of his influential cabinet ministers, one can identify certain principles and categories of social thinking which are close to ideas associated with the market-oriented economic system, profit or income incentives, and technical expertise as the principal and dynamic instruments of economic development and social change.

In the cabinet of twenty-two ministers that Rafsanjani presented to the parliament on August 19, 1989, were no more than four clerics, including Rafsanjani. The ministers of Information, Interior, and Justice were clerics. If one looks at the wider political structure, one finds that in addition to the speaker of the parliament (Mehdi Karrubi), the head of the Judiciary branch and the chief justice were also clerics. It was also significant that the Economics and Finance minister, Mohsen Nourbakhsh, and the minister of Commerce, Abdol-Hussein Vahaji, were well-known advocates of a market-oriented economic system and the private sector. The ministers of Agriculture, Higher Education, Education, Defense and Armed Forces Logistics, Health, Industries, Heavy Industries, Energy, and Housing and Urban Development were all more or less technocrats with appropriate expertise in their areas. The minister of Foreign Affairs, Ali Akbar Velayati, had the reputation of being a moderate.

Conflict Between Pragmatic and Militant or Radical Strategies

The term strategy has been used mostly in the art of war, where it refers to the planning of movements of troops to achieve certain military objectives. In the art of government, by strategy we mean a plan of action or policy in which economic, bureaucratic, and political resources are mobilized to attain certain well-defined goals.

This chapter has looked at the competing and conflicting strategies of the pragmatists and the militants or radicals in Iran. The central issue engaging the attention of the two competing groups is how to reconstruct the war-ravaged economy and provide more and better consumer goods and services to Iran's war-weary people. Pragmatists are recommending that there should be liberalization of both domestic and foreign policies. Domestic policies should be geared toward offering maximum opportunities to the private sector through profit and income incentives. As for external policies, they advocate improvement of relations with the West through certain tactical moves, like Iran facilitating the release of hostages. Radicals are opposed to such strategies because their contention is that Iran cannot abandon its revolutionary mandate and the guidelines of Imam Khomeini. Above all, they argue that, if the government were to relax its controls over key economic activities, such a policy would create gross economic inequalities leading to the enrichment of the few and the impairment of Islamic moral values. Similarly, any relaxation of Iran's opposition to Western attempts to penetrate the country culturally will bring in eventual de-Islamization of Iran's culture and spirituality as well as economic and political dependence.

To appreciate fully the polarized positions that the pragmatists and radicals have adopted on economic and foreign policy issues, one should have a clear picture of the economic situation that Iran is faced with in the postwar period. Soon after the revolution, the state brought under its control considerable sectors of the economy like ship building, aircraft and automobile industries, the entire banking system, and all insurance firms. In addition, a number of factories belonging to industrialists who had fled the country were nationalized. It seemed that neither the growth of the public sector nor the emphasis that the government placed on an Islamic economic system helped the lower income groups very much. According to the distribution of national income figures released by the government in July 1989, 40 percent of Iranians received an aggregate of about 3 percent of the income; another 40 percent slightly over 22 percent. The remaining 20 percent earned about 75 percent of the national income. If these figures were put together, it appeared that the top 1 percent of the Iranian population had a purchasing capacity 280 times more than the lower 40 percent.[14] The fact that government subsidies on foodstuffs and industrial production amounted to $2-3 billion indicated how the economy benefited the upper income groups and how much protection the lower income groups needed.

When the Five Year Plan was launched in 1990, Iran faced certain crucial decisions. What strategies should be adopted in attaining an average 8 percent real growth in GDP that the Five Year Plan contemplated? Could the government impose any hardships by bringing the highly overvalued exchange rate closer to the free market and thus unleashing inflationary forces and hardships on consumers because of the higher prices of imported goods? Could the government in the name of efficiency bring the living standards down by phasing out the subsidies of $2-3 billion on foodstuffs and industrial production? The government, since launching the plan, may have obtained some breathing apace because of the rise in oil prices as a result of the Gulf crisis. The plan by itself is an uncontentious issue. One of the major radical leaders, Mohtashemi, attacked the Five Year Plan by arguing that the plan was excessively concerned with narrow economics and paid no attention to Iran's revolutionary and Islamic mandate. This was by no means an impressive or coherent alternative to government policy.

Rafsanjani came under more systematic attack when he recommended certain specific measures to reflate the stagnant economy. He had placed certain key officials like Nourbakhsh in the Ministry of Economics, Vahaji in the Ministry of Commerce, and Adeli as governor of the Central Bank, all of whom regarded the private sector as vital for rapid economic growth. The strategy that Rafsanjani put forward was that the key to economic growth lay in providing maximum scope to the private sector; attracting foreign assistance, credit, and investment; lowering the exchange rate; and establishing private banks. Broadly speaking, in the majlis were 50 deputies who could be considered pragmatists, 50 were radicals, with the remaining 170 tending to stay in the middle and could be swung both ways. When in April 1990 it was announced by the radicals that the majlis should introduce the death penalty for those "economic terrorists," who had indulged in black marketeering, hoarding, and profiteering, Rafsanjani dubbed this attitude as narrow-minded thinking. He argued that people who were trying to bring prosperity to the deprived areas with their technical expertise and capital should be encouraged and not condemned.[15] The reaction of the radicals to what they considered the conservative policies of the government was expressed in an editorial of *Kayhan International*.

It is clear what effect this brand of economics will and has had on the whole of society. Obviously it has contributed strongly to the inequality in the distribution of wealth and income and consequently engendered a proportionate increase in the political power of these elements. This has come about in conditions wherein the nation was faced with a war, economic sanctions and the resultant shrinking economy. . . . In the context of these conditions, naturally the poor will become poorer, while the middle classes find themselves increasingly disempowered.

The *Kayhan* editorial went on to say that pursuit of such policies would promote "dependent capitalism" and lead to Iran becoming "a pawn of imperialist interests."[16]

The issue of foreign borrowing also generated considerable opposition from the radical group. According to the forecasts of the Five Year Plan, Iran needed external capital of about $17 billion over a period of five years. Ezatollah Sahabi, a former minister of Planning in the Bazargan government, thought that as much as $70 billion would be needed to meet the foreign exchange needs of the plan. He argued that resources of this magnitude would become available only if the government were to introduce a greater measure of democratization, invite outside entrepreneurs, and facilitate the return of Iranian businessmen and intellectuals living in exile.[17]

The prospect of raising foreign loans aroused hostile reactions and raised questions as to whether borrowing could be justified from a religious point of view. There was also opposition to foreign borrowing because it could bring about the penetration of Iranian society by foreign influence and values. When such questions were raised with an Iranian economist on deputation to one of the international agencies in Washington, we were told that the World Bank or a foreign country could get around the problem of interest by sharing the profit that might arise as a result of the investment of capital. The economist pointed out that a payment of this kind to the investing agency would "not be ex-ante but ex-post." An editorial in *Kayhan International* expressed alarm that, according to the governor of the Central Bank, Muhammad Husseini Adeli, the government of Iran was contemplating raising foreign loans to finance the implementation of certain productive projects. The editorial expressed its concern that Iran had been following certain policies recommended by the IMF and World Bank. "Prerequisites for coming to terms with the two major lending institutions have included curtailing the government role in the economy and increasing the private sector's share therein. In addition to this, the World Bank strategy calls for reducing the balance of payments deficit." The argument was that if the policies urged by these international agencies were followed, the social consequences in terms of curtailment of educational, health, and other expenditures relating to food imports would be detrimental to the living standards of the lower and middle classes.[18] In matters like this, which have a direct bearing on the Islamic ideology of Iran, the government should plan its strategy in such a way that the citizens in general are informed, educated, and persuaded that the government policy is not only in the interest of the country as a whole but also in accordance with its ideological and revolutionary tradition. Unfortunately, in the constant conflicts between the pragmatists in the government and certain radical groups there is not much time for educating and persuading the public. When people having been exhorted to follow a set of principles find that the actions of their rulers are at considerable variance with those principles, their initial confusion soon gives way to cynicism.

In the case of foreign policy, both groups, the pragmatists and the radicals, would subscribe to the slogan, neither East nor West. Nevertheless, one can discern that the two groups have evolved a specific strategy of their own. R. K. Ramazani divides the groups into revolutionary idealists and revolutionary realists. He thinks that their positions vary in terms of the relative weight that they attach to "Iranianness and "Islamicness" in formulating their foreign policy. Their differences also arise from the way they view the existing international system. "The idealists are world revolutionaries who want to establish an Islamic world order *now*, despite the fact that Khomeini has said, 'We hope this will gradually come about.' The realists, on the other hand, who also hope for an Islamic world order, are willing to come to terms with the realities of the existing international system. Hence, unlike the idealists, they are conciliatory in their policy orientation."[19]

We find that Ramazani has used this typology of idealists and realists because he thinks that the two groups have formulated their foreign policy positions in terms of an international system. We should take account of the fact that the two groups view the international system as one based on power and real politik. If one were to view the international order in such perspectives, the terms *idealists* and *realists* are not as helpful as the terms *pragmatists* and *radicals*. Both these groups think that the United States is determined to establish its hegemony over the Middle East and Islamic countries. Even though the two groups agree about the dangers that Iran faces with respect to American hegemonic objectives, they disagree about the means they should adopt to come to grips with this problem.

A clear indication of the differing means that the two groups advocated to counteract American objectives in the Middle East was provided by the hostage issue. The pragmatists wanted to

put an end to the hostage issue and in some instances used
their influence with the Lebanese factions like the Hezbollah and
others in getting two American hostages released in April and
May 1990. In response, President Bush expressed his thanks to
Damascus and Tehran. The radicals felt that the Americans and
others were as determined to dominate the Middle East and in
other instances to penetrate the Middle Eastern and Islamic culture that conciliatory policies, even with regard to the hostages,
should not be adopted. The pragmatists thought that, without
providing help in the matter of the release of hostages, Western
countries were not likely to provide any financial or technical
help for the economic reconstruction of Iran. In fact, the pragmatists tended to use every conciliatory gesture they came across
on the part of Western countries to impress upon the Iranians
that the government should seriously consider normalizing relations with some of these countries. A case in point was the reaction of the *Tehran Times*, which was considered close to the pragmatic wing of the regime, to some of the statements made by
British leaders expressing their great respect for Islam. "This
logical approach appears to have now lifted the obstacles facing
the Islamic Republic Foreign Ministry in restoring diplomatic
ties between the two capitals."[20]

The analysis here of the pragmatic and militant or radical
strategies of Iranian groups or factions suggests that these
groups have evolved mostly sectoral strategies rather than comprehensive or global strategies. For example, we have referred in
some detail to the economic strategy of the pragmatists in which
they emphasize components like the Islamic work ethic, the role
of the private sector, or the usefulness of developing private
banks. The pragmatists have been criticized by the radical group
for neglecting social justice in their economic strategy and thus
creating income inequalities with the consequential hardships for
the lower income groups. This criticism clearly indicates that
the pragmatists have not broadened their economic strategy and
cast it in societal terms. Similarly, the pragmatists criticize the
radicals for viewing foreign policy in such militant terms that
foreign credit and investment are discouraged. This suggests
that these groups should interrelate and even integrate their
sectoral strategies to include the larger societal dimension.

President Rafsanjani has expressed his concern and dissatisfaction that the Iranian society has not yet developed an
Islamic model attractive and workable enough to be emulated

by other societies. "We must build a society that, when looked at from outside, looks capable of delivering to humanity a model for emulation—a free, independent, and prosperous society. If we do so Islam will spread rapidly. If we imagine that with the existing way of working, with the existing level of production, with the existing level of work achieved, with the existing economic dependence, and with the existing multitude of problems afflicting our society we can be a model for other societies, then we are wrong."[21] In his book as well Rafsanjani expressed the hope that Iranians "inspired by the Qur'an and Islam and the fervor of their faith should be able to forge ahead. If we do that, we will have rendered a great service to the world. If we falter and fail, we will be doing grave injustice to human history."[22] These quotations tell us how Iranian leaders conceive of Islamic ideology in terms of a model of ideals. It is only when they start thinking in terms of precisely how these ideals of economy, society, and foreign affairs are interrelated and whether they can be achieved simultaneously or sequentially that the task of constructing an overall strategy will begin.

5

Islamic Opposition and the Stability of the Saudi State

It has often been argued that the West follows the secular tradition under which the state plays an autonomous role more or less independent of religious pressures. In the Islamic tradition, on the other hand, religion plays a pivotal and ideological role. We have seen that even in the case of Ibn Khaldun, who as a historian and sociologist assigned a primary role to asabiya (group solidarity), Islam became the inspiring force for Arabs to restrain or sometimes overcome their asabiya to move toward the Islamic umma. One discerns a similar interplay between the Islamic force of Wahhabism and tribal traditions and practices in Saudi Arabia. Wahhabis had been functioning as a proselytizing sect in central Arabia ever since the beginning of the eighteenth century, and as followers of Muhammad ibn Abd al-Wahhab (1703-1787), they denounced certain customs like veneration of saints as shirk (idolatry). It would not be fair to say that Abd al-Aziz ibn Saud (1881-1953), the founder of modern Saudi Arabia, deliberately organized the support of the Wahhabis in capturing Riyadh in 1902 and establishing his ascendancy over the whole of Nejd in 1921, because he himself was a sincere Wahhabi. He converted the puritanical zeal of the Wahhabis into the semi-military organization of the Ikhwan. Through a skillful combination of strategic matrimonial alliances with powerful tribes and the support of a dominant foreign power like the British, he extended his rule by 1925 over the Hijaz and the Holy Places. He became more and more aware that his political interests were paramount, and to pursue them, he had to keep the ideological or religious zeal of the Ikhwan under control. His first title was imam, which he changed later to sultan in 1921. In 1926 he was proclaimed malik or king of the Hijaz.

Abd al-Aziz entered into treaties with Iraq, Jordan, and Yemen to consolidate and demarcate his territorial power. Such policies sometimes could not contain the Ikhwan who raided Iraq and were subject to British military and aerial attacks. When Abd al-Aziz captured Mecca and Medina, he allowed the Ikhwan to eliminate what they considered as deviances in the form of shirk from the Holy Places. Again, the restraining influence of Abd al-Aziz was such that he removed the most zealous Ikhwan to certain remote areas of the interior. When the Ikhwan rebelled against some of his modern practices and policies involving motor vehicles, aircraft, telephones and telegraph, they were crushed through a military operation in 1929. The British writer, H. St. John Philby, who became a Muslim and his advisor, wrote: "Ibn Sa'ud's creation of the Ikhwan movement in 1912, on original lines of his own devising, was a master stroke of genius: only equalled by his courageous liquidation of the organisation eighteen years later, when it could be nothing but an obstacle to the consolidation of a position which he had built up so patiently and laboriously."[1] In suppressing the Ikhwan, in forging alliances with the West or entering into certain arrangements with the oil companies, the policies of Abd al-Aziz were based on a shrewd and unsentimental assessment of what he considered national advantage and the interests of the Saudi ruling family.

When we refer to the Saudi state, it would not be at all accurate to say that the state was emerging like its counterparts in the West, more or less detached from its religious moorings. Perhaps the Saudi rulers thought that even though they did not always follow the directions or advice of religious groups like the Ikhwan or advisors like the ulama, they were still pursuing certain Islamic interests or objectives as they conceived them to be. Pursuit of the Islamic objectives and the sense of legitimacy later diminished under a Saudi ruler like Fahd in the late 1980s and early 1990s.

During the reign of Abd al-Aziz, Saudi Arabia signed an agreement with the Arabian American Oil Company (ARAMCO) on November 30, 1950 under which profits were to be divided on a 50:50 basis. As a result of this agreement, Saudi oil revenues started increasing so rapidly that they amounted to $409.7 million in 1962 and $909.5 million in 1967. These enormously expanded resources of the Saudi state had to be channeled through the development of new state structures, budgetary systems, and social policies. When King Faisal (1905-1975) took command in November 1964, he introduced a considerable element of rationalization in state structures and administrative procedures, which were hitherto completely under the discretionary powers of the king. Under Faisal, the Council of Ministers emerged as the central decision-making body, with an oil minister like Zaki Yamani providing technical expertise and advice to the council. Similarly, the Central Planning Organization was reorganized to develop priorities for the investment of oil revenues in projects with the overall objective of the economic development of the country. Again, under Faisal an extensive educational program was launched, with education expenditures increasing at a rapid pace and constituting as much as 10 percent of the budget. Elementary schools for girls were set up but, to pacify those religious elements opposed to women's education, they were to function under religious control. Public expenditures were also directed towards the improvement of health facilities, so that during 1970-1975 hospitals, dispensaries and health centers increased at a phenomenal rate.

Rising oil revenues, accompanied by rising public expenditures, clearly indicated that Saudi Arabia was unlike most of the Third World or developing societies. It controlled a resource base like oil which was of vital importance to the United States and other Western countries. Second, it had a government, though a traditional oligarchy, which derived its support through tribal and other political links, from its people. Fred Halliday has pointed out that the dependent relationship which emerged between the United States and Saudi Arabia was vastly different "from that which the US had with its neo-colonial dependencies in Latin America and the Far East. . . . It is mistaken to see Saudi Arabia as just a US colony with the appearance of independence. The wealth of Saudi Arabia and the political character of the ruling family enabled it to forge an alliance with the US in which its ruling class wielded a degree of real power consonant with the preservations of US interests."[2]

Fred Halliday, however, did not seem to attach any weight to the Islamic factor, which made the U.S.-Saudi relationship different from American relationships with other dependencies. One could see that Saudi Arabia, even though a traditional society, occupied a pivotal position in the Middle East. It possessed the two most important sacred Muslim shrines, which enabled it to play the role of one of the most influential Muslim governments. In addition to being Islamic, it was Arab and also an extremely rich society. All these factors gave it certain built-in capabilities to play an important role in the Middle East, and because of its oil resources, it could cast its influence even in global matters. In the area of foreign policy, Faisal could demonstrate his ability to respond effectively to challenges of Arab nationalism under Nasser and also use the oil weapon in defiance of American interests. These policies transformed Saudi Arabia from being just a vast Arab principality with enormous oil resources into a major regional power in the Middle East.

During the 1960s, Arab nationalism under the dynamic leadership of President Nasser had become a militant movement. Arab monarchies like that of Saudi Arabia were denounced as corrupt, decadent, and servile instruments under Western hegemony. Charges of corruption and decadence could have been applied to the kind of chaotic rule that Faisal's predecessor, Ibn Saud, had established during 1953-1964. It was well known that some of the members of the royal family, who were known as "free princes," had come under the influence of Arab nationalism. During the civil war in Yemen between the Royalists and the Egyptian-supported Yemen Arab Republic, Egyptian aircraft bombed Royalist bases and also certain towns of southern Saudi Arabia. Faisal countered this movement of pan-Arabism by establishing a pan-Islamic movement called the Muslim World League. Faisal pointed out that Arabs had played a great role in world history entirely because they had presented to the world the Islamic faith and its civilization. Faisal's real success came only when Nasser's influence started declining as a result of the overwhelming victory of the Israelis against Egyptian forces in the 1967 war. The Yemeni crisis was also resolved with Egypt being unable to finance the war in Yemen and the Egyptians and Saudis agreeing to phase out their financial and economic backing of the rival forces in Yemen.

We have argued in Chapter 1 that Faisal's foreign policies leading to the imposition of an oil embargo soon after the outbreak of the Arab-Israeli War of 1973 were motivated by what he perceived as the desired adherence of Saudi Arabia to certain Islamic principles and Arab interests. By imposing the embargo, Faisal was trying to steer American foreign policy vis-à-vis Israel into less pro-Israeli and more pro-Arab or pro-Palestinian directions. Faisal was by no means highly successful in such a policy, but on the whole it has been conceded that his policy of an oil embargo did produce a "more pro-Arab stance in Europe, Japan and Africa and a shift of the U.S.A. from its usual pro-Israel policy to a more neutral position."[3]

These adjustments in Western policy toward Israel that had been induced by the Saudi oil embargo in 1973 did not amount to a sea change. In fact, after the Iranian revolution in 1979 one could see a hardening in Western determination to control the Middle East and particularly Saudi Arabia to ensure an uninterrupted supply of oil from the region. Since 1973, the American economy has become weaker and dependent on Germany and Japan, two of the main countries that have been investing funds in a debt-ridden American economy. The economic prosperity of Germany and Japan has become increasingly dependent on Middle Eastern oil. In addition, there are other factors, like the unwillingness of the American public to exercise self-discipline in the consumption of oil. This again suggests that the United States cannot relax its controls on the oil valves of Saudi Arabia. The United States simply cannot afford to let the pliant Saudi regime be overthrown the way the Shah's regime was overthrown by the Islamic radicals. It is noteworthy that ever since the days of Faisal, Saudi Arabia has had no leader who made any effort to assert Saudi independence and defy American domination.

Many observers of Middle Eastern societies seem to think that Islam plays a more or less static role in the social and political development of a Muslim society. Even some of the conservative Islamic thinkers are aware that their societies are being changed by foreign influences of science, technology, education and also by the cultural influence of dominant Western countries. These influences pose certain challenges, and even in a conservative society like Saudi Arabia, there tend to be varying responses. There are those traditional Islamic thinkers who subscribe to the view that the Qur'an has dealt with every conceivable social and scientific question and human societies have nothing new to add. Obviously there are others, even among conservative thinkers, who think that the Qur'anic values and principles are sufficiently flexible to be reinterpreted and applied to problems of modern times. Faisal was probably close to such thinkers.

Sheikh Abd al-Aziz ibn Baz, who currently heads the Supreme Religious Council of Saudi Arabia and has been the principal religious advisor of Saudi kings, thought that many Saudi universities had been intellectually infiltrated by heresies and one of them referred to the theory of the solar system. In an essay published by two newspapers, he took issue with the theory of the rotation of the earth around a fixed sun. "Hence I say the Holy Koran, the Prophet's teaching, the majority of Islamic scientists and the actual fact all prove that the sun is running in its orbit, as Almighty ordained, and that the earth is fixed and stable, spread out by God for his mankind and made a bed and a cradle for them, fixed down firmly by mountains lest it shake." Those who disagreed with this view could be accused of "falsehood towards God, the Koran and the Prophet."[4] Faisal, being concerned about the impact such views would have both home and abroad, was reported to have given instructions that all undistributed copies of the newspapers carrying these views should be destroyed.

Faisal was probably one of the most religious sons of his father, having been influenced by his maternal grandfather who was a direct descendant of the well-known Abd al-Wahhab, the initiator of the Wahhabi school, which became the official Islamic creed of the Saudi kingdom. Faisal's view on Islam was that the Sharia system was so comprehensive in its scope that it could absorb science and technology as well as social ideas of justice, freedom, and human development.[5] As already referred to, Saudi Arabia achieved rapid progress in matters of education and health under Faisal. These reforms and the fact that he pioneered the establishment of schools for girls must have alienated a number of ulama. During our visits to Saudi Arabia, some of the school teachers and preachers who were orthodox bemoaned some of the modernist tendencies in Saudi Arabia, which they thought were initiated by Faisal. These trends led some scholars to believe "that the influence of the ulama declined considerably under the rule of King Faisal."[6]

Faisal apparently believed that the process of modernization could be brought under Islamic influence. Here he disagreed both with the traditional ulama, who thought that science and technology had nothing to teach the Muslim world, as well as those Muslim secular liberals who subscribed to the view that Islam, apart from its rituals and prayers, had to make a retreat before the onward march of global modernization.

One of the outcomes of Faisal's conflict with Nasser was that Faisal encouraged a number of intellectuals and party workers, who were supporters of the Ikhwan al-Muslimun in Egypt and had been persecuted by Nasser, to seek refuge in Saudi Arabia. We noticed in visits to Saudi Arabia in 1983, 1985, and

1987 that some of the highly placed university officials in Mecca and Riyadh were former Egyptian members of the Ikhwan al-Muslimun. For example, the dean of the faculty of Sharia in Umm al-Qura University was al-Sheikh al-Sayyid Sabiq, a well-known author of a book on Islamic fiqh. Muhammad Qutb, the brother of the famous Egyptian leader and intellectual of the Ikhwan in Egypt, Sayyid Qutb, was teaching in Sharia College of Umm al-Qura University. Similarly, at the Islamic University of Imam Muhammad bin Saud in Riyadh and the Islamic University in Medina a number of senior positions were held by former members of the Ikhwan al-Muslimun. Several of these academics and university officials told us what a great and farsighted Muslim ruler Faisal had been and how they owed their appointments to his influence and the policies he had initiated in Saudi Arabia. The cumulative result of such appointments was that there emerged in Saudi Arabia a number of imams of mosques, schoolteachers, and religious activists who tried to increase the religious consciousness of the people at large as well as members of the lower income groups in several walks of life. This Islamic consciousness contributed to the general air of dissatisfaction bordering on hostility that existed among many circles in Saudi Arabia. The Saudi state claimed to be an Islamic state that enforced the Sharia and was influenced by the strict and spartan norms prescribed by the Wahhabis. In the eyes of Islamic groups there was a growing gap of contradiction between professions of loyalty to the Sharia and the actual practice as reflected in the consumption-oriented society at large and the corruption and ostentatious display of wealth and luxury at the top by the Saudi ruling family.

Against this state of affairs, Juhaiman ibn Muhammad Utaibi, the leader of the rebels who captured the Grand Mosque in Mecca on November 20, 1979, thundered. "Those who lead the Muslims with differing laws and systems and who only take from religion what suits them have no claim on our obedience and their mandate to rule is nil." As regards his former teacher, Sheikh Abd al-Aziz ibn Baz, his comment was, "Ibn Baz may know his Sunna well enough but he uses it to bolster corrupt rulers."[7]

The kind of intellectual and Islamic climate that Faisal's appointees in universities and theological colleges had created was not confined to extreme radicals like Juhaiman. It was reported that a number of students arrested in 1978 and 1979, when the unrest leading to the capture of the mosque was brewing, were students who had imbibed radical ideas at the theology schools in Mecca and Medina. It was perhaps more disturbing to the ruling circles that opposition to the regime had also infected those students in universities who were enrolled in disciplines like arts and sciences. The graffiti that could be seen in the toilets of King Saud University in spring 1981 read: "Juhaiman, our martyr, why didn't you storm the palaces? The struggle is only beginning."[8]

Middle Class Groups (Liberals and Muslim Radicals) and the Westernization Process

Western modernization theory, particularly its American version, has assumed that eventually the whole world is likely to be transformed into an industrialized, urbanized, consumption-oriented culture. Such changes will come about much more rapidly in a resource-rich country like Saudi Arabia. The middle class will be the main agent of change in this process of modernization. It is apparent that Saudi Arabia has been undergoing phenomenal urbanization as well as economic, educational, and technological development. The Saudi urban population starting at 30 percent of the total population in 1960 jumped to 77 percent in 1990 and was expected to reach 82 percent in the year 2000. Saudi Arabia spent $776 billion over the course of four Five Year plans; that is, during 1970-1990 or $65,000 for each of its 12 million citizens. In the Fifth Development Plan, which began in August 1990, another $200 billion would be spent. In the area of transport and communication, up to 1990 the mileage of roads expanded from 4,800 to 22,000. Telephone lines increased from 77,000 to 1.4 million. In education, the number of students (school and university) expanded from 545,000 in 1970 to 2.8 million in 1990. There were 23,000 teachers in 1970, and in 1990 the figure had gone up to 185,000. Altogether 8,631 primary schools, that is, more than one a day for twenty years (1970-1990), plus 2,947 intermediate and 1,206 secondary schools were opened. In 1970 the number of factories was 199 with 14,000 employees, which increased to 2,193 in 1990 with an employment of 145,000. The only problem was that so far as industrial development was concerned it depended upon 3 million foreign workers.[9]

In most societies, such rapid economic and social changes may produce cataclysmic consequences. Social scientists like

Karl Deutsch have pointed out that individuals in a traditional society, when faced with changes of urbanization and economic development, tend to give up their traditional or tribal loyalties in favor of new loyalties to either urban or political groupings. An Islamic society may not be such a fragile traditional society. Many Islamic groups, some conservative and others who may have a modernist outlook, do not view Islam as altogether dysfunctional to the new economic system that emerges in the urban areas. Muslim groups have argued that certain Islamic ideas of social justice are still relevant to the resolution of modern problems. Saudi society with its influential Islamic elements and enormous economic resources to cushion disruptive social changes was not likely to surrender entirely to the Westernization process. We have argued earlier that secular liberal groups in Saudi society were not strong enough to provide leadership to the modernization process. On the other hand, economic development and exposure to modern education had not only created a small, secular liberal class but also much larger groups of Muslim students and professors, both from religious and nonreligious universities in Riyadh, Mecca, and Medina, who were opposed to the Westernization process launched by the ruling Saudi family. The war against Iraq in 1991 and the presence of thousands of American troops in Saudi Arabia made them even more determined opponents of the West and its growing influence in their country. A moderate Ialamic scholar like Ahmad Tweijri, former dean of the faculty of Education at King Saud University, was of the opinion that considerable numbers of the Saudi people resented what they considered the cultural contamination from the West and therefore were likely to be swayed by those religious leaders opposed to contact with the West at all costs.

A powerful spokesman of this Muslim radical group was Safar al-Hawali, dean of Islamic studies at Umm al-Qura Univeraity in Mecca.[10] The following are a few extracts of his denunciation of the Saudi policy to seek American help in the Gulf War:

What is happening to us is because of our sins—women in beaches and markets in improper dresses.

We did not give the power to the Mutawwa [religious police.]

In our prayers, we ask for God's help and when we are in trouble, we ask the West for help.

If Iraq strengthens its grip on Kuwait, the West will strength its grip on us.

This crisis will last a long time. The crisis is not isolated. It is related to our being close to Allah or not.

Our hearts are bound to the West and not bound to God.

The West is our enemy from now until the day of judgment.[11]

Safar al-Hawali, as the dean of Islamic Studies, is close to students and preachers produced by religious colleges and universities. His entire mode of thinking is cast almost completely in an Islamic or Qur'anic mode. There are others whose exposure to Western social sciences has been much greater. Therefore, they have worked out their opposition to the Westernization process in a more systematic way. Thus, a book by Muhammad Ahmad Mufti and Sami Saleh al-Wakil, *Creating the Laws of Sharia in an Islamic State*, laments the fact that the rulers and the fragile polities of Muslim societies have allowed Western penetration of Islamic thinking to such an extent that not much of the Islamic identity will remain.

Dominant Western countries have made sure that Islamic laws are not introduced and they have done this by imposing their power on our regimes and by creating doubts in Muslim societies as regards the ability of Islamic laws to cope with changing circumstances. Writers like Ali Abd al-Razzaq have claimed that Islam confines itself to the realm of the spirit and has nothing to do with the political and economic development of the country. Under this massive Western influence, certain new secular trends have emerged. Under the notion that the Sharia is flexible, new movements of thinking have started suggesting that Islam and socialism, Islam and capitalism and Islam and democracy can also be integrated. The outcome is that Western culture has so captured our thinking process that laws which are contradictory to Islam are being presented as those consistent with Islamic thinking.

Our Sharia contains everything for the economic and social development of the country. Through ijtihad and through the rights of the Imam to adapt the laws, the

Islamic legal system will be able to deal with what is new in every society. It is not acceptable to adopt Western laws because their origins and goals are different. Western laws lead to the domination of Muslim countries by Western regimes and Western ideologies.[12]

The Gulf War (June 16-February 27, 1991) weakened the position of the royal family. Even though the government through massive propaganda was probably successful in persuading large numbers of Saudis that Saddam Hussein's occupation of Kuwait represented an immediate threat to the security of Saudi Arabia, two significant questions must have occurred with gnawing frequency to an average Saudi. How could the regime collaborate with the West and particularly with Americans in killing thousands of fellow Arabs and Muslims in Iraq, and what would this collaboration do to its traditional sources of legitimacy? There were reports that the speedy involvement of the Saudi government in the war against Iraq had aroused public discussions. Apparently many Saudis were disturbed by the consequences of the war in terms of increasing Saudi dependence on the United States. Some of the main points that emerged from these discussions were as follows: "The Americans should never have been invited here. We've become an occupied country." This drew the response, "Would you prefer to have been occupied by Saddam Hussein?" "Why was that our only choice?" asked the first Saudi. "What happened to the billions and billions we spent on defense?"[13]

The two petitions that were presented to the king in 1991 reflected the public concerns and criticisms that the country was dragged into the war against Iraq without prior consultation and consideration of all the related issues. The first petition was signed by forty-three intellectuals in February 1991 and the second by conservatives and some radical fundamentalists in May 1991. The liberal petition asked for the creation of a Consultative Assembly, which could be either a group of advisors or parliamentarians. The petition also demanded equality before the law of all citizens regardless of race, tribe, social status, or gender. As for the rights of women, the petition argued: "Notwithstanding our belief that caring for the new generation is the most sacred duty of the Muslim woman, we believe that there are various scopes for her participation in social activities within the limits of the Sharia." As for the interpretation of the Islamic law, the liberal petition pointed out. "It is influenced also by the times and surroundings. In other words, they [interpretations of Islamic law] are likely to be either flawless or erroneous and subject to lengthy discussions. This is why the scholars unanimously agree that no one, no matter how high his status is, can monopolize the explanation of the true meaning of the words of Allah and His Messenger nor can he impose his religious views as binding on the whole ummah."[14]

The petition submitted by fundamentalists and radicals in May 1991 was signed by about a hundred clerics and intellectuals. Among the signatories was Sheikh Abd al-Aziz ibn Baz, head of the Supreme Religious Council of Saudi Arabia and one of the most important advisers to the king on religious matters. The petition was also signed by Dr. Safar al-Hawali, dean of Islamic studies at Umm al-Qura University in Mecca, who has been quoted earlier. This petition was openly critical of the way the royal family was dispensing justice and dealing with economic matters and turned out to be much more influential than the liberal petition. Some of the university professors who signed this petition were from religious universities like the Islamic University of Imam Muhammad bin Saud and the Islamic University in Medina as well as professors of subjects like English and nuclear engineering from King Saud University. It was reported that another petition had been drafted by 200 university teachers (60 from King Saud University and 140 from the Islamic University of Imam Muhammad bin Saud).[15]

Some of the pointed demands of the petition submitted in May 1991 by radical fundamentalists were as follows:

Granting justice and equality to all members of the society to enjoy their full rights and perform their duties, without any favoritism to the elite or prejudice against the weak.

Using one's sphere of influence, no matter what or where, to evade performing one's duty or violate the rights of others, leads to the fragmentation and destruction of society, which the Prophet, peace and blessings of Allah be upon him, warned against.

Establishing justice in distributing the public wealth among all classes of society. Taxes must be abolished and government fees must be decreased as they have overburdened the people. The financial holdings of the state must be safeguarded against waste and exploitation, and to give priority to the dire needs of the country. . . . All forms of monopoly and illegitimate ownership must be removed. The ban on Islamic banks must be lifted, and all the public and private financial institutions must be cleansed of usury (interest), which is an assault against Allah and His Messenger and a reason for the disappearance of Allah's bounties and blessings.[16]

We have characterized the fundamentalists who formulated the petition as radical fundamentalists because the term fundamentalist is often used for certain Islamic groups who tend to hark back to the seventh century puritanical or idealiatic Islam of the Medina society. The fundamentalists whose thinking was represented in the petition were not merely thinking of the Islam of the seventh century. There seemed to be a conscious attempt to interpret or view certain Islamic values in such a way that they would become relevant to the concerns of modern Saudi Arabian society. This is confirmed by an analysis of the petition. Radical fundamentalists who formulated the letter seemed to think that Islamic values recommended that a Muslim society should be established on the principles of social justice and equitable distribution of wealth and taxation. They were also suggesting that certain forms of monopoly and legitimate ownership, which had crept into the corrupt society that had emerged under the Saudi ruling family, were inconsistent with Islamic principles and the Sharia. Similarly, they were demanding that the Saudi government should not place any obstacles against the establishment of Islamic banks and the abolition of interest. Another important element in the petition consisted of the constituency concerns of the radical fundamentalists. Specific references to taxes and government fees which overburdened the people indicated that they were trying to voice certain specific grievances of their constituents, who belonged to middle and lower income groups. Their strong opposition to the favoritism of elites and certain forms of monopolies and illegitimate ownership was clearly directed against certain princes of the royal family, who were using their privileged positions to amass wealth through corrupt or unfair means.

When the king responded to these demands, one could see how concerned he was that the radical fundamentalists were making serious inroads into what he probably considered the traditional constituency that supported the monarchy. It has been reported that the London-based Arabic newspaper *Al-Quds al-Arabi*, on August 1, 1991, published an explanatory memorandum which had been prepared at the request of Sheikh Abd al-Aziz ibn Baz.[17] Our interpretation of this development is that Abd al-Aziz ibn Baz was probably trying to get the fundamentalists to state their grievances in such a manner that the king could respond specifically to their concerns. Thus, in response to the complaints in the memorandum that driving and car licenses and certain charges relating to annual automobile inspections imposed undue burdens on the average individual, the king announced his decision of drastic reductions in fees for driving and car licenses and also made a concession that the inspection of vehicles would be carried out only every three years.[18]

In the concessions that the king was announcing, one could discern that such decisions would adversely affect the interests of a member of the ruling family who operated a company with monopoly rights over automobile inspections. It was also reported that in the explanatory memorandum specific reference was made to the monopoly rights in the area of international courier traffic that Prince Saud bin Naif exercised.[19] It seemed that instances of corruption involving other princes had become known to the public. Prince Muhammad bin Naif was given an exclusive right to import gas masks during the war against Iraq. It was also well known that a few of the senior princes holding highly important cabinet posts were recipients of commissions from foreign firms. Defense contracts were some of the principal sources of corruption. Even a brother-in-law of the king was often mentioned as one who enjoyed monopolistic profits through his ownership of a television company.[20] The public was outraged by the fact that, even though all the princes were being given rich stipends, some of them would resort to these practices to increase their already inflated incomes.

Some of the princes and liberal circles both in the bureaucracy and in the universities were unhappy about the concessions that the king had made to the radical groups. The king, however, was in a better position to realize how serious the situation had become in the sense that the radicals were winning support among low and medium income groups with an Islamic orientation who were supposed to be supporters of the government and therefore represented the king's constituency. In addition, the propaganda of the radical groups had penetrated another constituency of the king; namely, the armed forces. One of the petitions of the radical groups had urged the king to create a "modern, strong and independent Islamic army on the pattern of the prophet's armies."[21] Such a call would obviously create seeds of dissatisfaction among the ranks.

The king must have been aware of the general climate of discontent with future ominous overtones when he devised his adroit strategy of making specific concessions to the Islamic radicals and introducing gradualist reforms to create support throughout the country. Prince Abdallah bin Faisal bin Turki, former secretary-general of the Royal Commission for Jubail and Yunbu, pointed out to his liberal and foreign friends that the king had followed a prudent policy. If the king had adopted a tougher line against the Islamic radicals, such a course of action might have spelled disaster for the country.

How does one place these protests that Muslim groups launched against the Saudi regime in their broader and historical perspective? It seems that the protests represented at a deeper level an Islamic crisis or a turning point. From the very inception of the Saudi regime until the seizure of the mosque by Juhaiman in 1979, it looked as if Islam in its traditional, fundamentalist form was trying to shape the nature of the Saudi regime. Juhaiman and even Safar al-Hawali, who raised his criticisms after the Gulf crisis, seemed to express the idea that both Muslims and the regime had moved away from the strict Islamic path. Their argument was that instead of following the path of God, the regime was following the Western path and certain selfish strategies to preserve itself in power. The educated radical groups, on the other hand, were suggesting that it would not be enough to view the crisis only in terms of the Saudi regime not following the Islamic path and surrendering their Islamic sovereignty to foreigners. The educated Islamic radicals were groping toward something more positive. They were trying to define what the Islamic path was and not merely concerned with how the regime had not adhered to the traditional Islamic path. The arguments of the educated radicals were couched not only in negative terms, that is, they were not only against certain forms of injustice and corruption and the monopolistic hold of the economy by the princes, but were trying to define Islamic ideology in positive terms of social justice and an Islamic form of government. Glimmerings of this ideology can be seen in *Creating the Laws of Sharia in an Islamic State*, by Ahmad Mufti and

Saleh al-Wakil. Our interviews with some of the intellectuals in King Saud University also demonstrate the kind of thinking on an Islamic economy and Islamic polity that has been taking place in Saudi Arabia.

In interviews with Saudi economists and civil servants during January-February 1985, we were repeatedly reminded that many institutions and policies pursued in Saudi Arabia were very similar to those in the West. Therefore, the question arose, what was uniquely Islamic about these policies and institutions? A professor of economics at King Saud University raised the following questions:

> If the government of Saudi Arabia intervenes to enforce minimum wages for labor and maintains prices of essential commodities at certain levels, this intervention is being exercised in other countries as well. What is uniquely Islamic about it? They have developed some welfare institutions to follow the principle of zakat. This is Islamic. The general organization for social insurance operates under the Social Insurance Act in Saudi Arabia and covers two types of risks—employment risk and social contingencies. This is very much like the Social Security system in the U.S. What is Islamic about it? Rate of interest exists, commercial banking on Western lines exists. How can these be Islamic? The Saudi Arabian Monetary Authority (SAMA) regulates banks and also regulates interest. They maintain reserves in Western countries in the form of U.S. treasury bills which yield interest. This is not Islamic. The structure of the economic system is not competitive. Monopolies have been created in the import of goods.

Another professor of economics at King Saud University in Riyadh developed the following ideas in an interview:

> Western economic theory is predicated upon the rationality of the individual. It is difficult to assume rationality which is the basis of consumption theory. Islam, on the other hand, teaches us what is right and what is wrong. Certain goods are prohibited. Excessive consumption is condemned. Miserliness is also condemned. Ownership is derived from Allah. Some ownership is private and some public. Water, forests and minerals are in the public domain. We follow a

free market system. This is consistent with Islam. But we also have zakat and social security and public housing. Roads, education, health are all in the public sector. These activities of ours are not completely consistent with the capitalist system. In Islam, monopoly is forbidden. There has to be just redistribution of wealth. The spoils of war have to be divided—20 percent for Allah and for the Messenger and for the orphans and for the needy (Qur'an, Sura 8, verse 41). As regards prices, the Prophet was against controlling them when there was drought because such control would create more scarcity. But this does not mean that the state should not intervene if intervention would help the community.

In another interview with an official in the Ministry of Planning, we were told that because the Prophet was against price controls, therefore price controls were against an Islamic system. He was justifying a totally free enterprise system because the Prophet had spoken against price controls. These interviews and some of the books that radical Islamic intellectuals have produced suggest that they are moving in the direction of formulating Islamic ideas which may help the Saudis to develop a coherent social and economic program. In other words, the traditional fundamentalist approach that we have come across among people like Juhaiman and Safar al-Hawali cannot provide satisfactory solutions to many of the modern political and social problems that Saudi society is facing.

In contrast to some of the systematic thinking that radical intellectuals are engaged in, we find mostly rhetoric on the part of some of the influential princes in the Saudi royal family. An example of this kind of rhetoric may be seen in some of the pronouncements of the Saudi ambassador to the United States, Bandar bin Sultan. It is significant that some of these pronouncements are to be found in speeches that the ambassador made to persuade and impress American audiences. A few extracts will illustrate this point:

The Holy Koran is our constitution and the Sharia our main body of law . . .

Thus, His Majesty King Fahd is concerned with not just development—but development for a higher purpose and with ethical and human meaning . . .

Our legitimacy is valid so long as we work within
Islamic parameters . . .

The frequent Western view that material development
is dissolving long-accumulated, deeper identities is shallow
and self-deceiving.[22]

The first contradiction one notices in these statements is
that the ambassador claims that the Qur'an is the constitution of
Saudi Arabia and in the next statement addresses Fahd as His
Majesty King Fahd. According to one account, King Fahd's father
asked the Saudis not to address him as King or His Majesty as
there was only one sovereign and that was Allah.[23] Any observer
of Saudi Arabia would also be struck by the glaring contradictions that exist between the assertions of the ambassador that
development in Saudi Arabia should be viewed not just in terms
of material development but in terms of the Islamic ethical and
spiritual development and the profligate living styles of the Saudi
ruling family. The Qur'an enjoins simple living for the rulers and
redistribution of wealth not only among Muslims in one's own
country but throughout the Muslim community in the world.
The living styles of Saudi princes and the enormous control they
exercise over the country's almost inexhaustible resources stand
in sharp and cruel contrast to the misery that exists in neighboring countries like Somalia, Sudan, or in large parts of the
Middle East and Asia. Because Islam recommends redistribution of wealth and frowns on concentration of wealth in the
hands of the rich, how would King Fahd defend his estimated
wealth of $18 billion dollars built on a fee levied on every barrel of
oil extracted in Saudi Arabia before 1980?[24] *Fortune* magazine
refers to the king's gambling losses on the Riviera, incurred when
he was a prince, his palaces in London and on the French Riviera, and his $24 million Little Versailles overlooking Lake
Geneva. The same article mentions his yacht, the largest in the
world, with a 100-seat theater, a mosque, bullet-proof portholes,
antiaircraft guns, and accommodation for sixty guests.[25]

The concepts of property and wealth differ, particularly in
their public dimension, between Western and Islamic societies. In
Islam, property and wealth ultimately belong to God and are
held in trust by individuals or public authorities. From this perspective, the enormous oil wealth that King Fahd and his brother
princes are using both for public and private purposes is not
being utilized strictly from an Islamic point of view. The author

was reminded by a senior scholar of Sharia in Umm al-Qura University that the oil wealth that was in Saudi Arabia was a gift of God not just for the Saudi Arabs but for Arabs and Muslims all over the world.

The corrupt practices that have surfaced in Saudi Arabia under King Fahd are improper not only from certain ideal standards of Islamic conduct but are improper if we compare Fahd's administration with that of King Faisal or that of King Abd al-Aziz. Therefore, in view of such flagrant deficiencies, the sense of legitimacy in the eyes of the public of the present regime has undergone considerable erosion. This problem of legitimacy has been further compounded by the intrusion of American forces in Saudi Arabia, which both Saudi Arabs and Muslims across the world regard as holy and sacred. When, during public discussions, some Saudis raised the question as to how Saudi Arabia could have been defended from the impending threat of Iraqi aggression, other Saudis countered by pointing out that billions of dollars had been spent for the purchase of American-made weapons for the defense of the country.[26] This again brought to question the legitimacy of the regime because it had spent enormous sums of money on the country's defense without preparing it adequately for aggression from a country like Iraq.

Lord Acton said, "Power tends to corrupt and absolute power corrupts absolutely." We have seen in Iran that absolute power and enormous wealth brought the Shah's regime to a precipitous end. Iran and Saudi Arabia were the two main pillars of Western strategy. The Iranian pillar fell in November 1979 even though it had been bolstered by American support. One of our central questions is, Does the Saudi ruling family think that it will not share the fate that befell Iran?

The house of Saud can seek considerable comfort from the thought that its regime is quite different from the Iranian Shi'ite political system. In the latter, the clerics enjoyed enormous autonomous power because of their influence over considerable sections of the urban population like the bazaaris and the respect and prestige that they enjoyed among the Iranian population as a whole as authoritative transmitters of the Shi'ite theology. The ulama in Saudi Arabia do not enjoy the same kind of prestige because they are not autonomous and their role has been coopted by the regime. The Saudi state was established as a collaboration between the Saudi family and the Ikhwan. We have seen how King Abd al-Aziz in 1930 replaced this alliance with the absolute authority of the king with the influence of the Ikhwan being suppressed. The modern Saudi state controls the religious establishment through its network of religious patronage exercised by the Ministry of Pilgrimage and Religious Trusts. According to an announcement of the ministry, as many as 54,000 religious personnel were employed by the ministry in the country's mosques. In 1992, the ministry was planning to put 7,300 imams and muezzins (callers to prayer) on its payroll.[27]

U.S. Support for the Saudi Regime

Skillful and capable as the Saudi regime is in manipulating the internal variables, the Islamic factor, as we have seen throughout this chapter, can be both unpredictable and explosive. There have been sources of unrest in the form of Juhaiman's capture of the mosque in 1979 and periodic Shi'ite unrest in the eastern region. But a persistent factor is the smoldering nature of the dissatisfaction bordering on hostility that exists among the Islamic radicals. We have seen glimpses of these in the petitions to the king and his attempts to appease the radicals. It is not these manipulative and conflict management techniques that give a feeling of overweaning confidence to the regime in its capacity to stay in power for a long and indefinite period. A major source of this confidence is the American support for the regime. Caspar Weinberger, former secretary of defense, pinpointed the rationale for this American support. "The umbilical cord of the industrialized free world runs through the Strait of Hormuz into the Arabian Gulf and the nations which surround it."[28] President Reagan during his election campaign in 1980 used to attack his predecessor, Carter, for having allowed the Shah's regime to be overthrown by the hostile Islamic fundamentalists. As for the second pillar of strategy, he assured the Saudis that the administration under his leadership would never allow anything similar to happen in Saudi Arabia. In May 1980, he put forward the idea that the United States with its allies in Western Europe and Japan should signal a clear warning to the Soviet Union that the West "will not tolerate the overthrow of the Saudi Arabian government either by internal uprising or external aggression."[29]

A simple analysis of the Saudi traditional system would reveal that stability is maintained through "balancing competing forces, by paying off and playing off rivals, by rewarding friends generously and bribing enemies, also generously."[30] How has the Saudi government translated its traditional shrewdness into an elaborate and sophisticated modus operandi for pursuing its objectives in the complex American system with its constitutional system of separation of powers resting on an elaborate network of competing pressure groups? Probably no other embassy can equal the Saudi resources in hiring teams of lobbyists and advisors to help them understand and unravel the American political system. But to this detailed knowledge the Saudi leaders, and particularly the Saudi ambassador, Bandar bin Sultan, have brought their native shrewdness. Bandar bin Sultan became quite aware of the American needs. He knew that, even if the Saudis were to satisfy some of these needs, they would not be able to extract favors from the American system if they did not display an acute awareness of certain American constraints.

Under Reagan, because of his tendency to interfere excessively in Latin American affairs, the Congress often opposed the administration's attempts to extend military and economic aid to the Contras (an alliance of forces organized against the Sandinistas in Nicaragua). The State Department could get the kind of assistance from the Saudis that was denied it by the Congress. Bandar had also built his contacts with the CIA under Casey as well as with certain members like Robert C. McFarlane of the National Security Council. During the summer of 1984, when the Congress was not likely to grant immediate assistance to the Contras, Bandar persuaded his government to contribute $8-10 million to the Contras at the rate of $1 million a month. These transactions were completed at a time when Saudi Arabia was facing threats from Iran to its oil shipping in the Persian Gulf. The Saudi decision to provide help to the Contras was reciprocated by President Reagan writing a letter to King Fahd assuring him of American support in any confrontation with Iran. Similarly, the president used certain emergency procedures to bypass the congressional opposition to the sale of several hundred advanced antiaircraft Stinger missiles to Saudi Arabia.[31]

The American Israel Public Affairs Committee (AIPAC) was one of the most powerful pressure groups in the U.S. Congress. It was well known that no administration would like to provoke the hostility of AIPAC by pursuing any policies that could be interpreted as pro-Arab or pro-Palestinian. Bandar had been instructed by Fahd not to get entangled in the "rancor of the Arab-Israel dispute." Bandar, while promoting the sale of F-15s to Saudi Arabia, was reported to have told the Jewish lobbyists, "You want to talk about the Palestinians, you want to talk about the Middle East? I have nothing to do with that, I am a fighter pilot. I am telling you why we need this (F-15 sale) operationally, full stop."[32] Douglas Bloomfield, a former lobbyist for AIPAC, commented on Bandar's role as follows: "But I think Bandar is a daring personality. And from my pro-Israel point of view, he has made a significant contribution to try to ease the tensions."[33]

Bandar bin Sultan is aware that the course of real politik in the context of Saudi Arabia as an Arab and Muslim country with its role as a guardian of Islam's two sacred shrines proceeds along two courses of action. In the first course, every Saudi leader has to espouse certain motherhood principles about the unique role of Islam that Saudi Arabia has to fulfill. In the second, the reality of statecraft and survival takes over, so that both the Saudis and the Americans have to explore ways to ensure the survival of each society. American economic and global interests are inextricably interwoven with the uninterrupted flow of oil from Saudi Arabia to the Western world. It is crucial that the United States continues to be a dominant military power in the Middle East committed to the maintenance of the status quo in Saudi Arabia. This acute awareness of each other's needs, as far as Bandar is concerned, has grown out of his unique role as an insider in both the Saudi and American systems. This explains why he has tried so adroitly to create an interlocking relationship between the two countries.

An example of this role has been provided in the U.S.-led United Nations' operations against Iraq in 1991. Just before the outbreak of the war, Americans were pressuring Saudi Arabia to invite American forces because Saddam Hussein was massing his forces near the Saudi border. Fahd was reluctant to invite American troops, because this would mean Saudis were supporting Western military action against a fellow Arab country. Second, and above all, an invitation to enter Saudi territory would be strongly resented by Muslims across the world because the sacred territory of Saudi Arabia was out of bounds for non-Muslim troops. Perhaps as a delaying action, Fahd's initial response was to suggest that Saudis needed only air power with some equipment and that he would like to receive a briefing team to evaluate these options. President Bush seized on the idea of the team and thought that "a high visibility team" should be sent to Saudi Arabia with an offer Fahd could not refuse. Bob Woodward, in *The Commanders*, has provided some inside evidence as regards the nature of these discussions. According to this account, it was becoming increasingly clear to the Americans that the Saudi ambassador, Bandar bin Sultan, was actually helping the Americans tighten their hold on Saudi Arabia so that there would only be one outcome: the king would invite the Americans and overcome his "disinclination to accept U.S. ground forces." In these discussions it looked as if Bandar bin Sultan, as well as being the Saudi ambassador to the United States, was also functioning as the American ambassador to Saudi Arabia. According to Woodward: "When Powell heard about the Bush-Fahd conversation concerning a 'team,' he immediately saw Bandar's hand. The prince had been working overtime. Bush's inclination to help and Cheney's suggestion that Schwarzkopf be used to coordinate a possible operation had been transformed into a 'team' to make a presentation to the king. Powell called it 'convenient confusion' on Bandar's part. Bandar had once again cleverly moved the two nations into each other's arms."[34]

The real politik that the Saudis have pursued is not just based on riyal politik. As we have noticed, their policy of maximizing their friendship with the United States has been crafted after considerable planning and is based on an acute awareness or their needs and interests. The Saudis seem to be following the advice of Polonius to his son, Laertes, in Hamlet.

> The friends thou hast, and their adoption tried,
> Grapple them to thy soul with hoops of steel.
>
> *Hamlet*, Act 1, Scene 3

In the case of Saudi-American relations, F-15s, F-16s, the most recent tanks, and the AWACs represent the hoops of steel that have forged this relationship. These hoops of steel have conferred benefits to both sides: improvements in Saudi defenses against both external and internal foes, much needed funds for the American defense industry, and above all, an uninterrupted flow of oil to the Western world. The net outcome of this relationship is again described aptly by Shakespeare:

> For how can tyrants safely govern home
> Unless abroad they purchase great alliance?
>
> *Henry VI*, Act 3, Scene 3

A recent book on U.S. relationships with Third World countries referred to in Chapter 1 is also entitled *Friendly Tyrants: An American Dilemma.*

Islamic radicals and Arab nationalists view all such relationships with anathema. We have seen how Islamic radicals have organized their resistance against the Saudi regime by campaigning against it in terms of an Islamic society based on social justice. We have noticed that they are still struggling in defining their program of action in a coherent fashion. At this stage the principal weakness that one detects in Muslim strategy throughout the world is that Muslims do not seem to realize clearly that the "friendly tyrants" they face in their countries are not only supporters of the West but are integral components of the Western international political and economic system. Therefore, when Khomeini removes one tyrant in Iran, the West can regroup itself and construct other and even more formidable pillars of its strategy. This explains why Reagan issued a warning in May 1980 that under no circumatances would the United States allow the overthrow of the Saudi regime.

We have seen how the Saudi government under King Fahd and other princes has steadily consolidated its control over Saudi Arabia, and despite the continuous opposition of Islamic groups, it is doubtful whether the Saudi regime can be dismantled in the near future. The Saudi royal family feels quite confident that, with the political and military support it enjoys from the United States and the enormous resources it commands, it can overcome or neutralize social unrest and economic discontent. We have also seen how the Saudi regime has appeased the discontent that exists among the middle and lower middle classes with concessions.

The Saudi regime is aware that, given the nature of rapid economic development and social change taking place in Saudi Arabia, it has to plan ahead to forestall social movements arising as consequences of developmental change. The Saudi regime seems to have done considerable thinking and planning in the area of the news media, radio, and television, which are some of the principal instruments that the middle classes often use to mount their challenge against any regime. It is significant that the tentacles of Saudi control over such instruments may radiate from Saudi Arabia but extend to all the significant parts of the Middle East and Europe. In June 1992, it was announced that Middle East Broadcasting Limited, a British company owned by

Walid al-Ibrahim, King Fahd's brother-in-law, had acquired United Press International to extend the news-gathering scope of it's satellite television channel. This television channel covered large parts of Europe and the Middle East through its broadcasts in Arabic. Rafik al-Hariri, a Saudi billionaire and a friend of King Fahd, controls Radio Orient, which beams Arabic news and entertainment twenty-four hours a day not only to several million North African Arabs in France and Western Europe but also to millions of Arabs in Lebanon, Syria, and the Israeli-occupied West Bank. *Al-Hayat*, read by Arab intellectuals and government leaders, was started about four years ago by Prince Khalid bin Sultan, former deputy chief of staff of the Saudi army and the son of Prince Sultan, minister of defense. *Al-Hayat* reviews objectives of Saudi foreign policy but "more importantly, Al-Hayat's editors play down or omit negative news from Saudi Arabia or its Gulf allies." A more pronounced pro-Saudi newspaper, *Asharq al-Awsat*, is owned by Prince Ahmad, who is the son of Prince Salman, the governor of Riyadh and one of the king's most influential brothers. It is said that Prince Salman as the press overlord controls the press on behalf of the royal family.[35]

One can also see how successful the Saudi regime has been in exercising its press surveillance and particularly in influencing fundamentalists and leftist journalists. It has been reported that a well-known supporter of the Iranian revolution and another militant leftist have been influenced into toning down their former views and writing for Saudi-owned news magazines and newspapers. A senior editor at a Saudi-owned newspaper commented: "Every Saudi newspaper gets its orders from Riyadh." Muhammad H. Heikal, the famous former editor-in-chief of *Al-Ahram* in Cairo said: "There is nothing now which may be called a dialogue in the Arab world."[36] Given the extensive thought control that the Saudi regime is planning to exercise, the struggle that Islamic radicals are waging against the regime is likely to be protracted if not hopeless.

6

The Islamic State of Pakistan: Internal Conflicts and External Pressures

Very few states, either Muslim or non-Muslim, are as constantly beset with such internal tensions and external pressures as Pakistan. Its supreme objective, as a conservative philosopher Oakeshott said about every political activity, is "to keep afloat on an even keel."[1] Below the superstructure, Pakistan faces economic or class conflicts in which one witnesses conspicuous consumption matched by dire poverty. The ethnic conflicts between the Punjabis and Bengalis resulted in the dismemberment of the state in 1971 with East Pakistan emerging as the state of Bangladesh. In the present state of Pakistan, the conflicts between the Punjabis and the Sindhis or between the Punjabis and the Pathans, the Sindhis, and the Mohajirs (refugees from India) have continued. Because no clearly acceptable understanding or compromise has emerged between the advocates of an Islamic state and liberals or secularists, the battle between these forces continues with Islamicists having some sway over the masses whereas the liberals-cum-secularists seem to be more influential with the power wielders in the government.

At the level of the superstructure, the triangular struggle for power between the president, the prime minister, and the military has remained unabated. In May 1993 Nawaz Sharif had the dubious distinction of being the ninth prime minister to be dismissed by the head of the state out of the thirteen the country has had since 1947. The political parties or various pressure groups, instead of functioning as institutions which would resolve the triangular conflict, have been absorbed into the conflict.

External Pressures

Pakistan faces certain geo-political pressures because of its strategic location. It sits astride between the oil-rich Middle East and populous South Asia. It looks across to the north at the old Soviet Union and now a series of Central Asiatic Muslim republics. It shares some of its northern frontier with China and on its long eastern frontier, Pakistanis feel that their inveterate enemy, India, casts its malevolent eyes, having already grabbed the Muslim-majority valley of Kashmir. Pakistan's enmity with India ever since its formation in 1947 has remained the single preponderant preoccupation in foreign policy. To fend against India, it entered into U.S.-sponsored anticommunist military alliances in the 1950s, which in terms of economic and military assistance continued right until the end of the 1980s. But in the 1990s, the United States seems to have disengaged itself, partly because of differences over Pakistan's nuclear policies and partly because Pakistan has outlived its usefulness due to the Soviet withdrawal from Afghanistan and the subsequent disintegration of the Soviet empire. Another source of support for Pakistan has been Communist China, which Pakistan feels has checkmated Indian designs because of its own hostile relations with India.

No other external relationship has cast its shadows over Pakistan's economy and society as the way Pakistan was drawn into the Cold War conflict between the Soviet Union and the United States over the question of Soviet incursion into Afghanistan, which started in 1978. Pakistan became the conduit of both guerrilla forces and vital military weapons in the struggle that the Afghan guerrillas waged against Soviet occupation of their country. This struggle, for obvious reasons, was supported generously by Muslim countries like Saudi Arabia and Pakistan, because the supreme objective was to help the Islamic struggle as well as frustrate Soviet communist designs on the Middle East. It was significant that the United States, which is presently engaged in a systematic campaign against Islamic fundamentalism, supported with personnel, money, and CIA intelligence, the Afghan guerrillas who were fighting the Soviet occupation in the name of Islam.

Generous as the external help was, nevertheless the Afghan guerrillas became dependent upon the sale of drugs produced out of the luxuriant crop of poppies that was grown on Pakistan-Afghan border areas as well as within Afghanistan. It is significant that the United States has been continuously exerting pressure on Pakistan to close the guerrilla bases in Peshawar as well as control or even eliminate the flow of drugs from the border areas to Karachi for shipment abroad to Europe and the United States. Particularly Egypt has complained that a number of Islamic militants, who are bitterly opposed to the Egyptian government as an ally of the United States and at peace with Israel, were originally trained in Pakistan as Muslim guerrillas. Pakistan has closed a number of guerrilla bases in Peshawar and expelled many Arab mujahideen (guerrillas). But Pakistanis resent the American charge that Pakistan bears the sole responsibility for drug smuggling. Referring to a CIA document on the question of the Pakistan government's involvement in drug smuggling, a Pakistani newspaper, The Nation, has commented: "On the issue of drug smuggling from Pakistan, the CIA surely has not forgotten how it turned a blind eye to this activity even while it pumped in millions of dollars worth of arms and aid during the Afghan war. It may have been expedient then for Americans to focus only on Afghan resistance to the Soviets while ignoring these little 'misdemeanors' on the side. It appears expedient now to pillory Pakistan for a mess to which the American CIA can rightfully be considered to have contributed a major share."[2]

Pakistan had allowed itself to become a conduit of covert American military aid ($3 billion) being funnelled to Afghanistan to dislodge a pro-Soviet government there. In doing this, Pakistan had paid the price of allowing 3 million Afghan refugees to enter Pakistan and strain its resources. The net result was that the Pakistani economy was penetrated by drug money and its law and order situation imperiled by the inflow of Afghan refugees, some of them armed with Kalashnikov guns. Thus, Pakistanis could rightly argue that the cost that they had paid for improving the security position of the West and the United States vis-à-vis the Soviet Union had been enormous. It was well known that many American intelligence officials were of the view "that the Soviet loss in Afghanistan was a fatal blow to the Soviet Union."[3]

In this regard, the disclosure of General Mirza Aslam Beg, chief of staff of the Pakistan army during 1988-1991, regarding the real causes behind the American withdrawal of economic and military assistance to Pakistan in 1990 is significant. General's Beg's disclosure confirms the view that the United States was prepared to provide military and economic assistance to Pakistan as long as Pakistan was considered an important part of the American strategy of weakening the Soviet Union's influence in South Asia. According to General Beg, the reason behind American withdrawal of military and economic assistance to Pakistan in 1990 was not because Pakistan had developed a nuclear bomb. The Pakistani chief of staff revealed that Pakistan had already developed such capability in 1987, but the aid was withdrawn in 1990. The chief of staff in an interview to a London-based Urdu newspaper revealed that the U.S. administration "continued issuing a certificate that Pakistan had not crossed the line in its atomic program, but as soon as the Soviet Union was defeated in Afghanistan the situation changed immediately."[4]

The Kashmir problem had poisoned Indo-Pakistan relations ever since the two countries became independent in 1947. This conflict continued during the 1980s and 1990s and was further aggravated by the emergence of a Sikh movement in Indian Punjab for the establishment of a separate Sikh state. The result was that Pakistan was being accused by India of training guerrillas to wage war in Kashmir and supporting Sikh separatism in Punjab. Because the American strategy had also undergone a sea change as a result of the Soviet withdrawal from Afghanistan, the United States was no longer much interested in supporting Pakistan. Therefore, the Indian complaint about Pakistani complicity in training guerrillas for the Kashmir struggle and the alleged Pakistani support to Sikh separatists fell on sympathetic ears in Washington. Even after the Soviet withdrawal from Afghanistan, Peshawar continued to be a base for Islamic mujahideen. As we have seen, the Egyptian authorities had complained that a number of Islamic militants who were trying to dislodge the Egyptian government had been trained in Peshawar. In addition, Americans themselves felt threatened by the rise of Islamic militancy in the Middle East and South Asia and often took the view that these Islamic militants were anti-American.

Pakistan was therefore threatened by U.S. government spokesmen that it would be added to the list of states that sponsored terrorism like Iran, Iraq, Syria, North Korea, and Cuba. American pressure on Pakistan was exerted so that Pakistan would abandon its support of guerrillas in Kashmir and separatists in Indian Punjab. Pakistan was not actually placed on this list, yet it was clearly indicated in January 1993 that Pakistan would be placed on a watch list for 180 days. "While we are concerned about continuing reports of Pakistan's support for Kashmir and Sikh militants who commit terrorist acts in India, the secretary determined that the available information did not warrant a finding that Pakistan has repeatedly provided support for acts of international terrorism,' a subsequent statement said. 'The USA has raised this frequently with the Pakistan government at the highest level,' it went on, adding: 'We are keeping the situation under active, continuing review.'"[5] Pakistan, not being rich in oil resources and with its fragile economy, was extremely vulnerable to such American pressure. If declared a terrorist state, it would face certain catastrophic consequences like the drying up of aid and loans from American sources like the World Bank and the International Monetary Fund. It would further face severance of trade and air links with Western countries.

It was apparent that the United States was trying to justify certain "significant shifts" in its strategic thinking on South Asia. India and Pakistan had been fighting over Kashmir for almost half a century. The United States itself admitted that the Kashmir territory was a disputed area and that there had been abuses of human rights by India in that area. How would it be possible for any Pakistani government or a politician to abandon the Kashmiri cause without facing certain defeat in elections? Public opinion in Pakistan turned fiercely anti-American because of such periodic shifts in U.S. foreign policy on South Asia. Even though economic and military aid to Pakistan was suspended at the end of 1990, the government response to suspension of aid was "muted." Pakistan, as a weak state, was trying to accommodate itself to certain changes in American strategy in South Asia.

Behind the threats to declare Pakistan a terrorist state lay deep concern in Washington about the spread of Islamic militancy. Presumably it was not realized among American government circles that Pakistan, which professed to be an Islamic state, could not adopt the same kind of attitude toward Islamic militancy as the American government had adopted. Pakistan could soft-pedal its approach to Islamization or even renege on the support that it had promised to give to the Islamic mujahideen in Kashmir and Afghanistan. However, in pursuing such stances, it was also aware that it would end up alienating considerable public opinion in Pakistan and antagonize an influential member like the Jamaat-i-Islami of the alliance called the Islami Jamhoori Ittehad (IJI, Islamic Democratic Alliance). This alliance had brought Nawaz Sharif to power.

Internal Conflicts

Only a stable government can pursue a reasonably clear political strategy for the purpose of converting the diverse and sometimes contradictory pressures it faces from external and internal sources into a set of coherent policies. If such policies are pursued, the expectation would be that Pakistan as a state would continue and make at least some incremental or marginal progress in its economy.

Pakistan's original 1973 constitution, which followed a parliamentary form of government, was modified by General Zia-ul-Haq under the Eighth Amendment Act 1985. The result was that this amendment produced the worst features of the presidential and parliamentary systems. Under this system, there emerged neither a strong president nor an effective prime minister. The struggle for power between the president and the prime minister so riddled the central and provincial governments with feuds that Pakistan sometimes became ungovernable.

President Ghulam Ishaq Khan under this system tried to interfere with the day-to-day working of the government by planting his political and fellow Pathan supporters in the cabinet. Prime Minister Nawaz Sharif countered this by trying to establish his control over the cabinet but failed to make sure that the ministers would work under his authority rather than trying to seek presidential support in their conflicts with the prime minister. Another aim of Nawaz Sharif was to influence the appointment of the military chief of staff so that the army might be at least neutralized in his struggle against the president.[6]

In his struggle against the president, the prime minister suffered from certain disadvantages. President Ghulam Ishaq Khan was by origin a civil servant and his predecessors had been drawn from the army or the civil service. Members of bureaucratic organizations like the military and the civil service do not usually have the vision or the comprehension of the broader objectives of a state. Pakistan needed political leaders who had both the vision and political skills to reconcile ethnic, economic, and social conflicts through compromises and coalition building. For this, individuals were not enough. Pakistan needed vibrant institutions in the form of a parliament and parties, where such reconciliation and coalition building could be undertaken. President Ghulam Ishaq Khan lacked that vision and justified his personal, bureaucratic, and ethnic (Pathan) interests by invoking "rules and regulations." In a speech on April 18, 1993, dismissing the prime minister and dissolving the national assembly, he said: "In my life, I adhered to rules and regulations, and I cannot deviate from my principles for fear of anyone's displeasure."[7] The army command, also a bureaucracy, was often supportive of such a bureaucratic point of view and did not appreciate that the processes of state building and nation building could not be pursued within a bureaucratic straitjacket.

In the triangular conflict between the president, the prime minister and the army, the army through its chief of staff played the decisive role. The president was able to dismiss the prime minister in April 1993 because of the support he enjoyed through the army. Under the Eighth Amendment, it was the president who appointed the chief of staff. President Ghulam Ishaq Khan in his speech of April 1993 announcing the dismissal of the prime minister, revealed that perhaps one of the most important causes of the conflicts that arose between him and the prime minister was over the question of the appointment of the chief of the army staff.[8] Both the president and the prime minister constantly watched on whose side the chief of staff was going to throw his weight. The chief of staff, on the other hand, tried to insulate himself from these rival pulls and wanted to act independently. General Asif Nawaz, chief of staff 1991-1993, pinpointed the power of the chief of staff as follows: "They say I am not their man. I'm telling you . . . , they can have anyone they want in this seat and he'll be his own man. When you can move 500,000 men by gesture of your little finger, you have to be your own man."[9]

It is not quite accurate to claim, as General Asif Nawaz's statement suggests, that the chief of staff can exercise mono-lithic control over the army so that the army marches like a docile instrument on the orders of the chief of staff. During the fierce struggle for power that took place during April-July 1993 between the president and the prime minister, it was revealed that the chief of staff advised the president and the prime minister to patch up their quarrels and reach a compromise after consulting his corps commanders in Rawalpindi. In one of these meetings the corps commanders "are understood to have expressed reluctance for the military to intervene unless it is forced to do so by street violence or economic emergency."[10] Nevertheless, the army would support the chief of staff as a united organization once a decision were taken. This could certainly not be said about the prime minister, who had to wrestle with feuding factions in the central parliamentary party as well as with the ever-shifting alliances and defections that plagued his supporters in the provincial government and the assembly of Punjab. Similarly, the president in his attempts to establish his influence over the cabinet had to use as his agents certain members of the prime minister's cabinet. As may be seen later, in May 1993 the president resorted to horse trading by manipulating the Muslim League party in Punjab to dislodge the prime minister.

In April 1993 the struggle for power between the president and the prime minister had reached such a level of ferocity that the prime minister in a television speech denounced the president for using his office to disrupt the prime minister's cabinet by offering some of his colleagues the position of the prime minister and ministerial posts to others. A day later, on April 18, the president retaliated by dismissing the prime minister and dissolving the national assembly. The president used Article 48 (2b) of the constitution, which meant that in his view various acts of the prime minister and particularly his outright defiance of the authority of the president meant that the government of the country could not be "carried on in accordance with the provisions of the Constitution and appeal to the electorate is necessary."

The matter was referred to the supreme court. The supreme court decision of May 26 by a majority of 10 to 1 restored the prime minister in his office as well as the national assembly and declared the president's action as illegal and unconstitutional. In this judgment, the chief justice of the supreme court took the view that the president and not the prime minister had been instrumental in subverting the spirit of the constitution because "the president had ceased to be a neutral figure and started to align himself with his opponents and was encouraging them in their efforts to destabilize his government."[11] It was significant that the dissenting judge, Justice Sajjad Ali Shah, referred to the fact that the supreme court had accepted the decision of the president in dismissing the two previous Sindhi prime ministers (Benazir Bhutto and Junejo). "But when the turn of the Prime Minister from Punjab came the tables were turned." The dissenting judge added, "indications were given that the decision of the court would be such which would please the nation. . . . In my humble opinion decision of the Court should be strictly in accordance with law and not to please the nation."[12]

In addition to the struggle for power between the president and the prime minister, there was also a similar struggle for power between the prime minister and the leader of the opposition, Benazir Bhutto. This meant that the president could use the latter rivalry between the prime minister and the leader of the opposition to his own advantage. We have referred to the fact that Benazir Bhutto was also dismissed by President Ghulam Ishaq Khan in 1990. Both as prime minister and later as leader of the opposition, Benazir Bhutto often capitalized on the name and popularity of her father, Zulfiqar Ali Bhutto (the founder of the Pakistan People's Party), but lacked the political stature that her father had. When Nawaz Sharif was dismissed by the president, the central idea that guided her political behavior was "since my former enemy (the president) has emerged as the enemy of my enemy (Nawaz Sharif), my former enemy has become my friend." She hailed the president's action in dismissing Nawaz Sharif and forgot the fact that she had denounced the president for behaving in exactly the same way toward her.

During Benazir Bhutto's tenure as prime minister (1988-1990), she was obsessed with the idea of clinging to power and did not make any determined or systematic effort to pursue certain issues and principles that she had promised to the electorate. Here was the first woman prime minister of a Muslim country, but she did not proclaim a strong commitment to the cause of improving the status and conditions of women in Pakistani society. Second, her administration became tainted with gross corruption. Some of the criminal charges leveled against her husband, Asif Zardari, could be ignored as largely trumped up, but charges of his corrupt business practices could not be ruled out. After the dismissal of Nawaz Sharif, for a brief period Benazir Bhutto became the most influential person in determining the composition of the caretaker cabinet during April-May 1993. Even her supporters criticized her bitterly for the unwholesome influence of her husband. In the caretaker government, not only Zardari as Bhutto's husband was included, but also sons of some of the Sindhi leaders as well as the son-in-law of the president. Thus, a Pakistan People's Party (PPP) supporter complained bitterly, "This politics of husbands, sons, sons-in-laws and brothers is really sickening."[13] An equally alarming conclusion that *The Friday Times*. usually a supporter of Benazir

Bhutto, drew from Bhutto's conduct was: "Mr. Asif Zardari intends to be a force to reckon with in and out of the PPP in the future. People of merit and qualifications will find the going tough in the PPP unless they are prepared to become sycophantic and obsequious."[14]

In a society like Pakistan, which exists, as all Pakistani constitutions proclaim, to enable Muslims "to order their lives in the individual and collective spheres in accordance with the teaching and requirements of Islam," the speed with which political corruption has increased can truly be described as exponential. This complete contrast between ideals and actual political behavior not only makes Pakistan a special case study but has created in the minds of its citizens increasing disillusionment with the Islamic character of the state and perhaps cynicism with the very name of the state, Pakistan, which means "the land of the pure."

We cite the struggle that took place between the president and the prime minister and between the prime minister and the provincial government for winning control over Punjab, which constitutes the richest and most populous (60 percent) of the country's provinces, as a prime example of political corruption. Soon after the president dismissed the prime minister and dissolved the national assembly on April 18, 1993, the great majority of Prime Minister Nawaz Sharif's Muslim League supporters in the Punjab assembly swiftly transferred their political support to the president and rallied behind his newly appointed chief minister of Punjab. To bring about this political transformation of loyalties, the entire assembly was flown to Islamabad under presidential protection. During the three days of presidential guidance, the legislators were assured that their assembly would not be dissolved provided they moved a motion of no-confidence against Sharif's supporter, Ghulam Hyder Wyne, the provincial chief minister. They returned to Lahore and the great majority of them carried out these instructions.

As soon as the supreme court through its judgment reinstated the prime minister and restored the national assembly on May 26, 1993, the change in the political loyalties of the majority of the provincial legislators in Punjab was just as quick. The prime minister tried to have the chief minister of Punjab, Manzoor Wattoo, dismissed but did not succeed. The chief minister won the support of 75 members in a house of 248 members by including them in the provincial cabinet. The chief minister had the support of another 25 members. He needed another 25 members to have the majority support of at least 125 in a house of 248. The 25 members of the legislature were playing a double game. It was revealed that about 40 members were oscillating between the two camps and were weighing the offers of bribes from the two aides. "When the numbers game began, the rate of one MPA was said to be five lakh [500,000] rupees. Now with the dissolution case being dragged out in the high court, the rate has gone up to twenty lakhs [2 million]."[15]

There is not supposed to be too much rigidity about political principles in many democratic societies. But politicians once bought stay bought. This may be because they have sold their loyalties to certain political parties which enjoy a certain amount of durability. In the case of Pakistan, they have to engineer their allegiance in terms of how long what political actor, the president or the prime minister, is likely to continue at the top. However, it was ironic that the activities of the corrupters and the corrupted came to nothing when Pakistan's so-called democratic system collapsed on July 18, 1993. The powerful president resigned and his long bureaucratic and political career came to an inglorious end. The prime minister also resigned after advising the president to dissolve the assemblies and call for fresh elections in October 1993. The only satisfaction that the prime minister could extract from this unwholesome episode was that he had been instrumental in terminating the career of an autocratic president and that he would have another chance to improve his political fortunes through another election.

It would not be fair to suggest that Nawaz Sharif during his two years as prime minister was engaged only in political skirmishes with the president and the leader of the opposition, Benazir Bhutto. His political strategy centered around his economic policy of privatization, which he thought would not only reflate the stagnant economy of Pakistan but also create in this process a considerable sector of political support. The main weakness of his overall political strategy was that he expected that the growing middle class, consisting of some of the upper level civil servants, lawyers, and above all, traders, merchants, and growing number of industrialists, would be adequate by itself to provide him the main nucleus of a political movement. He had neither the experience nor the vision to realize that Pakistan needed a socio-political program with some Islamic emphasis to attract the enormous numbers of the lower income and have-not classes as well as those supporters of religious groups and parties, who would see in his movement both their economic interests as well as religious satisfaction. He thought that his main role in coming to power was to establish that in Pakistan a prominent member of a business class could make a serious dent into the elite political structure, which had hitherto been dominated by members of the feudal landowning groups. Perhaps as a representative of the business interests he could not see that his exclusive reliance on the growing middle class for political support would create room for corruption and thus alienate him not only from the lower income groups but also from those members of the middle class whose norms of probity were such that they could not see them disregarded for the sake of political gain or compromise.

One of the popular measures he thought would win support from the middle class groups was the privatization of the state-sector industries, which had expanded enormously under the Bhutto regime during 1971-1977. During the period 1991-1992, the government under the privatization program sold fifty-seven government-owned companies worth Rs. 9 billion (U.S. $360 million) to the private sector. During 1992-1993, the government was planning to sell another twenty-seven, which would have made a total of eighty-four companies. In the original list of November 1990, the government had listed 100 companies to be privatized.

When the government tried to privatize a public utility like the Water and Power Development Authority (WAPDA), the government of the North-West Frontier Province strongly opposed such a measure because it argued that the province would be deprived of the profits accruing to it from power generated by the hydroelectric plants of the utility located on its territory. The government, after consulting legal experts, decided not to go ahead with the privatization of WAPDA.

To provide better transport, particularly in urban areas, the government allowed the import of thousands of taxis and extended credit facilities to enable thousands of taxi owners to ply taxicabs in cities. This is reminiscent of a measure that made Indira Gandhi popular in India. These measures seemed to have considerably widened the support that Nawaz Sharif enjoyed among the middle classes. By providing taxicabs and building motorway projects linking Pakistani cities and thus providing employment to hundreds of thousands of people, Nawaz Sharif also seemed to have made a dent in the populist support that Benazir Bhutto enjoyed in Pakistan.

It may be noted that ever since the days of President Ayub Khan (1958-1969), the government strategy of accelerating economic growth by relying heavily on the role of the private sector had created in the public mind that such a strategy had resulted in enormous concentration of wealth in about twenty-two families. Questions were raised as to whether the private sector had been pandered excessively through taxation and tariff policies. Such policies had also resulted in gross economic inequalities. Zulfiqar Ali Bhutto characterized this process as "free loot" by the rich families like the Saigols, the Habibs, the Adamjees, the Sheikhs, the Fancies, and the Dawoods.

Under Zia-ul-Haq and later under Nawaz Sharif, the number of families who controlled the bulk of industrial wealth increased considerably. Among the newly rich groups, the family of Nawaz Sharif controlled the Ittefaq Group, a conglomerate of steel, sugar, and textile industries. In 1981-1982, the turnover of these industries was Rs. 337 million, which went up to Rs. 537 million in 1983-1984 and by 1986-1987 had reached as much as Rs. 2.5 billion. Since then, the Ittefaq empire included the biggest sugar mill in Asia, four textile mills, and a private hospital in Lahore.[16] During 1990-1993, the Ittefaq Group moved into the manufacturing of sugar-making machinery with capital assets running into over Rs. 1.3 billion. Prime Minister Nawaz Sharif was criticized for having used his official influence to sanction three sugar mills to be set up by the Ittefaq Group controlled by his family and also units for the manufacture of sugar machinery to be placed under the control of the same family industrial empire.[17]

Corruption in Pakistan was not confined to the matter of starting new industries or obtaining loans from banks. It had penetrated several other layers of Pakistani society. In Pakistan one is often told that the country is poor but its people are rich. This really meant that certain individuals had become extremely rich through corrupt practices. One of the major forms of corruption was tax evasion. Only about a million people paid income tax. Increases in custom duties were followed by increases in smuggling and bribes to custom officials. One of the reasons that public expenditures on welfare items like education and health were low was that the state was being constantly robbed through nonpayment of taxes. Thus, this partly explained why the country was so poor. Businessmen and industrialists had become experts in tax evasion. This expertise they had imbibed from government tax collectors. Excise duty could be reduced or evaded by making a deal with the excise collectors so that only half of the production was declared. As for old age benefits and social security taxes, the common practice was to understate the number of employees. Businessmen as well as private individuals who made numerous international telephone calls with some of the bills being as high as Rs. 20,000 a month, could have their bills reduced to Rs. 2,000 if the telephone operator were paid Rs. 1,000. Electricity charges would be drastically reduced because for a payment the meter man would fix the meter. Emma Duncan, who has narrated some of the previous instances, writes: "My friend was worried: the meter was sealed; wouldn't somebody find out? No, said the electricity man, the glass could be taken out carefully with a screwdriver. And what, said my friend, if he was transferred? Then the electricity man would introduce his successor to my friend. They made a deal."[18]

Our own interviews have confirmed these findings. One businessman expressed his helplessness against the working of the system by pointing out that to pursue one's business without too much harassment it often paid him to get the tax collector off his back by offering him the requisite bribe. According to the directories of income tax payers published by the Central Board of Revenue, Nawaz and Shahbaz Sharif, leading members of probably the richest business family in Pakistan, together paid only Rs. 3,577 or about $1,176 in tax in 1992-1993. Economists have estimated that the government of Pakistan has been losing as much as Rs. 100 billion or $3.3 billion a year in revenue because of nonpayment of taxes, duties, and utility bills.[19]

These corrupt practices were not confined to the rich. There were deals between postal clerks inside a post office and stamp sellers outside on the pavement. Because postal clerks lacked an adequate supply of stamps, the buyers were directed to the men outside "who charge fifteen per cent markup of which the men inside the post office get five per cent." Similar arrangements existed for obtaining application forms for passports.[20]

It seems that there is a general air of lawlessness in Pakistan. There is tax evasion on the part of the majority of the citizens. Drug money has created a huge black market economy. In a U.N.-sponsored drug abuse conference in Islamabad in 1993, the following admission came from the Pakistani delegates: "The massive inflows of money financed by drugs have given birth to a new political situation in Pakistan. . . . The profits generated from illicit narcotics activity have contributed to a huge black economy, half the size of the official one."[21] It has also been alleged that some of the politicians representing the tribal areas in the national assembly in Islamabad are drug smugglers. By 1989 it seemed that Karachi had become the second largest world center of the narcotics trade, the first being the golden triangle in the Southeast Asia peninsula.

One wonders as to how in the Islamic state of Pakistan this acquisitive habit of making money by legal or illegal means has become such an obsession on the part of so many Pakistanis. It may be argued that, in the cosmopolitan culture that has emerged under the world capitalist economy and the market system, Pakistanis cannot be blamed exclusively. However, there are historical and social reasons for the conspicuous-consumption culture that has emerged among the upper income groups in Pakistan. First, there is the legacy from the British raj. Particularly among the landowning ruling elites as well as the bureaucratic and military officers, flaunting expensive tastes and imitation of the British style of living became an integral part of the dominant culture. The British colonial culture was soon replaced by the American culture, in which the role of the merchant-cum-industrialist group set the tone of the new cultural pattern and the value system. In this regard some of the caustic comments by a former finance minister, Mubashir Hasan, may be quoted: "The new living style—dress, food and the whole style of living—was demonstrated in the cocktail, dancing and dinner parties held at hotels, clubs and private residences. In such gatherings, no matter how shallow the remark, since it was expressed in either an Oxford or Harvard accent, it acquired a profundity of its own. . . . Those who joined the high government or bureaucratic elite became Pucca Sahibs [upper class Anglicized gentlemen]."[22]

These observations of Mubashir Hasan are confirmed by the British journalist Emma Duncan. She writes: "The big Karachi and Lahore parties—200 to 300 people, any sort of alcohol you wish, staffed by uniformed servants handing round drinks and managing the open-air kitchen where whole fish simmer in four-foot-long pans—are one of the most popular ways of showing off money."[23] Ruling elites in other societies also practice hypocrisy. But the contradictions between what the rulers of the Islamic state of Pakistan preached and what they practiced had reached alarming proportions. It may be noted that Emma Duncan was writing about a Pakistan where General Zia-ul-Haq had prohibited the drinking of liquor as un-Islamic and illegal.

Mubashir Hasan's book draws our attention to another element of Pakistan's political culture and social behavior. He suggests that the ruling elites of Pakistan seem to be either unaware of or insensitive to the poverty and despair of their people "who sit and hear each other groan." "The well-to-do are not interested or concerned about the slums and hovels that exist in their cities, but they can talk for hours about Piccadilly Circus and Broadway. . . . There is a built-in racial inferiority complex among such people. Those who have become ministers or reached top positions in the bureaucracy have a tendency to reveal innermost secrets and details of their country to Western ambassadors and diplomats as if they were talking to their own parents or uncles."[24] It may be noted that those of us who talk to American officials in Washington are often told that they have seen certain cables on a given day which reveal that such and such a minister or leader of the opposition in Pakistan came to see the American consul general to disclose the latest vital information regarding government decisions. One can infer from the preceding analysis that there is a strong component of Westernization in Pakistan's modernization. This component may rob the modernization drive of the dynamism and nationalism necessary for modernization purposes. In addition, the dominant role of Westernized elites in Pakistan's decision-making structures has created class and regional disparities.

In Pakistan's budgetary priorities, one discerns again and again mounting defense expenditures but the problem of the rising debt is such that debt servicing constitutes the largest element in government expenditure. It has been estimated that debt servicing and defense expenditures appropriate over 90 percent of federal revenue. As for the overall development expenditures, even a government publication, *Economic Survey 1991-92*, admits: "The weakest area of the development process in Pakistan has been the slow moving social indicators, in particular literacy, nutrition, health, population, welfare, potable water, sanitation and sewerage. If these issues are not addressed urgently and squarely, it is not only the living conditions that would worsen, the process of economic progress itself would degenerate making prospects of social and political instability more palpable."[25] Similarly, the same government publication discloses that the national average health expenditure per person is as abysmally low as Rs. 79 or $3 per person.[26] When under IMF pressures the budget deficit was scaled down, it was significant that social sector allocations bore the entire brunt of the cuts. Allocations for education were reduced by 58 percent, health by 70 percent, with public works program being cut by more than 50 percent. In contrast to such draconian cuts in social sector allocations, the defense budget was raised by 11.6 percent.[27]

These grim facts were reflected year after year in the World Bank *Development Reports* and the U.N. *Human Development Reports*. In 1993 Pakistan was uniformly ranked twenty-first in areas like health, human deprivation, and wealth, poverty, and social investment among countries which the United Nations Development Program classified as indicating "low human development."[28] In the same report it was stated that Pakistan's military expenditure as percentage of GDP went up from 5.5 in 1960 to 6.6 in 1990. According to the same source, military expenditure as percentage of combined education and health expenditure was as high as 239 in 1990. Pakistan along with Ethiopia would be ranked as second and Somalia as first in the area of military expenditure as percentage of combined education and health expenditure among all the sixty-four countries with low human development.[29]

It is in the matter of the rights and social conditions of women that Muslim societies are often targeted for severe criticisms in the West. Some of these criticisms suggest that as long as Muslims follow the Qur'an strictly, the rights of women are not likely to improve. To buttress such criticisms, writers or journalists tend to be highly selective about certain Qur'anic verses. Thus, for example, it is often argued that the Qur'an states very clearly that men have been charged with the responsibility of protecting and maintaining women because God has given them more strength and the means for their maintenance. In their eagerness to score points in this regard, these writers often disregard both the specific and historical context in which these verses were revealed and many other verses where equality between men and women has been either stressed or recommended.[30] As Fazlur Rahman has pointed out, the Qur'anic pronouncements were accompanied by a *ratio legis*; that is, the socio-historical background that occasioned the revelation. "When the situation so changes that the law fails to reflect the *ratio*, the law must change. Traditional lawyers, however, while recognizing the *ratio legis*, generally stuck to the letter of the law . . ."[31]

Nevertheless, the problem of sexual disparity in Pakistan is probably more serious than class and regional disparity. The general literacy rate, low as it has been for males, has been even lower for females; According to government sources, the literacy rate in 1991-1992 was 34 percent (45.5 percent for males and 21.3 percent for females). This relative backwardness of women has been further compounded by the emergence of groups like small- and medium-sized trader-merchant elements in the urban scene. Such elements, though physically located in the urban areas, have their cultural and social roots in traditional rural cultures. When Zia-ul-Haq promulgated the Hadood Ordinances providing severe punishment for violating the Islamic code of behavior in a matter like rape, he presumably had the majority support of the new middle class groups. The problem that emerged in the Pakistani context was that the woman who lodged a complaint about rape to the authorities could find herself charged with adultery under these ordinances. As an American government report points out, "The predominantly male police force reportedly uses the Hadood Ordinances to threaten people on the basis of personal and political animosities. The Committee for the Repeal of the Hadood Ordinances estimates that 3,000 women are in jails in Pakistan awaiting trial under this law."[32]

Pakistan is supposed to be an Islamic state. But no political party has presented a coherent Islamic socio-political program to tackle some of the major issues that Pakistan's political system faces. Just as we have noticed that there is growing support for conservative or fundamentalist Islam among the small- and medium-sized trader-merchant elements, the Western-educated elites in urban areas and significant numbers of journalists and university students have become disenchanted with rigid, backward-looking Islamic conservatism. They probably feel that there is some correlation between Islamic fundamentalism and conservatism and periodic outbreaks of violent sectarian conflicts between Sunnis and Shi'as in central Punjab and parts of the North-West Frontier Province.

The Jamaat-i-Islami, which often represents Islamic fundamentalism, nevertheless is aware that Islam's fundamentalist ideas have to be converted into a socio-political program. Until the late 1980s, the Jamaat-i-Islami formulated its program in such conservative terms that it neither attracted the majority of the rural classes who consisted of small peasants, landless laborers, and tenants nor women and industrial labor in the urban areas. For example, in their electoral campaigns any emphasis on land reforms was conspicuous by its absence. The result was that in the 1985 election it won only 10 of the 68 contested seats to the national assembly and 13 of the 102 contested seats to the various provincial assemblies. In the 1990 election, its support slumped considerably because the Mohajir Qaumi Movement (National Movement of Refugees) was able to more or less eliminate it from its strong base in Karachi. The Jamaat won only 7 out of 207 seats in the national assembly and 11 out of 248 seats in the Punjab provincial assembly. Some of the major reasons for its lack of success was its inability to offer an attractive program to the lower and educated classes based on a reinterpretation of the Islamic Sharia.

It seems that a sense of political reality on the part of the Jamaat has made them realize that they cannot afford to be rigid in interpreting the Sharia. In their new strategy there is a growing realization, as one observer has noted, "Of the limits the emotive appeal of Islam had in the face of secular political issues—socioeconomic and ethnic concerns and democratic demands."[33] Under the initiative and leadership of the Jamaat, a new Islam-oriented or political organization called the Pakistan Islamic Front has emerged. The Islamic Front held its first meeting on May 23, 1993, attended by 4,000 people from all over the country. Among the names of participants released to the press there were as many as twenty retired senior officers belonging to the army, air force and navy. The Islamic Front announced a fourteen-point program that included certain items appealing to every Pakistani. These were steps to ensure provincial autonomy; elimination of ethnic, linguistic, provincial, and sectarian prejudices; an accountability system for president, prime minister, and all political leaders including members of the assembly; and working for the creation of an effective Islamic umma. In the fourteen-point program were also certain new issues and new phrases, which included creation of an exploitation-free society, equal distribution of wealth, and a respectable status for women.[34]

With its past ideological commitments as well as the presence of participants drawn from conservative and upper level military officers, it is not likely that the Islamic Front led by the

Jamaat would embark on a bold and dynamic socio-political program. In a program where there was no reference to the social implications of Nawaz Sharif's privatization policies and in what pragmatic ways the roles of the private and public sector would be blended in an Islamic system, phrases like *exploitation-free society* and *equal distribution of wealth* looked platitudinous. Both the Maliki and Hanifi schools in Islam have tried to come to grips with the desirability of placing areas relating to water, forests, and energy under public control. Muslim scholars have also referred to a Tradition of the Prophet in this regard. In addition, the provincial government of the North-West Frontier, though from a provincial point of view, had objected to the privatization of the Water and Power Development Authority. This again indicates that an Islamic movement like the Jamaat needs to display a new kind of thinking so that Islamic ideas and the requirements of a modern economy could move in tandem. In the light of this, how could liberals or progressive Muslims expect to see any specific content in the phrase *equal distribution of wealth* that the program of the Islamic Front states as the first plank in its program?

We are not criticizing the Jamaat alone for having been unable to embark on new intellectual initiatives. This is a failing of social thinkers in many Muslim countries. The United Nations' *Human Development Report 1993* pinpoints this general intellectual failing as follows: "Today, markets are much more popular. Indeed, some people claim that recent events prove the triumph of capitalism and the demise of socialism. This is too simplistic a view. If there is a triumph of capitalism, it need not be the triumph of personal greed. If there is a demise of socialism, it need not be the demise of all social objectives."[35] Thus, the question arises, what alternative would an Islamic socio-political program offer in this matter? How an Islamic system would combine the capitalist virtues of private initiative and the socialist emphasis on communitarian values is the challenge that Islamic thinkers face.

As regards the status and rights of women, all that the program of the Islamic Front states is, "A respectable status for women as provided in the Islamic system." The Jamaat knows that Muslims belonging to liberal, secular, and other points of view all agree that a new interpretation of the Islamic Sharia as regards the rights and status of women is needed. As already mentioned, the image of Pakistan has suffered as a result of the way the Hadood Ordinances is being implemented with respect to matters like rape. What new measure would the Islamic Front undertake, for example, as regards the traditional Islamic position that in credit transactions the evidence of women is equal to half that of men? Surely, Muslim women in terms of general and commercial education have advanced way beyond the time when the Qur'anic regulation (2: 282) was revealed. As noted earlier in this chapter, Fazlur Rahman has argued that when the situation which occasioned the Qur'anic regulation changes, the regulation needs to be reinterpreted in the light of changed circumstances.[36]

The case of Pakistan confirms the central theme of this book; namely, the overwhelming Western or American dominance of the Muslim world in the Middle East and South Asia. Pakistan, motivated and influenced both by Islamic and strategic interests, supported the Afghan guerrilla struggle against the Soviet presence in Afghanistan. Pakistan expected that, if the struggle were to conclude successfully, it would reap a good harvest. But now it finds that its investment has brought quite a few disastrous consequences. The Soviet Union has withdrawn from Afghanistan but instability and conflict have returned to that country. Pakistan's own territory has been ravaged by drugs, and it has had to face periodic outbreaks of lawlessness as a result of the introduction of weapons made available during the Afghan struggle.

It is true that as a superpower the United States had a right to wage ideological and even armed struggle against the Soviet Union. But it seems that as a dependent state, Pakistan cannot support the struggle for the liberation of Kashmir. Pakistanis would rightly ask, should they not be as committed to the liberation of Kashmir (a Muslim-majority area) as the Americans were in frustrating Soviet global designs? Pakistani bitterness in this respect has been expressed by Iqbal as follows:

> War is unhallowed, is not war unhallowed
> For Western arms? and if your goal be truth,
> Is this the right road,Europe's faults all glossed,
> And all Islam's held to so strict an audit?[37]

Similarly, the United States seems to follow a double standard in their policy of selling sophisticated planes like AWACs to Saudi Arabia despite Israeli opposition, but protesting vehemently against the alleged Chinese sales of parts for M-11 missiles to

Pakistan. Americans in their defense would argue that the availability of M-11 missiles in the hands of Pakistanis could contribute to the nuclear arms race between India and Pakistan because such a Pakistani capability would mean that Pakistanis would be able to carry a 1,750 pound payload 175 miles.[38]

It is clear from the checkered history of Pakistan that as a state it has been dominated by certain elites drawn mainly from the military and civil bureaucracies. Because this elite state has often run into political troubles, the bureaucratic and military elites have had to share power with political leaders. The latter group with few exceptions has not been able to emerge as a major power wielding group. Some observers have suggested that Pakistan is now ruled by a troika consisting of the president, a military leader like the chief of army staff, and the prime minister. The contention here is that the state in Pakistan throughout its recent history has been an elitist state in which the civil, military, and a few dominant political groups participate, with the bulk of the lower income groups and the masses of people being marginally involved with highly limited participation. However, the process of politicization of Pakistan's polity is continuing. With the entry of political groups into the decision-making process and with periodic elections, the bureaucratic and military elites are also becoming politicized. An example of this process is the military bureaucracy. Many observers have noted that the role of the army chief of staff has changed in the sense that the new military chiefs cannot impose their dominant power on the state. It is said that the army chief of staff will function more and more as a broker who tries to bring together the contending groups led by the president and the prime minister into some kind of a working alliance. What needs to be noted is the fact that ethnic divisions that exist in the society have penetrated the military as well. Thus, the nature and kind of compromise that the army chief of staff may be able to bring about depends upon the sort of pressures that the "Pathan and Punjabi components of the army high command"[39] are exercising on him. It is possible that in this process the Punjabi component with its larger numbers will become increasing influential. This is because with increasing politicization, the influence of Punjab with its majority population will become greater.

This analysis leads us to certain disturbing conclusions. Pakistan has always faced the problem of a leadership divided along both political and ethnic lines, with the army claiming that its intervention was necessary to keep the country intact. If the military structure also faces internal strains, Pakistan would have to find a new locus of political power. The only hope for Pakistan would then be that both certain economic changes and the continuing democratic political process from its present fragile form will crystallize into something more viable and stable.

This chapter started by suggesting that, because Pakistan faced such monumental external and internal pressures, it should settle for the conservative objective that Michael Oakeshott described as the essential characteristic of a political activity. This was "to keep afloat on an even keel." Perhaps a fuller quotation from Oakeshott would throw greater light on the predicament of Pakistan. "In political activity, then, men sail a boundless and bottomless sea; there is neither harbour for shelter nor floor for anchorage, neither starting-place nor appointed destination. The enterprise is to keep afloat on an even keel; the sea is both friend and enemy; and the seamanship consists in using the resources of a traditional manner of behavior in order to make a friend of every hostile occasion."[40] Islamicists and others would ask, What is the purpose of keeping afloat? By remaining afloat, for the time being the purpose may be to go somewhere later. If the state does not move in some direction, the stormy sea may drown it. In order to go somewhere, the country needs a purpose and a compass and a map.

This was precisely the major failing of the Pakistani leaders. They did not produce a coherent set of guidelines and a strategy or a plan to follow those guidelines. It is true that soon after the establishment of the state both the Westernized and the religious leaders got entangled in fierce controversies about the political character and ideology of the state. It was significant that both types of leaders seemed to be out of touch with the actual or concrete problems of their society. The Westernized elites waxed eloquent about the parliamentary form of government. The religious leaders produced lofty rhetoric about the glories of an ideal Islamic state. Neither side addressed itself to the concrete problems of the society. When Pakistan started, its society consisted of two parts. The rural areas still existed in a semi-feudal state, and in the urban areas the economy was largely in the hands of trading communities with faint glimmerings of a precapitalist society. Vast proportions of the population both in urban and rural areas lay steeped in poverty and illiteracy. The Islam that was practiced, particularly in the rural areas, was riddled with fatalism and superstition and thus laced with the content and customs of a semi-feudal society. The challenge that faced the founders and the builders was how to resolve the contradictions of such a society through a new social and political program with Islamic underpinnings. Jinnah, who represented perhaps the best among the Westernized elites, was a great founder but lacked the qualities of an imaginative builder. He could think only in terms of a strong centralized government guided by a governor-general at the center and governors in the provinces. As for the economic and social changes, his naval ADC told this author that the Quaid's vision of Pakistan was that of a poor Britain. Similarly, the religious leaders were incapable of measuring up to the task of how to defeudalize the rural society and unify the ethnic-ridden Pakistanis through Islamicization that involved progressivity. They talked only of instant Islamization. They could think only of the Islam of ibadat (religious worship). They neither knew how the complex world worked nor were they acutely aware of the actual concrete society of Pakistan that existed at the mass level.

Into such a state of political, cultural, and ideological confusion the Americans walked in with their handsome offers of military assistance through the SEATO and the CENTO with General Ayub Khan as their supreme representative. Americans had seldom heard anything more reassuring when Ayub declared in the U.S. congress, "We provide the manpower and you provide us with the means to do the fighting."[41] After that, the story moved along predictable lines—military rule for more than a decade (1958-1969) followed by an interregnum of 1970-1977 when the country broke up, and a democratic regime under Bhutto, the Bonaparte, emerged for seven years. This was again followed by military rule from 1977-1988 under Zia-ul-Haq.

The period following 1988 to the present has been described in considerable detail in this chapter. The same stark facts continue. Although Pakistan's men and women in the millions "sit and hear each other groan" both in the rural and urban areas, Pakistani elites—the new political groups dominated by the successors of the civil and military bureaucracies—have been trying to jerk the country forward through a philosophy that is a combination of social utility of greed and Islamic rhetoric. Western dominance has continued though in different forms. Pakistan's involvement in the Soviet Afghan war followed by an inflow of 3 million Afghan refugees, drugs and Kalashnikov guns have further worsened the already intractable political and social land-scape of Pakistan. Pakistan's attempts to develop some early forms of nuclear capability and its feeble attempts to continue the Kashmir struggle are often followed by the American threats to either declare it an outright terrorist state or place it on a "watch list" for 180 days.[42]

The reason for Western dominance of Pakistan through military aid to the Pakistan military and economic assistance to its weak economy was because Pakistan, due to its strategic location, would be a front line state to absorb or contain the Soviet threat. This explains why Pakistan was pressured into joining military alliances. That phase of Western dominance is over. But a new problem has arisen in the form of what the West regards as Islamic fundamentalism. In Western eyes, Islamic fundamentalism sits entrenched in Iran, a neighbor of Pakistan. The threat of Islamic fundamentalism emerging as a major force continues in Afghanistan. Similarly, in Western calculations Islamic fundamentalists lurk behind the Kashmiri struggle against India . As already pointed out, Pakistani involvement in the Kashmir struggle was viewed in that fashion and Pakistan was threatened that it would be blacklisted as a terrorist state . Thus, the threat of Islamic fundamentalism looms large in Western eyes because they see a real possibility of the fragile fabric of the Pakistani state being taken over by Islamic fundamentalists. The friends of the West like liberals and secularists in Pakistan also view the situation along similar lines. They welcomed the election of Benazir Bhutto as the prime minister of Pakistan.

We have tried to indicate that the weak state of Pakistan is not a sovereign state controlling either its domestic policies or in a position to shape its foreign policies. It needs life jackets "to keep afloat." Pakistan is an Islamic state which should be able to decide how to contain or control extreme forms of Islamic fundamentalism, whether such threats stem from internal or external sources. We have said that Saudi rulers, who control such abundant economic resources, have to depend upon external alliances to maintain themselves in power. The Pakistani prime minister would go to any length to consolidate her position, which is based on neither a sound economy nor strong political support within the country.

However, it can be argued that Pakistan—its government and the people—have the capacity to extract from a seemingly inclement environment certain political and ideological resources that can give it relative autonomy to move the country forward in ways that are expected of an Islamic polity. Third World countries like India, Pakistan, and Algeria, to name a few, waged their struggles for independence with the help of national movements and not political parties. Pakistan also needs a national Islamic movement. To pursue such a course of action, Pakistani elites would have to make a conscious decision to change their living styles from excessive or conspicuous consumption to one that their own legitimate earnings and the resources of the country can afford. This involves a whole series of ideological commitments, and we have been at pains to point out that such a strategy differs from that of the fundamentalists. It involves the formulation of a socio-political Islamic program designed to modernize the economy and society of Pakistan by combining Islamic ideology and Western technology.

An equally important part of this movement would be the social and attitudinal transformation of the people who live surrounded by despair and poverty, both in the rural and many parts of the urban areas. They also believe in Islam, but as Ali Shari'ati pointed out, their Islamic belief and poverty can be transformed dialectically to make them aware of how their conditions can and must improve. This involves a long-term process that can be pursued through a movement. This is Islamicization: making Muslims progressively Islamic. Islamic fundamentalists often opt for instant Islamization accompanied by violence and removal of their rulers.

Thus, Pakistani intellectuals and leaders have to decide as to how they want their country to develop. Should it drift and stumble along, hoping at best, as the quotation from Oakeshott suggests, "to make a friend of every hostile occasion"? Or should the leaders and people of Pakistan be clear and committed in their minds to a national and ideological destiny of Pakistan that is different from but not necessarily hostile to the West? To reach that destiny, the intellectuals and the leaders along with the people would have to embark on a cooperative enterprise for community development at the grassroots level. Such community development would be the foundation with the objective being national development. It may be recalled that Zulfikar Ali Bhutto used to harangue his people by offering them roti, kapra, aur makan (bread, clothing, and housing), but after winning their support would retire to his palatial surroundings. Obviously this cosmetic form of Mao's mass line did not strike roots.

Pakistan's version of politics has produced its own canons. Both Pakistani civil and military bureaucrats are centralizers and often tend to disregard Pakistan's cultural and ethnic diversities. The military leaders have consistently followed the strategy that Pakistan can buy maximum insurance for its defense against India only through external dependence. Politicians seem to think that maximum accumulation of power without civil or military checks would somehow maximize public benefit. None of these power wielders and power seekers have learned from Pakistan's political history that the political fabric of the state can be built not through unitarian strategies and coercive methods but through federal consensus. It is significant that in the exercise of coercive centralization that Pakistan's power wielders have pursued they have found their allies in the ulama.[43] Since the ulama subscribe to the ideal of the unity of the entire Muslim umma, it is difficult for them to face the reality that very often not even a united Muslim umma exists in Pakistan. We come back to the same problem that Pakistan has faced ever since its inception. The fabric of this state cannot be built on a long-term basis merely through the military and bureaucratic structures that Pakistan has inherited from its colonial past. Both political realities and a reappraisal of its Islamic resources would suggest that only through new vibrant Islamic and political movements can this country build bridges of understanding and working relationships between the elites and the common people and between Islam and federalism. Bridges between Islam and federalism can be built only by those leaders and intellectuals who have developed a deep knowledge of and confidence in the Islamic process as well as a profound understanding of the cultures that underpin the regional forces.

7

Islamic Political Theory
and Human Development

Political theory refers to those concepts, ideas, and principles which have been formulated through deduction and empiricism to explain how a political society and its institutions function. David Miller thinks:

> Perhaps the best approximation is to say that political theory is an attempt to understand political and social relationships at a high level of generality, and in light of that understanding to advocate a certain practical stance towards them. At one extreme, a theory may portray existing relationships as the perfect embodiment of rationality and consequently recommend conserving them in their entirety; at the other extreme, a theory may highlight the gulf between existing institutions and rational principles, and describe in some detail an alternative social and political order which would better realize the principles in question.[1]

Islamic political theory suggests that if human beings were to follow the Sharia (certain mandatory prescriptions derived from the Qur'an and the Traditions of the Prophet), they would obtain both God's approval and maintain social justice in their community. This is, on the face of it, a highly normative theory which urges Muslims that they should follow certain principles of human behavior. But this normative theory is grounded in some empiricism in the sense that the Qur'an argues that those people who did not follow these principles as conveyed to them by God's messengers or prophets came to grief. Thus, the Qur'an reminds all human beings about how certain communities who did not follow these laws were destroyed. For gaining an empirical insight into what happened, the Qur'an suggests: "Do they not travel through the land so that their hearts (and minds) may thus learn wisdom and their ears may thus learn to hear? Truly, it is not their eyes that are blind but their hearts which are in their breasts" (22: 45-46). Thus, the Qur'an is recommending an empiricism of a profound nature through which human beings will learn to hear, see, and discern both the events as well as their meanings and implications.

Many Muslim writers and observers have argued that Islamic political ideas form a part of an ideological framework. Islamic ideology in this sense may be compared to "a total ideology which as an all-inclusive system of comprehensive reality . . . is a set of beliefs . . . and seeks to transform the whole of a way of life. . . . Ideology, in this sense, . . . is a secular religion."[2]

In what ways does an Islamic ideology promote human development? Human development is a process which expands and widens people's choices. It is in a democratic community where the citizens through the exercise of certain political freedoms and human rights can determine and shape their own futures. Traditional Islamic theory, on the other hand, may emphasize that social justice and an enriched human life can be attained through following certain Islamic commandments. This implies that human happiness is brought about more through obedience to certain commandments rather than through a process of making choices.

Islamic rulers are enjoined to use certain consultative mechanisms for the betterment of the community. The question that arises is, Will such a community produce sufficient political energy to enable the citizens to attain higher and higher levels of human self-realization? This explains why some Muslim thinkers have emphasized that the shura (consultative process) should be anchored in an elected assembly. Muhammad Iqbal is such a thinker. We would argue that an equally important element in an Islamic democracy are a grassroots, participatory kind of local or mosque democracy as sometimes attempted by organizations like the Ikhwan in Egypt.

In contrast to the kind of normative theory that Islam recommends where the emphasis is on the umma (Muslim community) as a whole, we find that the reality is that the Islamic world has been divided for a long time into nation states and within nation states certain ethnic and linguistic communities and groups. It is here that we find Ibn Khaldun's concept of asabiya (group solidarity) very useful. Ibn Khaldun (1332-1406) was the author of the well known work, *The Muqaddimah* [*An Introduction to History*]. His social theory was based on certain social laws derived and developed from the observations of facts which were found as concomitances and sequences. These facts, in addition to revealing certain causal relationships between events which could be both past and current, could also be explored to see if there were certain hidden or inner meanings of historical change in them. Thus, his methodology did not constitute simple empiricism. The Qur'an had also referred to the hidden meaning of events. Ibn Khaldun wrote: "The inner meaning of history, on the other hand, involves speculation and an attempt to get at the truth, subtle explanation of the causes and origins of existing things, and deep knowledge of the how and why of events. (History,) therefore, is firmly rooted in philosophy. It deserves to be accounted a branch of (philosophy)."[3]

The great contribution of Ibn Khaldun was to draw the attention of the Muslims to the study of sociology and history as interrelated subjects so that they could understand their past greatness and present predicament. He said: "The past resembles the future as water resembles water."[4] Another point that he emphasized was that masses of human beings influenced the currents of history more than isolated individuals.

This kind of thinking runs counter to traditional Muslim thinking, which argues that, if they were only to return to certain forms of Islamic piety, God would set everything right and the community would be extricated from its present plight. The historical process does not distribute its rewards on the basis of only individual religious piety. It is a cosmic process in which those nations which combine individual ethics with appropriate social behavior and maximize the use of material and nonmaterial resources for national purposes emerge as ascendant with others lacking in such qualities declining. If in the historical process the United States has emerged as dominant, it is difficult for Muslims to admit that this is perhaps God's will, which implies that in the cosmic scale Muslims may have been found lacking in certain qualities. Thus, if Muslims decide to resist American domination, they would have to reorganize certain social forces to meet this challenge. The Qur'an suggests something similar when it declares: "God does not change a nation until they change what is in their hearts" (13: 11). According to Fazlur Rahman, the most fundamental point that needs to be grasped is: "That a God to whom it is, in the final analysis, indifferent whether He is effective in history or not is certainly not the God of Muhammad and the Qur'an. If history is the proper field for Divine activity, historical forces must, by definition, be employed for the moral end as judiciously as possible."[5]

Ibn Khaldun's social theory of how Arabs developed into a great power and civilization followed certain sequential stages and concepts. These were asabiya (group solidarity), mulk (royal authority), and khilafa (Islamic rule). Ibn Khaldun was more a realist than an Islamic idealist though his devotion to Islam cannot be questioned. Scientific observation based on facts as they were and not as they should be suggested to him that asabiya was a primary and vital source of energy for establishing political power. The dictionary meaning of *asabiya* includes positive connotations like tribal solidarity leading to national consciousness and nationalism. *Asabiya* also implies zealous partisanship, bigotry, clannishness, and racism. Obviously, Islamic normative theory would perhaps frown on both the negative and positive connotations of asabiya because they negate the very concept of the umma and its development. A historian or sociologist, on the other hand, would have to face the fact of asabiya and the pride that goes with it as something embedded in human nature. Ibn Khaldun as a historian and sociologist could see that even though Arabs were steeped in their asabiya, they were capable of developing their larger Islamic loyalties if inspired by a religion and the leadership of a prophet or a saint. Thus, his perceptive observation was, "But when there is religion (among them) through prophecy or sainthood, then they have some restraining influence in themselves. The qualities of haughtiness and jealousy leave them. It is, then, easy for them to subordinate themselves and to unite (as a social organization). This is achieved by the common religion they now have. It causes rudeness and pride to disappear and exercises a restraining influence on their mutual envy and jealousy."[6]

There is a dialectical struggle between asabiya (tribal solidarity, pride or nationalism) and an Islamic order, which aspires for an international umma. The Saudis built their modern state with the twin principles of asabiya and Islam, the latter force coming from their adherence to the Wahhabi doctrines as represented by the Ikhwan (the military-religious brotherhood of warriors). The political rhetoric of the Saudis is Islamic, and some of their generosity, though limited and shortsighted, is influenced by Islam. As the Saudi involvement in the U.N. war against Iraq has demonstrated and as William B. Quandt has pointed out, "The Saudis appear to have come to realize that Islamic solidarity may prove to be as fragile a notion as Arab unity. Therefore, faced with specific choices the Saudis seem to weigh their security concerns first, their ideological preferences second."[7] Indeed, many Islamicists have noticed that the very term *Saudi Arabia* indicates how the asabiya notion has edged out the Islamic concept.

The failure of Khomeini's strategy to radicalize the entire Muslim umma both against local rulers and against the American domination of the Middle East and the Muslim world again demonstrates the enormous and continuing strength of the asabiya relative to the Islamic factor in the Muslim world. In contrast to Khomeini's annual exhortations to the Muslim pilgrims assembled in Mecca to use the occasion as an opportunity to rid the Muslim world of foreign and particularly American domination, we find his chastened successor, Rafsanjani, admitting that the umma is not even united enough to start its month of fasting in Ramadan on a common day and ruefully conceding what serious national, sectarian, and political divisions plague the Muslim umma. Similarly, in the case of Pakistan one can argue that the Punjabi asabiya of the ruling political and military groups provoked Bengali nationalism, and these two factors were jointly responsible for the secession of Bangladesh from the state of Pakistan in 1971.

Many Muslims do not recognize that the community of believers is a confederal community that has within it nations, subnations, and ethnic and cultural groups. They regret that the single solidified community (umma) does not exist but think that a few bold moves in that direction and overcoming the divisive machinations of the enemy forces would create this community. They forget that the Qur'an itself refers to the fact that God has created nations and tribes for purposes of classification and distinction. Thus, assabiya is present as a distinguishing or divisive factor even within what are recognized as single Muslim nation states like Pakistan or Iraq or Turkey. The asabiya of which a Sindhi or a Kurd is proud can contribute to human development. Cultural or linguistic consciousness can very often lead to the multicultural enrichment of a federal or a confederal state. Suppression of these forms of pluralist consciousness can very often lead to the disintegration of the hitherto recognized nation states.

The lesson that can be extrapolated from Ibn Khaldun's ideas is that Muslim communities first need to combine their respective asabiya with vibrant Islamic social and political programs as a possible strategy to convert the soft states that exist now into strong and cohesive states. Muhammad Iqbal as early as the 1930s urged Muslims that, "For the present every Muslim nation must sink into her own deeper self, temporarily focus her vision on herself alone, until all are strong and powerful to form a living family of republics."[8]

The challenge for each of these Muslim states that Iqbal is referring to is how to develop an Islamic polity within its respective territory. How does it develop an Islamic social and political program in its respective national context? Iqbal suggested that a transfer should take place of the power of ijtihad (creative interpretation of the law) from individual representatives of schools to a Muslim legislative assembly, which in view of the growth of opposing sects would be the only possible form ijma (consensus of the Muslim community or scholars for a legal decision) could take in modern times.[9] In the Shi'i view, ijma is a consensus of imams.

Because Islam is considered to be a political religion with an ideology, which is often termed Islamic ideology, the great majority of Muslims subscribe to the view that such an ideology should govern every category of human activity. Therefore, the central question is, How all-encompassing is the Sharia (Islamic law)? Broadly speaking, two categories of human activities are governed by the Sharia: ibadat (religious worship) and mu'amalat (interpersonal affairs). The rules of ibadat with no significant variations tend to be the same among the various sects and schools of law. Among these schools of law, a principal one is the Hanafi school, which influences the largest number of Sunni Muslims, who are concentrated in the eastern Mediterranean areas and Pakistan and India. The adherents of the other Sunni schools like the Maliki school are concentrated in North and West Africa. The members of the Shafi school are to be found in coastal areas of East Africa, Ceylon, Malaysia, and Indonesia. The fourth Sunni school is the Hanbali school, with most of its followers living in central Saudi Arabia. The principal Shi'ite school is the Twelver school, with most of its followers in Iran. There is considerable agreement as regards the fundamental rules of ibadat among all these schools.

The main differences between the sects and schools arise in the matter of the second category of the Sharia; namely, the

mu'amalat, which pertains to the conduct of interpersonal relations rather than the relationship of the Muslim to God. Therefore, the question that the Muslim community is faced with is
how the Sharia pertaining to mu'amalat will be legislated in Muslim states. For legislation dealing with this aspect of the Sharia,
the two important governing concepts are ijma (consensus of
the Muslim community or scholars for resolving legal questions)
and ijtihad (individual judgment necessary for a legal ruling
through creative interpretation of the existing body of law). As
regards ijma, the debate is between those who think that ijma
implies universal consensus of all the ulama and those who take
the more realistic view that there is no universal agreement either
in the entire muslim community (the umma) or among all the
ulama. In other words, ijma may exist either in different countries or among different schools and sects inhabiting these countries. In addition, there is the view of the modernists who think
that ijma and ijtihad can be exercised by a Muslim legislative
assembly.

The famous Muslim scholar from India, Shah Wali Allah,
was of the opinion that it was simply not possible for universal
agreement to emerge regarding the Sharia pertaining to interpersonal matters in either the community as a whole or all the
ulama of the community. "Ijma," according to Shah Wali Allah,
"is the consensus of the ulema and men of authority in different
towns and localities. In this sense, ijma can be held anywhere at
any time."[10] The argument put forward by Muhammad Iqbal
runs along similar lines with the additional weight that he
assigns to the necessity of the Muslim community developing
and reinterpreting the Sharia in response to the needs of modern times.

> I know the Ulama of Islam claim finality for the popular
> schools of Mohammedan Law . . . but since things have
> changed and world of Islam is today confronted by the
> extraordinary development of human thought in all its
> directions, I see no reason why this attitude should be
> maintained any longer. Did the founders of our schools ever
> claim finality for their reasonings and interpretations?
> Never. The claim of the present generation of Muslim liber-
> als to re-interpret the foundational legal principles, in the
> light of their own experience and the altered conditions of
> modern life is, in my opinion, perfectly justified.[11]

Iqbal was again quite clear that the power of ijtihad in the form of interpreting Islamic law should rest with the popularly elected legislative assembly. "The transfer of the power of Ijtihad from individual representatives of schools to a Muslim legislative assembly which, in view of the growth of opposing sects, is the only possible form Ijma can take in modern times, will secure contributions to legal discussion from laymen who happen to possess a keen insight into affairs."[12]

Muhammad Asad, a European and a Jewish convert to Islam, was deeply influenced by Muhammad Iqbal, who persuaded him "to help elucidate the intellectual premises of the future Islamic state."[13] In spite of his close relations with King Abd al-Aziz of Saudi Arabia, Asad emerged as a protagonist of an Islamic state which would respond to the needs of modern Muslims. He was of the opinion that the scope of the Sharia was relatively small thus providing to a modern Muslim state considerable autonomy to legislate about social and economic matters. Muhammad Asad, in *The Principles of State and Government in Islam*, wrote:

> Because it is restricted to commands and prohibitions expressed in self-evident terms in Qur'an and Sunnah, the real shari'ah is extremely concise and, therefore, easily understandable; and because it is so small it cannot—nor, as I have pointed out, was it ever intended to—provide detailed legislation for every contingency of life. . . . To be more precise, the legitimate field of the community's lawmaking activity comprises (a) details in cases and situations where the shari'ah provides a general principle but no detailed ruling, and (b) principles and details with regard to matters which are mubah, that is, not covered by shar'i laws at all. It is this method that the Quran has referred to in the words: For every one of you We have ordained a Divine Law and an open road.[14]

Fazlur Rahman, in *Islam and Modernity*, has suggested a highly innovative method of Qur'anic exegesis. This involves processes of thinking in which the skills and qualities of a historian, a social scientist, and an "ethical engineer" are combined. The first task is that of the historian, who examines the specific situations that the Qur'an presents to elicit from it "certain general principles, values and long range objectives." To this process, the social scientist brings to bear a knowledge of the socio-historical situation that exists in modern times. The task of the social scientist is to make a careful analysis and assessment of the present situation to "change the present to whatever extent necessary, and so we can determine priorities afresh in order to implement the Qur'anic values afresh."[15]

It seems that the task of the social scientist is intertwined with that of the "ethical engineer," because the social scientist is both analyzing and diagnosing the present situation to rectify it. He does this to change it so that the Qur'anic values may be implemented. Fazlur Rahman's thesis clearly indicates that he has in mind a committed Muslim social scientist who analyzes and assesses the present to change it through the implementation of Qur'anic principles and values. Those who would raise questions as to how impartial or professional a social scientist is in functioning as a social engineer of a Muslim society are likely to face equally valid criticisms from Fazlur Rahman and Muslim scholars. The latter would point out that Western social scientists have used their knowledge and skills of social sciences to assist their political leaders in pursuing certain domestic and foreign policies of their governments.

We propose to examine how suitable and adaptable are the Western or American models of democracy and the free market system in Muslim societies. First we will deal with the democratic model and what changes need to be made in it so that it may suit the social conditions and intellectual traditions of a Muslim society. Chapter 2 suggested that some of the major ideas of Muhammad Abduh in Egypt and Sir Sayyid Ahmad Khan in India were challenged by some of the Muslim leaders, including the leader of the Ikhwan al-Muslimun in Egypt and the Jammat-i-Islami in Pakistan. Their argument was that Abduh and Sayyid Ahmad Khan had gone so far in incorporating Western ideas into their suggested Islamic reforms that perhaps the spirit and vigor of Islam had been compromised. In addition, it could also be argued that the liberal and modernist followers of the two reformers had not been able to produce viable political systems because of frequent military interventions in Muslim societies.

Our analysis of modern Muslim history suggests that the dissatisfaction with some of the orthodox Muslim ideas that started during Abduh's and Sir Sayyid's times has persisted. Thus, we have writers like Muhammad Iqbal (1876-1938) in

India, Ali Shari'ati (1933-1977) in Iran, and Fazlur Rahman (1919-1988) in Pakistan who have emphasized that there should be some kind of progressive movement within Islamic thought so that the ideas of liberal democracy that were first presented during the time of the Prophet and his first four successors may be reinforced and updated to meet the Muslim challenge. In addition, one could see that these writers were also concerned about human development so that the concept of Islamic social justice would be interpreted more imaginatively and profoundly to improve the lot of the poor as well as the rights of women in a Muslim society.

The question, therefore, arises that when these ideas have been a part of Muslim thinking for such a long time, why have they not become politically popular and acceptable in Muslim societies? The problem has been that political leaders have not been able to develop an institutional framework for persuading Muslim societies to accept Islam's liberal tradition. There are several reasons as to why this has occurred. First, political leaders in Muslim societies tend to manipulate the devotion that the Muslim masses have for Islam and have not developed their own profound understanding of Islamic ideas and institutions because they have used mostly the Muslim mullahs and sometimes the ulama as well in mobilizing support for their political programs. The result has been that the Muslim masses were very often swayed by Muslim religious leaders who presented Islam by emphasizing religious piety and not the other component of social justice. Sometimes the religious leaders went so far as to lull the masses into a supine acceptance of whatever fate (taqdir) had destined for them under feudal systems.

If Muslim leaders had tried to reinterpret the Islamic message in terms of human development rather than in pursuing their own narrow political ends, they would have presented the shura concept to the masses not just in terms of consultation but in terms of both representative and participatory democracy. The reason why Muslim leaders failed to interpret the Qur'anic ideas in terms of social equality and social democracy was that the Qur'anic ideas came into conflict with the social and power structures and interests of the leadership and Muslim governments. It is significant that the Qur'an anticipated this problem when it enjoined the Prophet not to disregard the pleas of a blind, poor, and powerless man for instruction in the Qur'an and be deferential to the powerful and influential personalities in

Mecca who had also come to see him. The Qur'an states: "The Prophet frowned and turned away, because there came to him the blind man (interrupting). But what could tell thee but that perchance he might grow (in spiritual understanding)? Or that he might receive admonition, and the teaching might profit him? As to one who regards himself as independent, to him dost thou attend" (80: 1-6). Some of the commentators have argued in defense of the Prophet that the Prophet was being deferential only to the important people who were present in the meeting because they had been using their power and influence to prevent the Islamic cause from spreading. He was hoping to persuade them to join the faith.

Thus, the question is raised, How can Qur'anic ideas of egalitarianism overcome certain existing and formidable social and power structures? Democracy could emerge in other societies only when economic and capitalist development could dissolve or overcome feudal structures of the landed gentry. Should Muslim societies also wait until this happens or should certain Muslim leaders with the help of Islamic ideas accelerate the process of social change and human development? Perhaps believing in the triumph of ideas over interests, intellectual leaders like Iqbal, Shari'ati, and Fazlur Rahman have argued that the Qur'an is an uncompromising advocate of social justice. The argument here is that Muslim countries cannot strengthen their societies and state structures unless they commit themselves to representative and participatory democracy. If Muslim societies do not make a strong effort in strengthening and developing their social and political institutions, they will continue to be "soft states" and thus ineffective in their responses to the Western challenge.

When Third World societies are told that they should follow the Western democratic system, what is often implied in this advice is that they should develop a competitive party system. It is not realized that the party system in the West very often amounts to a system of competitive electoral instruments and the parties function mostly as electoral devices to get a group of leaders elected. Because in many Western societies governments are not supposed to control the bulk of the social sectors, parties tend to become dormant for several years after their respective leaders have been elected. This book is suggesting that the political party, particularly in a Muslim society with its emphasis on Islamic ideology, has to function not just as an electoral instrument but as a social service organization engaged in activating local governments, composing ethnic differences, and above all, providing leadership and initiative in developing rural and urban services in areas like education, health, and so forth.

The Gandhian model of activating village economies through cottage industries and other social services satisfied some of the characteristics of a social service organization. A more dynamic model was that of Mao's mass line where the leadership was from the masses to the masses. To win over the masses, Mao argued, "take the ideas of the masses (scattered and unsystematic ideas), then go to the masses to propagate and explain these ideas until the masses embrace them as their own, hold fast to them, and translate them into action, and test the correctness of these ideas in such action."[16] When a political party functions as a transmission belt in which ideas bubble from bottom upward and then are refined and communicated to the masses by party cadres, the party and the mass line create political consciousness that becomes a precondition for generating economic development. As Mao put it succinctly, "a great spiritual force becomes a great material force."[17] It was astonishing that a Marxist had become aware of what latent spiritual energy the masses possessed and how enthusiastically they would work for national development in a participatory democracy. The Gandhian and Maoist models have to be supplemented by a tireless and systematic campaign to educate the masses to make them aware of how great socio-economic changes are afoot and how they should participate in and respond to them. The laudable efforts that Akhter Hameed Khan has made in Pakistan to improve the living conditions and promote social development at the local level will be noted later in this chapter.

In a Muslim society, Islam could act as an inspiring and instructive model. It was in this area that Ayatollah Khomeini made his unique contribution. He pointed out that Islam "is a religion where worship is joined to politics and political activity is a form of worship."[18] Unlike other religious leaders in other Muslim societies, he constantly preached to his people that they had to participate in a massive socio-economic revolution. In fact, the great socio-economic revolution was as important as the political revolution. He asked Iranians to wake up from the sleep that had been imposed upon them for several hundred years— not so much for performing prayers but for initiating rapid economic and industrial change.

They injected this sleep and you have to wake up. You are the same humankind and realize that other races, countries and regimes are not superior. They have made us this way by propaganda and made us such that our hands are stretched towards the West or East: whatever we need comes from these countries. . . . If we want to produce those things which we need in ordinary life, we will be able to produce them by our efforts and after a while we will become industrialized. Those who developed industries are just like us—one hand and two ears. But the difference is that they woke up before us and they put us to sleep and used their forces to keep us in that situation. . . . In every revolution in the beginning there are slogans. But after the revolution we have to act. Your hand should not be stretched to either East or West. We don't want to be dependent. First, we have to wake up.[19]

What we are suggesting is that before the democratic plant strikes roots in the soil of some of the Muslim societies, some of its roots will have to be enriched and its branches pruned before the plant as a whole starts flourishing in an Islamic environment. We have, therefore, recommended that some of the attempts made under the Gandhian model in India, the Maoist mass line in China, and the public educational campaign that was undertaken during the Nehru era would all be useful in nurturing the plant of democracy. We have also indicated how Islamic ideas are an essential element in the nourishment of democracy.

As for the usefulness of the free market system, it seems that equally major modifications are needed before it becomes adaptable and productive in a Muslim environment. Capitalism with its consumption-oriented society is penetrating Third World societies. The free market system and the capitalist structure of the economy have been recommended to Third World societies because the functional inequality and social utility of greed, despite the danger of increasing economic inequality and even poverty in the short run, are supposed to accelerate economic growth in the long run. Capitalism by itself is such a doctrine of cold calculus that it can neither legitimize itself through any system of social justice nor can it alter the parameters of the social equation that exists in Third World societies. "Modern capitalism," wrote Lord Keynes, "is absolutely irreligious, without internal union, without much public spirit, often, though not always a mere congeries of possessors and pursuers."[20] In Third World societies too many people are chasing too few goods. Therefore, the fundamental question is, How does such a society control its growing population and at the same time increase its per capita GNP without a mechanism of social and distributive controls?

Political scientists have tried to develop a model of macro socio-economic change on lines similar to that of the Keynesian theory in economics. The line of reasoning put forward by Karl Deutsch, Samuel Huntington, and others is that rapid economic change and urbanization invariably result in the erosion of certain traditional loyalties like those of caste, tribe, and religion. This theory has been applied to the Middle East, and it has been suggested that Islam will also face a similar erosion of loyalties. Daniel Lerner has written:

> As we shall show, the Western model of modernization exhibits certain components and sequences whose relevance is global. . . . The model evolved in the West is an historical fact. That the same basic model reappears in virtually all modernizing societies on all continents of the world, regardless of variations in race, color, or creed. . . . The point is that the secular process of social change, which brought modernization to the Western world, has more than antiquarian relevance to today's problems of the Middle East transition. Indeed, the lesson is that the Middle Easterner modernizers will do well to study the historical sequence of Western growth.[21]

The Islamic revolution in Iran disproved this sequential model in the sense that industrialization and urbanization did not bring about any marked decline in the loyalty of Iranians to Islam. Chapter 3 indicated that the Shah's policies of rapid industrialization and urbanization created considerable social injustice among the lower middle and working class groups. This resentment was further compounded by some of his capitulatory policies toward the West and also his frontal assault on the bazaar and the clerics. All these policies enabled Khomeini to organize a massive opposition to the Shah resulting in his overthrow.

What some of the Islamicists have not appreciated is the fact that the replacement of a secular regime is by itself not enough. This has to be followed by a systematic attempt to set up a polity that satisfies the needs of the deprived population in rural and urban areas. The revolutionary regime in Iran made an earnest effort to introduce certain structural changes, like bringing basic industries under state control and land reforms and other measures to bring about income redistribution. Some of these measures in vital areas like land reform could not be implemented because of the war with Iraq and also because of the internal opposition that the regime encountered from some of the influential clerics. As regards land reform, Ayatollah Baha ad-Din Mahallati, one of the prominent ulama of Shiraz, declared that "the law for agrarian reform which has been called Islamic contains provisions which are in clear contradiction to the criteria of Islam, to Ja'fari fiqh, and to the consensus of 'ulama of both early and late times. . . . I pronounce it forbidden to implement his bill." Similarly, Ayatollah Abdullah Shirazi of Mashhad stated that "numerous provisions of the law are contrary to the essential bases of Islam, the Ja'fari school, the practice of the Prophet and the Twelve Imams, and the view of all the jurisprudents of Islam." On the other hand, the three authors of the bill on land reforms defended it as consistent with Islamic law. Ayatollah Muhammad Husayn Bihishti pointed out that "the understanding of Islam held by certain well known fuqaha does not sufficiently accord with the understanding of Islam that is the basis of our revolution."[22]

This goes to show that Khomeini did not exercise monolithic control over the ulama and that the clerical leaders at the top level were by no means united in their commitment to social reforms. Khomeini's constant reiteration that the Islamic revolution was created to maximize certain social benefits to the mustazafin (deprived and exploited) was not carried out in practice. In fact, the gap between revolutionary declarations and their implementation widened as the Iranian regime, faced with the hard reality of reflating the economy after the ravages of war, resorted to certain pragmatic measures like privatization of industries and scaling down of social expenditures.

Some grim estimates indicate that the standard of living in Iran has fallen to 50 percent in real terms of what existed when Khomeini came to power. Uncontrolled rise in population plus an influx of refugees in cities like Meshed have swollen the population and increased overall misery. Similarly, it has been estimated that as many as 15 million Iranians are unemployed and

75 percent of them under the age of twenty-five are underemployed. Seventy-five percent of Iranians live in poverty, making about $1.00 a day. The annual rate of inflation seems to be galloping at about 40 percent.[23]

It seems that the urban ghettos and slum areas, which existed during the Shah's period, continued under the new regime. How some of the slum areas around the city of Meshed erupted into violent demonstrations against the local government in June 1992 was described in the following account in *The New York Times*:

> Witnesses in Meshed said residents of Tolab, a low-income neighborhood near the Imam Reza Shrine, a destination for many Shiite pilgrims, stormed and torched police stations to protest the demolition of their homes by municipal workers.
>
> Residents had been warned to vacate their dwellings on property owned by Astan Qods, Iran's most powerful religious establishment, which administers the shrine and has holdings in real estate, banking, industry and agriculture worth billions of dollars. The dwellings reportedly were erected without building permits . . .
>
> Saturday's riots, along with earlier protests in Teheran, Khorramabad, Shiraz and Arak—in which hundreds of people have been wounded or arrested—constitute the most serious urban disturbances in Iran in 12 years.[24]

We have seen in the case of land reform that some of the conservative clerics were not in favor of redistribution of land. Similarly, in the case cited from Meshed, we find that the religious establishment with investments in real estate, banking, industry, and agriculture worth billions of dollars came into conflict with squatters who had built dwellings on its property. These cases suggest that, in spite of the Islamic revolution and the call for an egalitarian economic and social system, many Islamic clerics find it difficult to overcome their property and class interests. Referring to Islamic, Christian, and Buddhist principles of compassion for the lower income and underprivileged groups, Maxime Rodinson writes: "But these same principles have up to now most often served to justify societies based upon privilege, and this has inevitably weakened their power to mobilize men in the direction indicated. In any case, this circumstance shows that it is vain to count upon these principles alone to transform the world."[25]

It has been argued that the chief strength of the market system and the nascent capitalism it generates is that it produces consumer goods for the middle class. When the middle class in Third World societies watch American TV shows on their networks (and it has been reported that sometimes as many as 30 to 70 percent of such shows are American in origin),[26] they would also like to enjoy some of the comforts and luxuries like TV sets, washers and dryers, and of course, automobiles. This middle class has already risen to 160 million in India and is expected to grow to 300 million by the turn of the century. A society which has started enjoying Pepsi Cola, Wrangler jeans, and Barbie dolls starts caring less and less for the plight of the poor. "Consumerism has raised both expectations and a sense of deprivation," says Devendra Gupta, a New Delhi economist. "If that brings new frustrations and tensions, it could lead to more instability."[27]

Production in a free enterprise economy is propelled by the reward of maximum profits. In this consumption-oriented society, increasingly dominated politically and economically by middle class groups, it is obviously much more profitable to produce for these classes rather than wage goods for the lower income groups. In societies like Pakistan and probably Saudi Arabia, the middle class groups are also dominated by politically powerful bureaucrats and army officers. These groups, although paying their ideological homage to an Islamic society, would like to have their savings invested in banks to earn attractive interest rates. When threats appear that riba or interest will be banned, these groups get alarmed or, in the case of Saudi Arabia, divert their savings to banks in Bahrain. In Pakistan, we were faced with a strange situation when a government, which had campaigned for the enforcement of the Sharia, put advertisements in American newspapers to attract funds from both Pakistani and American investors. An alarming situation arose when the ads assured the buyers of bearer bonds yielding higher than the international market rates of interest that no questions would be asked "of source of funds" and that the bonds would be subject to no income tax. When government officials were asked whether funds made through illegal activities like drugs would also be welcome, the bold, blunt answer was that the purpose of such operations was to convert black money into white money.[28] This, some Islamicists and perhaps radicals would argue, is the insidious influence of capitalism. It has the capacity of making not only individuals dishonest but even governments duplicitous.

In another context, a perceptive writer like Galal Amin of Egypt has pointed out that during the month of Ramadan the ads that the pious were exposed to constantly reiterated at the time of the breaking of the fast or just after the call for evening prayers the message, "We hope that in the breaking of the fast the faster will accept the compliments of Schweppes. The free market system and infitah," Galal Amin complains, "has insured the entry of Schweppes into a Muslim's fast and his prayers."[29] In other words, he suggests that Schweppes has penetrated the innermost relationship of the fasters with their God.

The Qur'an constantly refers to man's ingratitude to his creator. He prays to God fervently when he is in trouble and constantly forgets him when he is out of trouble. The Qur'anic view of man is not very complimentary. "Lo, man is an ingrate unto his Lord. . . . And, lo, in the love of wealth he is violent" (100: 6 and 8). "Rivalry in worldly increase distracteth you until ye come to the graves" (102: 1 and 2). "Woe unto every slandering traducer, who hath gathered wealth (of this world) and arranged it. He thinketh that his wealth will render him immortal" (104: 1-3). Is the Qur'an thundering against accumulation of wealth in fewer and fewer hands and arguing in favor of the circulation and distribution of wealth through zakat? Savings created through interest and contributing to investment in goods which produce maximum and quick profits may lead to prosperity at the top. Does this unrivaled capitalism lead to human development? Are the poor expected to wait until they receive their crumbs through the trickling down process? The Prophet warned that poverty may lead to disbelief.

Under the welfare state in the West, an active role for the state has developed so that the excesses of capitalism may be moderated through the transfer of resources and services to lower income groups. Many Islamic scholars have argued that there is a role for the public sector in an Islamic polity. There is a hadith (Prophetic Tradition) that states: "Muslims share alike in three things: water, herbage and fire."[30] According to the Maliki school, minerals, including oil, cannot be privately owned, but belong to the state irrespective of how they are extracted or mined, that is, by the individual with or without the consent of the state. When the authorities license a person to search and extract minerals, they do not surrender the ownership for minerals remain vested in the state. The Hanafi school specified that minerals could be owned and extracted by private individuals but such individuals had to pay the treasury one-fifth of the total proceeds, that is, royalty. Similarly, Muhammad Baqir as-Sadr has argued that if the ruler (authority) deems it necessary to place activities like reclamation of land, mining minerals, and digging canals within his sphere, he can do so to pursue the Islamic ideals of the society.[31] One can argue that the hadith just quoted may also be used by Muslims states to preserve the environment through public control of water, herbage, and fire.

As indicated in the early part of this chapter, the Sharia tends to divide human activities into two categories: ibadat (religious worship) and mu'amalat (interpersonal affairs). An Islamic fundamentalist by and large tends to take the view that, if Muslims were to attend in a devout manner to their ibadat, their mu'amalat with God's help would automatically be set right. Khomeini in revolutionary Iran had a more dynamic view and argued that there was a political and social dimension to ibadat that would shape and determine the mu'amalat. In his conception of mu'amalat, he again took a much more radical view than the Saudi religious leaders and also a religious group like the Jamaat-i-Islami in Pakistan by arguing that the West, because of their interest in oil and the strategic location of the Middle East, were determined to put their stamp on Islam. This he characterized as "American Islam." But there is an economic power structure in the Middle East and the Third World that can disable even a dynamic or revolutionary Islam from translating some of Islam's ideas of social justice into appropriate policy legislation. This has surfaced very clearly in postrevolutionary and particularly in post-Khomeini Iran. First, the clerics were opposed to any scheme of radical redistribution of land. Now they are hesitant to redistribute economic power and income even in the urban areas. This explains the urban riots that have taken place in Iran as well as the glaring disparities in income that have continued relatively unaltered since the days of the Shah.

When we look at Saudi Arabia, the conservative cast of Islam becomes much more pronounced. The hard realities are that Western interests dominated by the United States keep the Saudi royal family in power. The Saudi royal family in its turn makes sure both in terms of its own interests and the interests of external powers that Saudi Arabia is free of any social turbulence. This became crystal clear in the case of the Gulf War in

1991. Sheikh Abd al-Aziz ibn Baz, the head of the Council of Ulama in Saudi Arabia, issued a fatwa (religious decree) blessing not only Muslim participation in the war but also the alliance that the Saudi regime had forged with non-Muslim powers to evict Iraqi forces from Kuwait.[32] In the Gulf War, the Islamic factor was being manipulated both by Saddam Hussein of Iraq and King Fahd of Saudi Arabia. Saddam Hussein argued that King Fahd's alliance with the Americans and the United Nations was in essence an anti-Islamic alliance that had brought about the presence of non-Islamic "infidels" in Saudi Arabia. King Fahd, as the custodian of the two holy mosques in Mecca and Medina, mobilized the support of a conference of some of the most prominent religious scholars extending all the way from Egypt to Nigeria. This was followed by the fatwa of Abd al-Aziz ibn Baz.

During the aftermath of the Gulf War, it was clear that the more moderate and younger scholars and professional groups in Saudi Arabia, who by and large supported the fundamentalist line, were disturbed that the Saudi alliance with the Western powers had gone too far and resulted in Muslims of Saudi Arabia and Egypt waging war against Muslims of Iraq with Arabs and Muslims in the Middle East and South Asia being alienated by such developments. Therefore, they submitted a petition to the king urging him to introduce certain reforms like the formation of an independent consultative council to give guidance on the internal and external affairs of the country. It was significant that the petition asked for the establishment of justice in distributing public wealth among all classes of society and also "to make the foreign policy of the country serve the interests of the ummah and to avoid making illegitimate alliances." As for economic reforms, the petition urged "all forms of monopoly and illegitimate ownership must be removed. The ban on Islamic banks must be lifted, and all the public and private financial institutions must be cleansed of usury (interest), which is an assault against Allah and His Messenger."[33]

We held extensive interviews with Iranian clerics in 1983 and 1988 and with Abd al-Aziz ibn Baz in Saudi Arabia in 1987. In Iran, we felt that even though the revolutionary regime was interested in promoting redistribution of economic and political power in favor of the mustazafin (deprived), the levers of actual power that remained in the hands of conservative clerics were enough to frustrate the main thrust of social reforms. In Saudi Arabia, the impression one gathered was that the ulama headed by Abd al-Aziz ibn Baz were so engrossed in ensuring the observance of the ibadat that they lacked interest in social problems. They were so conservative, so unaware of the socio-economic change afoot in the world, and above all, so closely aligned with the power structure of the Saudis that their interest in social reforms was practically nonexistent. The only source for change in Saudi Arabia are the growing middle class and professional and academic groups who signed the petition to the king in 1991. But these groups tend to take a simplistic view of social change. They think that dissemination of certain Islamic social and political ideas through the media and universities is likely to result in appropriate policy changes. They seem to be unaware that a power structure stands in the way of a simple translation of ideas into policies.

One of the major questions that a Muslim society needs to explore is how and what sort of mediating mechanisms are necessary to translate Islamic ideas into appropriate behavior. For this it has been suggested that the role of a party in an Islamic polity should be not just that of an electoral instrument but a social service organization. Similarly, the Western concept of the free market system has to be modified by setting up certain distributive and public sector controls over an economy which relies on the private sector and private initiative. The reader may wonder why some of the intellectual and institutional changes suggested here should be introduced only within an Islamic framework. Why cannot a Muslim society bring about these changes just as any other society in a secular setting? The answer would be that a Muslim society in which the great majority of people are motivated intensely by religious considerations may perhaps agree to accept such changes if they are couched and communicated in Islamic terms.

What is truly amazing is that Muslims keep complaining about Western dominance and how Islam should resist and even overcome this dominance by creating an Islamic society, but as yet no model of Islamic democracy or any other acceptable form of Islamic polity has been produced. Many Muslims also claim that an Islamic political system is vastly superior to the Western democratic system but among a billion Muslims that exist in this world an Islamic society based on social justice and Islamic democracy has yet to come into being.

It is suggested that there are several reasons why Muslims have not started thinking systematically as to how an Islamic social and political system should be constructed. First of all, Western dominance is so overwhelming that most of the time Muslims are busy reacting to this phenomenon. The response of the fundamentalists is to keep emphasizing certain vital Islamic values and principles without much critical analysis because Muslim society can best be galvanized into resistance only through certain raw and broad principles of Islamic religion and polity. It is suggested here that a more effective response would be through the formulation of an Islamic socio-political program. Even Khomeini, whose role in setting up the revolutionary regime in Iran was described as not strictly fundamentalist because of his attempts to convert Islamic ideas into constitutional principles and public policies, tended to lapse into the fundamentalist mode of thinking. In 1970 he declared: "The entire system of government and administration, together with the necessary laws, lies ready for you. If the administration of the country calls for taxes, Islam has made the necessary provision; and if laws are needed, Islam has established them all."[34]

Similarly, this simplistic thinking is reflected in the understandable but romantic yearning of many Muslims for the immediate establishment of a single, united Islamic umma. It is well known that such a united Islamic umma does not exist. This explains why we have endorsed the proposal of Muhammad Iqbal that Muslims should first think of converting their respective communities into vibrant Muslim republics before joining the umma as an international or confederal entity. This requires a series of systematic socio-political programs in various Muslim countries and mobilizing support for them before such an objective can be realized. The same thing needs to be done for converting the Islamic ideas of shura (consultation) and the ideas of participatory democracy into an Islamic system suggested in this chapter. Political Islam through a socio-political program can accomplish this much better than the fundamentalists, who tend to rely mostly on raw and emotional ideas.

This chapter has tried to explore the relationship between Islamic political theory and human development. A growing number of Muslims believe that Islam does not advocate inequality of status and rights between men and women. Some Western observers tend to highlight only those verses of the Qur'an where it is stated that men are the protectors and maintainers of women and where, in the event of disloyalty and ill conduct, men have been given the right to punish women.[35] Such verses are torn out of their particular and historical context. Many other verses in the Qur'an emphasize equality between believing men and women. This issue of women's rights is an example of how the fundamentalists do not seem to realize that a literal interpretation of the Qur'anic verses would leave them behind because Muslim society, particularly in the concrete urban setting, is developing rapidly. One of the pioneers for social change in Pakistan, Akhter Hameed Khan, has pointed out: "The mullahs want to return to the past, and we can't. The big cities are like a crucible for change. It's cities like Karachi where change will happen. And the real change that is occurring is the emergence of women from segregation."[36] It is significant that in Orangi, a lower income, suburban area of Karachi, as many as 10,000 women have started working and 90 percent of girls are in schools. The trend is that not only more and more women are joining the work force, but that in a few instances, women are earning more than their husbands.[37]

If human development is a process in which through better living conditions and participatory democracy people's choices are widened, then an Islamic system will have to demonstrate that it facilitates and accelerates such a developmental process. If socio-political Islam through its programs and policies exemplifies human development, it will score two impressive gains over Islamic fundamentalism for winning public support. There will be greater social discipline and public support in Muslim states so that they may be converted from "soft states" into more cohesive and strong states. Soft states cannot mount an effective response to Western dominance. Second, at the broader international level where a battle is taking place for winning minds, an Islamic system by promoting human development will present itself as a viable rival to the Western social and political system.

8

Epilogue

The central questions raised in this chapter are twofold. First, what kind of intellectual and ideological reconstruction are Muslims undertaking to meet the Western challenge? Such a strategy is of a long-term nature. The second question concerns itself with the policy and political responses that the three states we have chosen for analysis—Saudi Arabia, Iran, and Pakistan—are devising to meet some of the short- or medium-term problems they are encountering. It has been suggested that the strategy of the secular West has been developed and followed by the practitioners of real politik, "that blend of cold realism and power-oriented statecraft that tended to be, to use Kissinger's description of Bismarck, 'unencumbered by moral scruples.'"[1] Walter Isaacson in his biography of Kissinger reports that Nixon, while engaged in a conversation with Golda Meier, the prime minister of Israel, "twisted the golden rule into a power game, telling her, 'My rule in international affairs is, 'Do unto others as they would do unto you.' At which Kissinger interjected: 'Plus ten percent.'"[2] One of the seminal questions that has been explored in this book is, Can political Islam with its religious ideology respond effectively to the dominance of the secular West? The analysis in this book, which has examined certain major Islamic ideas as interactions with a series of political events, clearly indicates that some of these ideas need to be reinterpreted so that a new socio-political program may be constructed as a response to Western dominance. Without a reinterpretation of Islamic ideas and a reconstruction of Islamic thought, it would simply not be possible for Muslim countries to develop an effective response either singly or collectively to Western dominance. It has to be realized that Western dominance does not rest merely on military hegemony. Its origins lie embedded in the way the West has advanced intellectually and scientifically during the last two centuries, with Muslim countries handicapped by following certain stagnant ideas drawn from a political and social culture in which a traditional mode of Islamic behavior and thinking were intertwined with a semi-feudal society.

Three Modern Interpreters of Islamic Thought

Tracing the growth of Islamic thought in this century, previous chapters have indicated how the ideas of al-Afghani, Sayyid Ahmad Khan, and Muhammad Abduh followed by the Ikhwan movement came to shape the nature and direction of the Islamic struggle in the Middle East and the subcontinent of India and Pakistan. The same struggle at an intellectual level was pursued by Muhammad Iqbal during the 1930s in the Indian subcontinent. Iqbal's great contribution lay in his attempts to understand the nature and thrust of global forces as manifest in Western cultural and intellectual dominance. His response was both intellectual and institutional. He argued that, "The claim of the present generation of Muslim liberals to re-interpret the foundational legal principles, in the light of their own experience and the altered conditions of modern life is, in my opinion, perfectly justified."[3] He thought that both the institutions of ijma (overall consensus of the community) and ijtihad (creative judgment) could be lodged in a Muslim assembly. If such an assembly were to develop its own knowledge and expertise in Islamic law, there was no need for the ulama to exercise their veto on the deliberations of the assembly. Another contribution of Iqbal was to move the community in certain strategic directions by emphasizing that the unity of the entire umma should be built by progressive stages through each Muslim community first attaining its own national or subnational unity. "For the present every Muslim nation must sink into her own deeper self, temporarily focus her vision on herself alone, until all are strong and powerful to form a living family of republics."[4]

Fazlur Rahman belongs to the same liberal mainstream initiated by Iqbal. In his hermeneutical method there is "a double movement, from the present situation to Qur'anic times, then back to the present."[5] The idea was that the guidance for the current global Muslim predicament would be sought through a systematic understanding of the macro situation that existed in seventh century Arabia and how it was transformed by Islam. He thought that the present problem of Muslim weakness and dependence could be tackled by developing certain general guidelines from the Qur'an. He recommended that a systematic historical method would enable Muslim historians to generalize certain specific answers that the Qur'an had given and "enunciate them as statements of general moral-social objectives that can be 'distilled' from specific texts in light of the sociohistorical background and the often-stated *rationes legis*."[6] According to Fazlur Rahman, the central task was to determine how the present situation could be changed by the application of appropriate Islamic values and priorities. "For if the results of understanding fail in application now, then either there has been a failure to assess the present situation correctly or a failure in understanding the Qur'an."[7] Thus, for Fazlur Rahman, the processes of interpretation and reinterpretation continue as the world situation changes and Muslim understanding of the world and the Qur'an improve. The fundamentalists tend to adopt a once-for-all approach, suggesting the Qur'an has not only spoken for all times to come but that their understanding of Qur'anic prescriptions is also final and irrevocable.

In Iran, which is a Shi'ite country, religious scholars or the clerics can play a much more powerful role in blocking any attempts at reinterpretation or reconstruction of Islamic thought. Ali Shari'ati put forward the view that only enlightened intellectuals and not the traditional ulama could undertake the mission of an Islamic resurgence based on a reinterpretation of Islamic thought. For Shari'ati, the two types of Islam that had confronted one another in Islamic history were "the degenerate and narcotizing religion" and "the progressive and awakening religion." Obviously, such a conflict could be resolved in favor of progressive Islam through scientific research and logical analyses of religious, political, and philosophical factors. Because of such pronouncements Shari'ati created the impression, both on conservative clerics and on Khomeini, that he advocated an "Islam minus the religious scholars."[8]

Abd al-Karim Surush, who has emerged as one of the prominent leaders of the Islamic reconstruction movement in postrevolutionary Iran, is continuing the tradition of questioning and challenging the role of clerics in interpreting Islam. In his seminal work, *Quzb va Bast-i-Ti'urik-i-Shariat* [*Contraction and Expansion of the Theory of Sharia*], Surush has pointed out: "There must be something wrong with the Muslims that in this modern age they are lagging behind in the fields of science and technology and modern civilization."[9] Surush states boldly, "Religion is sacred but the knowledge or interpretation of the religion is not sacred."[10] He is obviously referring to the interpretation that the clerics have put forward for centuries. His main contention is that human knowledge during the last two centuries has advanced enormously, and his complaint is that the clerics have so narrowly confined themselves to the interpretation of the Sharia that they have not made themselves conversant with the advances that modern science and social sciences have made. He writes:

> Today, when we look at the sky, stars, water and earth, we don't see the same objects as our ancestors did, for our perception of them is coloured by our theories which are different from theirs. . . . Even our description of our vision has changed. We no longer talk in terms of the emission of light from our eyes onto objects but in the reverse direction. Such differences would affect the meaning of sentences. Consider the following sentence: "I looked at the sun today." What we now understand by this sentence is the following: "Today, some light rays hit my eyes from a great mass of gases around which the Earth circles." This very sentence was understood differently by our ancestors.[11]

Surush thinks that the Qur'an contains certain immutable but hitherto undiscovered truths which human beings will be able to understand and grasp as their knowledge improves. He refers to a hadith that states that the first few verses of sura "al-Hadid" ("The Iron") will be intelligible to thinkers born toward the end of time.[12]

Surush is aware that many Muslims, and particularly religious leaders, find this kind of thinking extremely dangerous because they think that, if religious thinking becomes a hostage to change, then religion and tradition will be destroyed, with people denying their whole past. In our conversations with many Iranians, they have also expressed the fear as to what will remain of Islam if Muslims keep on making concessions to the demands of change. Therefore, Surush suggests that a formula should be devised for preserving and protecting the unchangeability of religion, on the one hand, and, on the other hand, accepting change within the framework of continuity so that progress can be maintained.

A comprehensive way to develop such a perspective is epistemological. Under such a perspective, it is important to realize that human understanding of the Qur'an has by no means become complete or perfect. The Qur'an is yet to yield many aspects of the truth which have not been reached in the various forms of religious knowledge like tafsir (exegisis), fiqh (jurisprudence), kalam (theology), and akhlaq (ethics). One of the indicators of this incomplete stage reached by the religious sciences is the differences of opinion that one comes across regarding religious matters among the ulama (learned authorities on Islam).[13]

One of the most important theoretical perspectives with enormous practical implications that Surush has developed is through the interaction that he strongly urges between religious knowledge and various branches of human knowledge. Surush's central point is that religious scholars have always been influenced in interpreting the Qur'an by certain ideas derived from other sources of knowledge like philosophy, science, or astrology of the period in which they lived. Thus, he writes: "Nobody starts understanding the Qur'an and Sunna without having a point of view. All points of view are time bound. I have a specific point of view at the present time and another person ten centuries ago had a different point of view. All these points of view are influenced by one's non-religious knowledge. All tafsirs are from a specific personal point of view."[14]

In Fazlur Rahman's hermeneutics, the main thrust of changes in the interpretation of the Qur'an seems to have been triggered by the global modernization process. Under Surush, the perspective of change is epistemological. If one combines the changes in the Islamic system of Qur'anic interpretation suggested by Fazlur Rahman as a result of the modernization process and those changes in the interpretation of the Sharia through epistemology suggested by Surush, then we are in the midst of certain changes of climacteric proportions. However, what is still lacking in the methodologies suggested by Fazlur Rahman and Surush is a political strategy which addresses itself to some of the concrete political and policy issues some of the Muslim countries face.

AbuSulayman, a Saudi intellectual, is not prepared to go as far as reinterpretation and reconstruction of Islamic thought. In his book the *Crisis in the Muslim Mind*, AbuSulayman's central concern is that the Muslim thinking processes have moved away from the basic principles and values that can be deduced from the Qur'an and the Traditions of the Prophet. If Muslims were to Islamize their thinking processes, they would certainly be able not only to meet the Western challenge but put forward their own view as to how the future of the world civilization should be shaped. AbuSulayman traces the origins of the present crisis to that which surfaced during the regimes of the third and fourth caliphs who, along with the first two caliphs, constituted the Rashidun (the Rightly Guided caliphs). His view is that during the regimes of the third and fourth caliphs, Uthman and Ali (644-661), the ranks of the close followers of the Prophet were so depleted as a result of a series of wars that the Muslim armies came to be dominated by the new beduin recruits. During this period the Muslim society faced a fundamental crisis when the pure Islamic values and modes of behavior taught by the Prophet ceased to be the guiding force and were replaced by the selfish and material interests of the beduin tribal majority. The umma (Muslim community) came under the influence of "a mixed pre-Islamic and Islamic style" of leadership and politics. This view challenges the traditional belief held by Muslims that Islam's glorious age lasted from the time of the Prophet to the end of the regimes of the first four caliphs. This crisis was further compounded when large numbers of Iranians, Indians, Turks, and Africans entered the fold of Islam, and continued right through the Ummayad, Abbasid, and Ottoman dynasties. What AbuSulayman wants is for the Muslim community to return to the original values and principles of Islam.

According to AbuSulayman, the heart of the crisis that the Muslim community faces lies in the ways Muslims think, perceive, and reason. Thus, when he prescribes his reformist remedies, he focuses almost entirely on the intellectual process which can transform the secular components of Muslim society by religious principles, values, and guidelines. The process of transformation may be difficult but the principles and means which can bring about this transformation are crystal clear. The educational institutions, which will set in motion the process of reformation, will start from the "universal truths, convictions and purposes." "In this process only the teachings of *wahy* [divine inspiration in the form of the Qur'an and the Traditions of the Prophet], the laws of nature, and the needs and requirements of the Ummah are to be taken into consideration."[15] AbuSulayman emphasizes again and again that unlike Islam, the West by setting aside revelation has deprived itself of spiritual and moral guidance and has been trapped by the shackles of materialism. Therefore, he urges the launching of a well-organized and world-wide Islamization movement which is no less than the Islamization of the entire field of knowledge embracing methodology, epistemology, and philosophy, and the setting up of departments in universities in fields like social sciences, communications, and Islamic civilization. His argument is that Islamic knowledge agrees with rationalist and materialist knowledge but the advantage that a Muslim has is that "Islamic knowledge puts both empirical and inductive knowledge together with the sources of *wahy*."[16] A major purpose of restoring Islamic political thought and institutions along the lines that this thinker recommends is to "deliver the *Ummah* from the failings and humiliation that have left it with a clearly discernible slave mentality, bereft of free will and independent action."[17]

We discern certain major problems in the proposals that AbuSulayman has put forward. His logic is based on the premise of there being a united umma when he is aware that the task of forging united links between different Muslim countries with their varying and sometimes conflicting cultures and historical experiences has become enormously difficult. By setting up the International Institute of Islamic Thought in Herndon, Virginia, which has become a major influence in the establishment of the Islamic University in Kuala Lumpur, Malaysia where AbuSulayman has been appointed as the rector, he can claim to have launched the beginning of the Islamization movement. The International Institute of Islamic Thought seems to have close relations with the intellectual circles associated with the Jamaat-i-Islami movement in Pakistan. All this is impressive. But in addition to the conflicts and divisions that exist in the Muslim umma, the growing influence of secular nationalists in Muslim countries represents a formidable obstacle to conservative reformers like AbuSulayman. Another major missing element in AbuSulayman's logic is that when he refers to the Qur'an and the Sunna as sources of divine inspiration and guidance for the Muslim community, he does not tell us as to whether these seminal sources of Islamic knowledge need to be reinterpreted to meet the challenges of modern times. However, one can discern from the tenor of the logic that he follows in his book that he is likely to be averse to the kind of systematic efforts of reinterpretation and reconstruction of Islamic thought that Fazlur Rahman and Abd al-Karim Surush have recommended.

Political Capabilities of the Three Regimes
and the New Challenges

It seems that Muslim countries as a whole lack political and ideological resources to cope with the problems of external dominance as well as in tackling some of the major internal crises they have to face from time to time. To take the example of Saudi Arabia, one of the world's richest societies, possessing financial reserves of $121 billion amassed less than a decade ago, finds itself with depleted reserves of only $12 to $15 billion in 1993. It has been pointed out that since June 1990 the Saudis have signed arms contracts with the Pentagon to the tune of $30 billion, "roughly equal to the amount spent by the American military on major weapon systems this year."[18] The present position is such that one of the world's wealthiest countries has been reduced to a state of indebtedness to the United States. Due to a cash flow crisis, the payment of $16 billion that Saudi Arabia owed to the Pentagon by May 1992 had to be stretched out to ten years from four. On July 31, 1991, Richard G. Darman, the budget director under President Bush, told the congress that the Saudis "are now, for the first time, borrowing considerably to service their own needs."[19]

Americans also became dependent upon this spending spree of the Saudis. In September 1992, President Bush, whose reelection campaign had run into grave difficulties, offered guarantees in an election meeting in St. Louis, where the manufacturer of F-15 fighters, McDonnell Douglas, was located, that the Saudis would buy seventy-two F-15 fighters. "Some of the Pentagon officials argued that the purchase was unwise from a military standpoint, and that the Saudis would have been better off buying larger quantities of cheaper planes."[20]

In the realm of foreign policy, Saudi choices were predetermined by the Cold War logic of the Americans and the West. The logic was that, because the Soviet Union cast its predatory eyes on Saudi oil, the simple strategy that the Saudis were urged to follow was to align themselves completely with the West. In addition, the situation in the 1980s had become even more dangerous because Iran, having moved out of the Western orbit, was capable, either with Soviet connivance or by its own decision, of posing a serious threat to Saudi security. In such a situation, the Iraqi invasion of Iran in 1980 presented itself as a golden opportunity for both the West and the Saudis to pursue certain common courses of action. In the war the West provided intelligence aid to Iraq but the Saudi support for Saddam Hussein was in the form of hard cash resources of $23 billion. The irony was that the same Iraq at the time of the Desert Storm in 1990 became an enemy country with the Saudis providing $55 billion as their contribution to the cost of the war. This was according to a 1991 study by the International Monetary Fund, which stated that, of the $55 billion, the Saudis paid $12.8 billion to the United States.[21] These expenditures, first in support of Iraq and later against Iraq, drained Saudi resources. It was significant that such expenditures were a part of a secret budget that only the king and a handful of technocrats were aware of and controlled.[22]

The internal system in Saudi Arabia is plagued by a system of patronage of unconscionable largess to the 4,000 princes which looks like zakat on a lavish scale, ironically for the benefit of the rich princes. The banking system faces billions of dollars in uncollected loans to members of the Saudi royal family. There is no income tax, and a Saudi can buy a house on an interest-free loan of up to $80,000. He pays 9 cents a litre for his gas, and his air conditioners keep running through the summer months for about $10 a month. "'We are talking about a government,' said a foreign expert, 'which ten years ago could lay its hands on realisable reserves of a good hundred billion dollars, but is now down to $12 or $15 billion.'"[23]

All Muslim societies in varying degrees face an ideological and political crisis. In our view a Muslim society faces an ideological and a political crisis when its intellectual, ideological, and political resources have been outstripped by challenges and problems stemming from external pressures and those relating to demography, political incapabilities, and mismanagement. In the case of Saudi Arabia, in the short run its economic resources are probably more than adequate to tackle the problems that have been created by external pressures and internal mismanagement. But problems do not constitute the entire configuration of a crisis. Crisis lies embedded in the history and political culture of a system. Economic resources alone cannot tackle the problems that have been created by the historical development and political culture of a society. As already suggested, a society like Saudi Arabia may have more than adequate resources, but the expectations generated by its Islamic political culture are such that certain significant sections in the Saudi Arabian community are opposed to the way the country's economic resources are being managed under external pressure by the Saudi ruling family. This indicates that per capita GNP or even its distribution may not be the only factors which create stability if significant sections in the society strongly believe that the country should be independent in managing its own resources.

Pakistan is also faced with a political and ideological crisis but of quite a different kind and magnitude. Here one of the major problems is a grave paucity of economic resources as compared to the enormity of the political and economic problems that the country faces. Pakistan suffers from a fundamental disequilibrium of historic proportions. Pakistan as a political and social system faces problems of a protracted and persistent nature which have outpaced the country's political, economic, and ideological resources.

Following the breakdown of the central government in August 1993 because of the struggle for power between the president and the prime minister, an interim government was installed for three months under a former vice-president of the World Bank, Dr. Moeen Qureshi. The interim government introduced a series of measures including agricultural income taxes on the rich farmers and feudal landlords, repayment of loans of over a billion dollars that politicians had borrowed from state-owned banks, withdrawal of subsidies on wheat and edible oil, and a number of other measures designed to eliminate corruption as well as drugs from Pakistani society. These reforms and radical measures that the government introduced could tackle Pakistan's problems only in an incremental way. The moral question that arises is, How did a society that declared itself to be Islamic allow such problems to fester for such a long time? It seemed no government, including a number of martial law regimes, had the courage to impose agricultural income tax on rich landowners when the country was often short of tax revenue. Pakistan, being dominated by certain classes and interests, could not introduce any radical reforms. This deficiency was bad enough, but the dominant classes compounded it by raiding the resources of their country to maintain a style of conspicuous consumption. A cynic would argue that Pakistan, an Islamic state, was pursuing not a process of Islamicization but a process of de-Islamicization. Therefore, how could a society which was at odds with itself possibly counter Western domination?

The Islamic revolution in Iran, like several other revolutions, seems to have blazed the trail for both purists and pragmatists. The Khomeini line is the purist line. Some of the major hardliners in Iran regard themselves as its authentic followers. Because the implacable and unalterable opposition to what Khomeini considered as the imperialist designs of the West did not produce the intended results, Rafsanjani set in motion his pragmatic strategies when he became the de-facto leader of his country after Khomeini's death in 1989. Rafsanjani's line of reasoning was that Iran with its depleted economic resources could not afford to wage ceaseless ideological and other forms of struggle against the West. The Iraq-Iran war as well as certain revolutionary emphases on developing the public sector had almost exhausted the country's economy, which could undergo radical restructuring and reflation only through a new strategy of maximum encouragement to the private sector.

The argument of the hardliners led by the former minister of interior, Ali Akbar Mohtashemi, was that Rafsanjani's policies had produced enormous economic hardships for the people and were also weakening the ideological defenses of the country against the likely American cultural penetration. In several issues of an Iranian newspaper, *Salam*, the central argument put forward against the government's economic policies was that they had created such economic inequalities that there was lack of effective demand on the part of the great majority of Iranian consumers. The paper produced figures to show that, in terms of the average annual cost for food and tobacco for urban and rural families during March 1991-March 1992, 70 percent of Iranian families or 38.5 million out of a population of 55.8 million were living below the poverty line. The paper further estimated that about half of Iran's gross national revenue went to 20 percent of its families with high incomes with the other half going to 80 percent of families with average and low incomes.[24] Western sources reported that roughly 20 to 30 percent of the work force in Iran was unemployed and the population was growing at 3.5 percent a year. Such unofficial figures estimated the foreign debt to be $30 billion.

Rafsanjani was first elected president in 1989 with a majority of 94.5 percent of the vote when he faced only one challenger. In the June 1993 presidential election, Rafsanjani was opposed by three challengers and his electoral support dropped to 63 percent. These figures were not the only barometer of the erosion of support taking place toward both the government and the revolution. Another indicator was that the opposition to the presi-

dent inside the majlis as well as in public forums was intensify-
ing. One of the major causes of the poor results in the April 1993
general elections of the hardliners led by Ali Akbar Mohtashemi;
the former speaker, Mehdi Karrubi; and the former revolutionary
prosecutor general, Muhammad Musavi-Kho'iniha, was the intervention of Ali Khamene'i, the supreme guide of the revolution, in
support of President Rafsanjani. Later, it seemed that Khamene'i
had switched his support to the ideologues, and this factor
explained why Rafsanjani's political support started declining
both in the assembly and outside.[25] The hardcore opposition of
the hardliners was centered around the Militant Clerics Association, which was planning to open offices in 157 cities.

Mohtashemi seemed to think that the government led by
Rafsanjani was pursuing a long-term strategy of persuading
influential sections of Iranians to concentrate on economic affairs
and not get engrossed in political matters. The expectation was
that if such a strategy were to succeed, people would take less
interest in ideological and political matters like the danger of
Iran getting closer to the United States. Thus, Mohtashemi
pointed out that unlike Khomeini, who wanted to increase the
political awareness of the bazaar merchants and students and
their knowledge of international affairs, the Rafsanjani government was trying to depoliticize students by not letting them
demonstrate against the U.S. government. "Ever since the government of Hashemi-Rafsanjani was established, one of the
issues that was propounded was that the trend of depoliticizing
should reign over the country."[26]

The fears of some of the ideologues were confirmed when in
July 1993 Raja'i-Khorasani, a well-known member of the majlis
and a former member of the Iranian mission to the United
Nations, circulated a letter addressed to Ali Khamene'i in which
he emphasized the need to resolve Iranian differences with the
United States. This led to a series of criticisms and outbursts
against the Rafsanjani government, because many members in
the majlis and other ideologues suspected that the government
was thinking of improving Iran's relations with the United States.
Ali Reza Sadra, a member of the Foreign Policy Committee of
the majlis, launched an attack against such a policy and pointed
out that there could be no meeting ground between the two con-
tradicting cultures of Western materialism represented by the
United States and Islamic civilization led by Iran. He further
argued that the United States was interested in "establishing a

uni-polar system with U.S. on the top and Europe, Canada and Japan in the middle and the Third World at the bottom." Sadra emphasized that Iran and the Islamic world would oppose such a unipolar world order and would make efforts "to set up a kind of multi-polar system by the Islamic world as the major part of it."[27]

Iranian leaders were deeply worried that in spite of some of the reverses the United States was suffering in international affairs, the American economic and cultural system was spreading and was likely to make serious inroads into Iran itself. In a Friday sermon in Qom in October 1993, Ayatollah Javadi-Amoli exhorted the audience along the following lines: "The message of the religion is this: The oppressed have tasted the sweet sherbet of martyrdom. They will fight while they are alive and when they are dead, then whom is America going to rule over? How long does America want to go on killing? Who does it want to kill? How many does it want to kill?"[28] An indicator of Iranian alarm that the penetration of Iranian society by Western culture had reached disturbing proportions was the statement by Ali Larijani, the minister of Islamic Culture and Guidance. He pointed out that certain studies indicated that Iranian youths spent "most of their time on watching television, entertainment and sports" and devoted "the least amount of their free time on religious affairs and worship." Referring to the result of a study launched by the Supreme Council of Youth, Minister Larijani considered "the spread of this indifference by youth toward religion the result of cultural invasion by the West and its efforts to take away the faith of Iranian youth."[29]

Larijani's criticism falls under the rubric of the Western cultural infiltration of Iran's Islamic society. How can the ruling circles and higher income groups resist the blandishments of the most attractive gift that Western society has conferred on the indigent East; namely, a consumption-oriented way of life? Therefore, Larijani's criticism of the youths should be extended to the clerics who claim to be the custodians of the revolution. The cynicism of the common man toward the purity of the revolution is best reflected in the remark that one hears about the life-styles of the leaders in Iran. Many of the clerical leaders are described as Ashab-i-Bunuz (Their Eminences with Mercedes Benzes).

As for the criticism of the Rafsanjani government by the leader of the radical ideologues, Mohtashemi, that a systematic attempt was being made to depoliticize Iranian society, one needs to pursue this criticism at a deeper level. It seems that, for Mohtashemi and many other clerics, the term *depoliticization* carried the simple connotation that the masses were being persuaded to move away from raising political slogans against the threats of American domination and cultural penetration of Iranian society. The political style of clerics in a country like Iran often tends to be that the main guidelines would come from the top with the masses being reduced to rallies of the faithful. It is difficult to imagine at this stage that the clerics would be imaginative enough to realize that political awareness can strike roots only if it is deepened and extended to the masses in such a way that, instead of the people being mere recipients of guidelines from the top, they would develop the capacity to initiate demands of their own on the government. This was referred to as mass line democracy in Chapter 7, and it has been argued that such a concept of democracy is consistent with the Qur'anic principles and Traditions of the Prophet.

We are witnessing today a confrontation between two sets of fairly rigid attitudes and positions on the part of a dominant power like the United States and Islamic fundamentalists. The West, as represented by the United States, is constantly preaching the political gospel of market democracy. American political leaders are not noted for appreciating how the historical process works. Theirs is the relatively simplistic approach which suggests that since the competitive party system and the market economy have created American prosperity, so will such a recipe produce similar results in the Islamic and the Third world. We have argued that the American and Western dominance, accompanied by more or less stagnant thinking patterns in the Muslim world, have created political dependence and economic underdevelopment resulting in economic deprivation for the great majority of the people, particularly in Pakistan and also in Iran. Muslim liberal secularists mimic the Western political culture and Western living styles. The clearest example is Pakistan where mimicry of the West has failed to tackle the fundamental class and regional contradictions as well as what we have characterized as the fundamental disequilibrium between intellectual and political resources and the economic and political problems.

It is significant that the Islamic fundamentalists also adopt a rigid and unhistorical attitude. They think that the problems of dependence and cultural humiliation arising from Western dominance will disappear through an Islamization strategy which implies almost instantaneous changes in Muslim societies through the capture and exercise of political power by authoritarian Islamic regimes. We have argued all along that the process of Islamic change involves Islamicization, that is, gradual change and not instant Islamization. A Muslim society has to work with the existing economic and class differences and contradictions and devise ways and means to promote a process of Islamicization both through reconstruction of Islamic thought and the development of certain political structures within the larger Islamic framework. In this regard we have considered at some length the ideas of Iqbal, Fazlur Rahman, Ali Shari'ati and Abd al-Karim Surush, who have recommended reinterpretation of Islamic ideas leading to a possible reconstruction of Islamic thought. Their central argument is that the timeless message of Islam can be adapted for their own needs by timebound Muslims of a given generation if the latter were to bring to this intellectual challenge more systematic thinking and deeper insights.

We have argued that reinterpretation of Islamic ideas leading to new thinking processes needs to be supplemented by Muslims building and developing new political structures of participatory democracy within an Islamic framework. There is some hope that the recent activities of the Ikhwan al-Muslimun (Muslim Brotherhood) in Egypt may turn out to be a significant initial step in this direction. As opposed to the violent and simplistic political activities of the Islamic fundamentalists, the Ikhwan in Egypt has tried to harness and maximize political power by winning support among municipalities, professional and labor associations, and university faculties. Sensing that there is a possibility of the Ikhwan capturing majority political support in Egypt, the Egyptian president Hosni Mubarak, who typifies the "friendly tyrants" aligned with the West, has unleashed a new wave of oppression against the Ikhwan.

It may be emphasized that the Ikhwan for quite some time has been committed to establishing an Islamic state by peaceful means. Secondly, in an open competition with the government political party it succeeded in winning political support from a number of professional groups. It may be noted that among these professional groups there were many who did not support the Islamic ideology. Some of the Ikhwan's supporters were drawn from the Socialist Labor Party. The only problem that one can see is that its women members are required to wear the hejab or head scarf if they want to join certain unions. This is a part of the Egyptian or Islamic social culture and such a culture cannot be eliminated by force. It may change only with the passage of time and in response to the concrete requirements of a professional society. The social and cultural values of a society are not tailor-made to certain norms or specifications dictated from outside. These values evolve from within a society. It will be up to Muslim women to develop ways and means to change those values or modes of life that they find restrictive in the pursuit of their professional activities.

Is it not possible for the United States to see that the Ikhwan is trying to integrate liberal and democratic values into an Islamic framework rather than being unimaginative and simplistic in trying to set up a market democracy on Western lines? It is only when the new thinking processes that we have referred to are further combined with attempts to develop political institutions which are both liberal and Islamic that the Muslim world will initiate an effective and sustainable challenge to Western dominance.

Notes

Chapter 1.
Islamic Resistance to Western Hegemony
in the Middle East

1. Leonard Binder, *Islamic Liberalism* (Chicago: University of Chicago Press, 1988), p. 83.

2. Rosemarie Said Zahlen, *The Making of the Modern Gulf States*. Cited in Simon Bromley, *American Hegemony and World Oil: The Industry, the State System and the World Economy* (Oxford: Polity Press, 1991), p. 108.

3. We have chosen Yusuf Ali's translation as perhaps the best example of what many Muslims have in mind. Other translators, like Arberry, have merely used the word *religion*. Pickthall uses the term *creed*. A thinker like Maudoodi would find the term *form of religion* more suggestive of his point of view, which is subscribed to by a great majority of Muslims on this particular question. He argues that Islam, unlike Christianity, is opposed to a secular state because it is opposed to any bifurcation of human activities into religious and political.

4. Hamid Algar, trans., *Islam and Revolution: Writings and Declarations of Imam Khomeini* (Berkeley: Mizan Press, 1981), p. 39.

5. *Projet de Programme Politique du Front Islamique du Salut* [Political Plan of the Islamic Salvation Front] (Algiers: March 7, 1989).

6. Robert O. Keohane, *After Hegemony: Cooperation and Discord in the World Political Economy* (Princeton, N.J.: Princeton University Press, 1984), p. 168.

7. Ibid., p. 169.

8. Ibid.

9. *President Gamal Abdel-Nasser's Speeches and Press Interviews* (Cairo: Information Department, 1959), p. 527.

10. Daniel Yergin, *The Prize: The Epic Quest for Oil, Money and Power* (New York: Simon and Schuster, 1991), p. 598.

11. Ibid., p. 559.

12. Jeffrey Robinson, *Yamani: The Inside Story* (London: Simon and Schuster, 1988), p. 87.

13. Ibid., p. 89.

14. Ibid., p. 90.

15. Ibid., p. 91.

16. Ibid., p. 94.

17. Keohane, *After Hegemony*, p. 32.

18. Ibid., p. 140.

19. Robinson, *Yamani*, p. 123.

20. Maxime Rodinson, *Islam and Capitalism* (New York: Pantheon Books, 1973).

21. Joseph Kostiner, "Shi'i Unrest in the Gulf," in Martin Kramer, ed., *Shi'ism, Resistance and Revolution* (Boulder, Colo.: Westview Press, 1987), p. 181.

22. Richard Nixon, *Seize the Moment: America's Challenge in a One-Superpower World* (New York: Simon and Schuster, 1992), p. 204. See also Seymour M. Hersh, "U.S. Secretly Gave Aid to Iraq Early in Its War AGainst Iran," *New York Times* (January 26, 1992).

23. George P. Shultz, *Turmoil and Triumph: My Years As Secretary of State* (New York: Scribner's, 1993), pp. 240-241.

24. Ibid., p. 235.

25. *Foreign Broadcast Information Service* (FBIS)-*NES, South Asia* (November 1, 1988), pp. 54-59.

26. Richard Nixon, *The Real War* (New York: Warner Books, 1980), p. 74.

27. Nixon, *Seize the Moment*, p. 214.

28. Daniel Pipes and Adam Garfinkle, eds., *Friendly Tyrants: An American Dilemma* (New York: St. Martin's Press, 1991), p. 262.

29. Nixon, *Seize the Moment*, p. 216.

30. Ibid., p. 219.

31. Ibid., p. 220.

32. Ibid., p. 221.

33. *Wall Street Journal* (March 11, 1992).

34. *New York Times* (March 25 and 26, 1991).

35. "Excerpts from Pentagon's Plan," *New York Times* (March 7, 1992).

36. *German-Iranian Talks*. March 28-30, 1988, in Haus Rissen/Hamburg (typescript), pp. 7-8.

37. Ibid., p. 9.

38. Karl Marx, *The Eighteenth Brumaire of Louis Napoleon* (Moscow: Progress Publishers, 1972), p. 10.

39. Pipes and Garfinkle, *Friendly Tyrants*, pp. 221 and 242.

40. Joseph S. Nye, Jr., "The Company We Keep," *New York Times Book Review* (December 15, 1991), p. 16.

41. Lewis H. Lapham, "Brave New World," *Harper's Magazine* (March 1991), p. 12.

42. James E. Akins, "The New Arabia," *Foreign Affairs*, vol. 70, no. 3 (Summer 1991), p. 48.

43. Ibid., p. 45.

44. Youssef M. Ibrahim, "The Arabs Find a World in Which They Count Less," *New York Times* (April 5, 1992).

45. *New York Times* (March 30, 1992).

46. Cited in *The Christian Science Monitor* (March 16, 1992).

47. *Wall Street Journal* (March 18, 1992).

48. Gunnar Myrdal, *The Asian Drama: An Inquiry Into the Poverty of Nations* (New York: Pantheon Books, 1968), vol. 1, p. 66.

Chapter 2.
The Intellectual Challenge of the West
and the Faltering Islamic and Arab Response

1. Albert Hourani, "How Should We Write the History of the Middle East?" *International Journal of Middle East Studies*, vol. 23, no. 2 (May 1991), p. 129.

2. Cited in "Ahmad Khan," *Encyclopaedia of Islam*, 2nd ed. (1953), p. 288.

3. Cited in Malise Ruthven, *Islam in the World* (Harmondsworth: Penguin Books, 1984), p. 305.

4. Cited in Angus Maddison, *Class, Structure and Economic Growth: India and Pakistan Since the Moghuls* (London: Allen and Unwin, 1971), p. 41.

5. "Shamloo," comp., *Speeches and Statements of Iqbal* (Lahore: Al-Manar Academy, 1948), p. 33.

6. Albert Hourani, *Arabic Thought in the Liberal Age 1798-1939* (London: Oxford University Press, 1962), p. 144.

7. Albert Hourani, *A History of the Arab Peoples* (Cambridge: Belknap Press, 1991), pp. 345-346.

8. Karl Marx and Friedrich Engels, *The Communist Manifesto* (Harmondsworth: Penguin Books, 1967), p. 82.

9. These are free translations of passages in Sayyid Abul Ala Maudoodi, *Musalman aur Maujuda Siyasi Kashmakash [Musulman and Present Political Conflict]*, vol. 1 (Pathankot: Dar-ul-Islam, 1938), p. 90.

10. Ibid., vol. 3 (Lahore: 1955). The argument against nationalism is spelled out in pp. 141-149.

11. Dr. Sir Muhammad Iqbal, *The Reconstruction of Religious Thought in Islam* (Lahore: Sh. Muhammad Ashraf, 1960), p. 159.

12. Cited in Muhammad Asad, *The Principles of State and Government in Islam* (Gibraltar: Dar al-Andalus, 1981), p. 91.

13. Richard P. Mitchell, *The Society of the Muslim Brothers* (London: Oxford University Press, 1969), p. 14.

14. Ibid., p. 8.

15. Ishak Musa Hussaini, *Moslem Brethren (Al-Muslimin)* (Lahore: The Book House, n.d.), pp. 56-57.

16. Ibid., pp. 57-58.

17. Mitchell, *The Society of the Muslim Brothers*, p. 328.

18. Ibid., p. 329.

19. Mahmoud Hussein, *Class Conflict in Egypt* (New York: Monthly Review Press, 1973), p. 80.

20. Cited by Yvonne Y. Haddad, "Sayyid Qutb: Ideologue of Islamic Revival," in John L. Esposito, ed., *Voices of Resurgent Islam* (Oxford: Oxford University Press, 1983), p. 71.

21. Gamal Abd El-Nasser, *The Philosophy of the Revolution* (Cairo: Dar Al-Maaref, n.d.), pp. 5 and 54-56.

22. Adeed Dawisha and Karen Dawisha, *Soviet Union and the Middle East: Policies and Perspectives* (New York: Holmes and Meier, 1982), p. 13.

23. Joel S. Midgal, *Strong Societies and Weak States* (Princeton, N.J.: Princeton University Press, 1988), p. 230.

24. Cited in ibid., p. 231.

25. For this part of our analysis, we have relied on Migdal, ibid., who has drawn on works like Raymond William Baker, *Egypt's Uncertain Revolution Under Nasser and Sadat* (Cambridge, Mass.: Harvard University Press, 1978) and John Waterbury, *The Egypt of Nasser and Sadat: The Political Economy of Two Regimes* (Princeton, N.J., 1983).

26. Mohammed Heikal, *Autumn of Fury* (New York: Random House, 1983), p. 123.

27. Baker, *Egypt's Uncertain Revolution*, p. 26.

28. Ibid., p. 105.

29. Sayyid Qutb, *Maarakat al-Islam wa-al-Rasmaliyyah* (Beirut: Dar al-Shuruq, 1975), p. 36. Cited in Esposito, *Voices of Resurgent Islam*, p. 95.

30. Baker, *Egypt's Uncertain Revolution*, p. 40.

31. Nasser, *The Philosophy of the Revolution*, pp. 55 and 73.

32. Mounah A. Khouri and Hamid Algar, eds., *An Anthology of Modern Arabic Poetry* (Berkeley: University of California Press, 1974), p. 189.

33. Hourani, *A History of Arab Peoples*, p. 420.

34. Raymond William Baker, "Afraid for Islam: Egypt's Mulsim Centrists Between Pharaohs and Fundamentalists," *Daedalus*, vol. 120, no. 3 (Summer 1991), pp. 43-46.

35. Raymond William Baker, *Sadat and After: Struggle for Egypt's Political Soul* (Cambridge, Mass.: Harvard University Press, 1990), p. 235.

36. Ibid., p. 258.

37. Galal Amin, *Misr fi Muftaraq al-Taraq [The Parting of the Ways]* (Cairo: Dar al-Mustaqbil al-Arabi, 1990), p. 138.

38. Ibid., pp. 138-139.

Chapter 3.
American Dominance and Islamic Defiance in Iran

1. Henry Kissinger, *For the Record* (Boston: Little Brown, 1981), pp. 176-177. Ervand Abrahamian, *Iran Between Two Revolutions* (Princeton, N.J.: Princeton University Press, 1982), p. 427.

2. Samuel P. Huntington, *Political Order in Changing Societies* (New Haven, Conn.: Yale University Press, 1968), p. 137.

3. Abrahamian, *Iran Between Two Revolutions*, p. 441.

4. Huntington, *Political Order*, p. 338.

5. Abrahamian, *Iran Between Two Revolutions*, p. 442.

6. Ibid., p. 444.

7. Ibid.

8. Hamid Algar, trans., *Islam and Revolution: Writings and Declarations of Imam Khomeini* (Berkeley, Calif.: Mizan Press, 1981), pp. 205-208.

9. Khomeini's "Proclamation," cited in Abrahamian, *Iran Between Two Revolutions*, p. 445.

10. Ibid.

11. Hamid Enayat, *Modern Islamic Political Thought* (Austin: University of Texas Press, 1982), p. 194.

12. Ali Shariati, *Man and Islam* (Mashhad: University of Mashhad Press, 1982), p. 229.

13. Ibid., p. 256.

14. Ibid.

15. Ibid., p. 243.

16. Algar, *Islam and Revolution*, p. 271. Algar thinks that this slogan was first put forward by Shari'ati but later used by people who were not in the Islamic mainstream, p. 316 n. 94.

17. Dr. Ali Shari'ati, *What Is to Be Done* (Houston: Institute for Research and Islamic Studies, 1986), p. 63.

18. Ibid.

19. John Simpson, *Inside Iran* (New York: St. Martin's Press, 1988), pp. 102-103.

20. Cited in ibid., p. 103.

21. V. G. Kiernan, trans., "The Way of Islam," *Poems from Iqbal* (London: John Murray, 1955), p. 65.

22. Said Amir Arjomand, *The Turban for the Crown* (New York: Oxford University Press, 1988), p. 94.

23. Edward Mortimer, *Faith and Power* (London: Faber, 1982), pp. 326-327.

24. Algar, *Islam and Revolution*, p. 29.

25. Arjomand, *The Turban*, p. 98.

26. *Iran, A Country Study*, 4th ed. (Washington, D.C.: Department of Army, 1989), p. 119.

27. Algar, *Islam and Revolution*, p. 182.

28. Arjomand, *The Turban*, p. 95.

29. Karl Deutsch, "Social Mobilization and Political Development," *The American Political Science Review* 60, no. 3 (September 1961).

30. Arjomand, *The Turban*, p. 96.

31. Ibid., p. 97.

32. George W. Ball, *The Past Has Another Pattern: Memoirs* (New York: W. W. Norton, 1982), pp. 454-455.

33. William Shawcross, *The Shah's Last Ride: The Fall of An Ally* (New York: Simon and Schuster, 1988), p. 163.

34. Ibid.

35. Ibid., p. 27.

36. Asadollah Alam, *The Shah and I: The Confidential Diary of Iran's Royal Court, 1969-1977* (London: I. B. Tauris, 1991), p. 538.

37. Ibid., p. 552.

38. Ibid., p. 386.

39. Oswald Spengler, *The Decline of the West* (New York: Alfred A. Knopf, 1962), p. 20.

40. Fred Halliday and Hamza Alavi, *State and Ideology in the Middle East and Pakistan* (London: Macmillan, 1988), pp. 32-33.

Chapter 4.
Pragmatic versus Militant Strategies
in Post-Khomeini Iran

1. Hamid Algar, "Social Justice in the Ideology and Legislation of The Islamic Revolution of Iran," in Laurence O. Michalak and Jeswald Salacuse, eds., *Social Legislation in the Contemporary Middle East* (Berkeley: University of California, 1986), p. 40.

2. Ibid.

3. Ibid., p. 43.

4. *Crescent* (July 16-31, 1987).

5. *Crescent* (June 16-30, 1988).

6. *FBIS-NES* (July 30, 1987), p. 1.

7. *FBIS-NES* (November 1, 1988), p. 55.

8. For this interpretation, see Richard Cottom, *"Revolutionary Iran,"* Middle East Journal (Spring 1989), p. 181.

9. William James, *Pragmatism: A New Name for Some Old Ways of Thinking* (New York: Longmans Green, 1967), Lecture 1.

10. Akbar Hashemi Rafsanjani, *Amir Kabir Ya Qahreman-e-Mobarezeh Ba Iste'mar [Amir Kabir or Champion of the Struggle Against Colonialism]* (Qom: Entesharat-e-Farahani, 1346 (1967/8).

11. *FBIS-NES* (November 27, 1989), pp. 57 and 59.

12. Scheherazade Daneshkhu and Andrew Gowers, "Iran Must Bridge Gap Between Moslem and Economic Fundamentalism," *Financial Times* [London] (August 31, 1989).

13. *FBIS-NES* (April 17, 1989), pp. 1-3.

14. Arnold Hottinger, "New Era in Iran," *Swiss Review of World Affairs* (October 1989), p. 12.

15. *FBIS-NES* (April 25, 1990), pp. 36-37.

16. *Kayhan International* (June 30, 1990).

17. The Economist Intelligence Unit, *Country Report: Iran*, no. 2 (1990), p. 11.

18. *Kayhan International* (July 28, 1990).

19. R. K. Ramazani, "Iran's Foreign Policy: Contending Orientations," *Middle East Journal* vol. 43, no. 2 (Spring 1989), p. 211.

20. Editorial, "British Stance Acceptable," *Tehran Times* (August 6, 1990).

21. *FBIS-NES* (November 27, 1989), p. 60.

22. Akbar Hashemi Rafsanjani, *Inqelab va Difa-e-Muqaddis [The Revolution and Sacred Defense]* (Tehran: Chapkhana-e-Kutbiya, 1347 [1989/90]), pp. 404-405.

Chapter 5.
Islamic Opposition and the Stability of the Saudi State

1. H. St. John Philby, *Sa'udi Arabia* (New York: Arno Press, 1972), p. 313.

2. Fred Halliday, *Arabia Without Sultans* (Harmondsworth: Penguin, 1979), p. 57.

3. The Economist Intelligence Unit, *Country Profile: Saudi Arabia 1986-87*, p. 4.

4. Cited in David Holden and Richard Johns, *The House of Saud* (New York: Holt, Rinehart and Winston, 1981), p. 262.

5. See the text of Faisal's speech in Gerald de Gaury, *Faisal: King of Saudi Arabia* (London: Arthur Barker, 1961), Appendix II, pp. 165-169.

6. Joseph A. Kerchichian, "The Role of the Ulama in the Politics of an Islamic State: The Case of Saudi Arabia," *International Journal of Middle East Studies*, 18 (1986), p. 60.

7. Joseph A. Kerchichian, "Juhaiman 'Utaibi's 'Seven Letters' to the Saudi People," working paper presented to the Middle East Studies Association, November 21, 1986, pp. 16 and 19.

8. Edward Mortimer, *Faith and Power: The Politics of Islam* (London: Faber, 1982), p. 183.

9. Figures disclosed by Hussein al-Segini, deputy minister of planning for Saudi Arabia, in his interview with *The Christian Science Monitor* (May 15, 1990).

10. Many Muslim and Saudi students in the United States who belonged to this group invited him to North America for lectures, but for various reasons he could not come.

11. Translation of Safar al-Hawali's Arabic speech on cassette. There is a reference to Safar al-Hawali's cassettes and his speeches in U.S. House of Representatives, Task Force on Terrorism and Unconventional Warfare, "The Rise of Popular Fundamentalism" December 4, 1990.

12. This is not a literal translation, but by following the text in a careful way we have conveyed the essential meaning and thrust of the argument. Muhammad Ahmad Mufti and Sami Saleh al-Wakil, *Al-Tashri wa San al-Quwanin fi al-Dawlat al-Islamiah [Creating the Laws of Sharia in an Islamic State]* (Riyadh: Research Center of the Faculty of Administrative Sciences, King Saud University, 1990), p. 66.

13. Judith Miller, "The Struggle Within," *The New York Times Magazine* (March 10, 1991), p. 27.

14. "A Memorandum to the King," *Kayhan International* (February 9, 1991).

15. *Kayhan International* (June 29, 1991).

16. Ibid. The petition of radical fundamentalists represents an attempt to combine certain Islamic values with some modern concerns of social justice and equitable distribution of wealth and also contains certain grievances of the middle and lower income groups—a milestone in Saudi Arabian history. Therefore, we have tried to make sure that the English version reproduced from *Kayhan International* is an accurate translation of the original Arabic petition. It is an interesting commentary on the compactness of Arabic prose that the original Arabic petition, which was about half a page in length, became a much longer piece when translated into English.

17. The Economist Intelligence Unit, *Country Report: Saudi Arabia*, no. 4 (1991), p. 7.

18. Ibid., p. 8.

19. Ibid., p. 7.

20. Miller, "The Struggle Within," p. 39.

21. The Economist Intelligence Unit, *Country Report: Saudi Arabia*, no. 3 (1991), p. 8.

22. HRH Prince Bandar bin Sultan, "Saudi Arabia and the Middle East," address to the Carter Center for Emory University, November 6, 1983 (Washington, D.C.: Embassy of Saudi Arabia), pp. 5-7.

23. Ahmad Hasan Ahmad Dahlan, *Dirasa fi'l-Siyasa al-Dakhiliya li'l-Mamlaka al-Arabiya al-Saudiya [A Study of the Internal Policy of the Saudi Arabian Kingdom]* (Jeddah: Dar al-Shuruq, 1981), p. 36.

24. *Time* (November 24, 1990), p. 29.

25. *Fortune* (October 12, 1987), pp. 167-168.

26. Miller, "The Struggle Within," p. 27.

27. The Economist Intelligence Unit, *Country Report: Saudi Arabia*, no. 1 (1992), p. 9.

28. Simon Bromley, *American Hegemony and World Oil* (Cambridge: Polity Press, 1991), p. 221.

29. *The New York Times* (May 10, 1980), Section 10, p. 1.

30. Miller, "The Struggle Within," p. 31.

31. For details of these deals and transactions, see Bob Woodward, *Veil: The Secret Wars of the CIA 1981-1987* (New York: Simon and Schuster, 1987), pp. 352-354.

32. Patrick E. Tyler, "Double Exposure," *The New York Times Magazine* (June 7, 1992), p. 80.

33. Ibid.

34. Bob Woodward, *The Commanders* (New York: Simon and Schuster, 1991), p. 35.

35. This information has been derived from *The New York Times* (June 29, 1992).

36. See ibid. for both quotations.

Chapter 6.
The Islamic State of Pakistan:
Internal Conflicts and External Pressures

1. Michael Oakeshott, *Rationalism in Politics and Other Essays* (New York: Basic Books, 1962), p. 127.

2. *FBIS-NES* (March 1, 1993), p. 69.

3. *The New York Times* (July 24, 1993).

4. The interview with the Urdu language newspaper *Awaz* was quoted in *The New York Times* (July 25, 1993). A day later *The New York Times* quoted the general as saying that he had been misquoted. The misquotation referred to the "cold test" that Pakistan had successfully carried out in 1987 and not other parts of the general's interview.

5. The Economist Intelligence Unit, *Country Report: Pakistan*, no. 1 (1993), p. 22.

6. Ibid., p. 15. See also *FBIS-NES* (April 19, 1993), p. 61, in which the president alleges that the prime minister had opposed the president's decision to appoint the last two chiefs of staff.

7. *FBIS-NES* (April 19, 1993), p. 60.

8. Ibid., p. 61.

9. *The Friday Times* (January 14-20, 1993).

10. *The Times* [London] (July 7, 1993).

11. *The Friday Times* (July 8-14, 1993).

12. Ibid.

13. *The Friday Times* (May 6-12, 1993).

14. Ibid.

15. *The Friday Times* (June 24-30, 1993).

16. Emma Duncan, *Breaking the Curfew* (London: Michael Joseph, 1989), p. 96.

17. *The Friday Times* (May 20-26, 1993).

18. Duncan, *Breaking the Curfew*, p. 42.

19. The Economist Intelligence Unit, *Country Report: Pakistan*, no. 4 (1993), pp. 19 and 29.

20. Duncan, *Breaking the Curfew*, p. 42.

21. *Financial Times* (June 16, 1993).

22. Mubashir Hasan, *Shahrah-Inqillab [Highway to Revolution]* (Lahore: Ripon, n.d.), pp. 350-351.

23. Duncan, *Breaking the Curfew*, p. 45.

24. Hasan, *Shahrah-Inqillab*, p. 351.

25. Finance Division, Government of Pakistan, *Economic Survey 1991-92* (Islamabad: Government of Pakistan, 1992), p. xxiv.

26. Ibid., p. 152.

27. Rais Ahmad Khan, "Pakistan in 1992: Waiting for Change," *Asian Survey* vol. 33, no. 2 (February 1993), p. 133.

28. United Nations Development Programme, *Human Development Report 1993* (New York: Oxford University Press, 1993), pp. 159, 141, and 171.

29. Ibid., p. 177.

30. Judith Miller, *The New York Times*, December 27, 1992.

31. Fazlur Rahman, *Major Themes of the Qur'an* (Minneapolis: Bibliotheca Islamica, 1980), p. 48.

32. Committee on Foreign Relations and Foreign Affairs of the Senate and House of Representatives, *Country Reports on Human Rights Practices for 1990* (Washington: U.S. Government Printing Office, 1991), p. 1588.

33. Seyyed Vali Reza Nasr, "Islamic Opposition to the Islamic State: The Jama'at-i-Islami, 1977-88," *International Journal of Middle East Studies* 25 (1993), p. 272.

34. *FBIS-NES* (May 26, 1993), pp. 55-56.

35. *Human Development Report 1993*, p. 51.

36. Rahman, *Major Themes*, p. 48.

37. V. G. Kiernan, trans., *Poems from Iqbal* (London: John Murray, 1955), p. 63.

38. *The New York Times* (July 26, 1993, and August 7, 1993).

39. The Economist Intelligence Unit, *Country Report: Pakistan, Afghanistan*, no. 2 (1993), p. 8.

40. Oakeshott, *Rationalism in Politics*, p. 127.

41. *Congressional Record—House* (July 12, 1961), p. 12394.

42. The Economist Intelligence Unit, *Country Report: Pakistan*, no. 1 (1993), p. 22.

43. Anwar H. Syed, *Pakistan: Islam, Politics, and National Solidarity* (New York: Praeger, 1982), p. 78.

Chapter 7.
Islamic Political Theory and Human Development

1. David Miller, "Political Theory," *The Social Science Encyclopedia* (London: Routledge and Kegan Paul, 1985), p. 618.

2. Daniel Bell, *The End of Ideology* (Cambridge, Mass.: Harvard University Press, 1988), pp. 399-400.

3. Franz Rosenthal, trans., *Ibn Khaldun: The Muqaddimah*, vol. 1 (New York: Pantheon Books, 1958), p. 6.

4. Charles Issawi, *An Arab Philosophy of History* (London: John Murray, 1963), p. 7.

5. Fazlur Rahman, *Islam*, 2nd ed. (Chicago: University of Chicago Press, 1979), p. 21.

6. Rosenthal, *Ibn Khaldun*, p. 305.

7. William B. Quandt, *Saudi Arabia in the 1980s* (Washington, D.C.: Brookings Institution, 1981), p. 45.

8. Dr. Sir Muhammad Iqbal, *The Reconstruction of Religious Thought in Islam* (Lahore: Sh. Muhammad Ashraf, 1960, p. 159.

9. Ibid., p. 174.

10. Mohammad Hashim Kamali, *Principles of Islamic Jurisprudence* (Cambridge: Islamic Texts Society, 1991), p. 190.

11. Iqbal, *The Reconstruction of Religious Thought*, p. 168.

12. Ibid., p. 174.

13. Muhammad Asad, *The Road to Makkah*, 2nd ed. (Lahore: Caravan Book House, 1982), p. 2.

14. Muhammad Asad, *The Principles of State and Government in Islam* (Gibraltar: Dar al-Andalus, 1980), pp. 14-15.

15. Fazlur Rahman, *Islam and Modernity* (Chicago: University of Chicago Press, 1982), p. 7. It may be noted that Albert Hourani, in *A History of the Arab Peoples*, has mentioned only one non-Arab writer and that is Fazlur Rahman.

16. Cited in Jerome Ch'en, *Mao: Great Lives Observed* (Englewood Cliffs, N.J.: Prentice-Hall, 1969), p. 25.

17. Stuart R. Schram, *Authority, Participation and Cultural Change in China* (Cambridge: Cambridge University Press, 1973), p. 116.

18. Hamid Algar, trans., *Islam and Revolution: Writings and Declarations of Imam Khomeini* (Berkeley, Calif.: Mizan Press, 1981), p. 275.

19. Our translation of Khomeini's speech in Farsi. Ayatollah Khomeini, *Payamha wa Sokhanraniha-i-Imam [Messages and Speeches of Imam Khomeini]*, vol. 2 (Tehran: Intasharat Noor, 1980), pp. 285-286.

20. Cited in R. H. Tawney, *Religion and the Rise of Capitalism* (West Drayton: Penguin, 1948), p. 280.

21. Daniel Lerner, *The Passing of Traditional Society* (London: Free Press of Glencoe, 1958), p. 46.

22. For all quotations, see Laurence O. Michalak and Jeswald W. Salacuse, eds., *Social Legislation in the Contemporary Middle East* (Berkeley: University of California Press, 1986), p. 43.

23. *The Times* [London] (June 6, 1992). Some of the figures in *The Times* have been derived from *The Wall Street Journal.*

24. *The New York Times* (June 1, 1992).

25. Maxime Rodinson, *Islam and Capitalism* (New York: Pantheon Books, 1973), pp. 183-184.

26. Paul Harrison, *Inside the Third World* (Harmondsworth: Penguin Books, 1987), pp. 56-57.

27. *The Christian Science Monitor* (January 6, 1989).

28. See *The Wall Street Journal* (March 16, 1992) and *The New York Times* (May 7, 1992).

29. G. A. Amin, *Mihnat al-iqtisad wa'l-thaqafa fi Misr [The Plight of the Egyptian Economy and Culture]* (Cairo, 1982), pp. 180-181.

30. Ibn Abbas reported God's Messenger as saying this. Abu Dawud and ibn Majah transmitted it. James Robson, trans., *Mishkat al-Masabih [Select Traditions of the Prophet]*, vol. 1 (Lahore: Sh. Muhammad Ashraf, 1975), p. 640.

31. Muhammad Baqir as-Sadr, *Iqtisaduna [Our Economy]*, vol. 1, part 2 (Teheran: World Organization for Islamic Services, n.d.), p. 58.

32. *The New York Times* (January 20, 1991).

33. For the text of the petition, see *Kayhan International* (June 29, 1991). A summary of the petition appeared in *The New York Times* (May 26, 1991).

34. Laurence O. Michalak and Jeswald Salacuse, eds., *Social Legislation in the Contemporary Middle East* (Berkeley: University of California, 1986), p. 40.

35. Judith Miller, "Women Regain a Kind of Security in Islam's Embrace," *The New York Times* (December 27, 1992).

36. "Crusader vs. Mullahs: What Is a Women's Place?" *The New York Times* (August 10, 1992).

37. Ibid.

Chapter 8.
Epilogue

1. Walter Isaacson, *Kissinger* (New York: Simon and Schuster, 1992), p. 139.

2. Ibid.

3. Dr. Sir Muhammad Iqbal, *The Reconstruction of Religious Thought* (Lahore: Sh. Muhammad Ashraf, 1960), p. 168.

4. Ibid., p. 159.

5. Fazlur Rahman, *Islam and Modernity* (Chicago: University of Chicago Press, 1982), p. 5.

6. Ibid., p. 6.

7. Ibid., p. 7.

8. Hamid Algar, trans., *Islam and Revolution: Writings and Declarations of Imam Khomeini* (Berkeley, Calif.: Mizan Press, 1981), p. 271.

9. Abd al-Karim Surush, *Qabz va Bast-i Ti'urik-i-Shariat [Contraction and Expansion of the Theory of Sharia]* (Tehran, 1992), p. 366.

10. Ibid., p. 375.

11. A. Surush, "The Word and the Speaker: A Hermeneutic Circle," *First Joint Theological Symposium: Christians and Muslims in Dialogue* (July 6-8, 1992), Selly Oak Colleges, Birmingham, U.K., p. 2.

12. Ibid., p. 5.

13. Surush, *Qabz va Bast-i Ti'urik-i-Shariat*, pp. 373-375. We are not merely translating. We are summarizing rather than translating the views of Surush in this passage. We are grateful to Faroq Jahan Bakhsh

for helping us to translate this work. These passages contained many religious and mystical allusions not easily understandable even to Iranian university students.

14. Ibid., pp. 378-379.

15. AbdulHamid A. AbuSulayman, *Crisis in the Muslim Mind* (Herdon, Virginia: International Institute of Islamic Thought, 1993), p. 136.

16. Ibid., p. 157.

17. Ibid., p. 133.

18. *The New York Times* (August 23, 1993).

19. Ibid.

20. Ibid.

21. *The New York Times* (August 22, 1993).

22. *The Manchester Guardian Weekly* 149, no. 9 (week ending August 29, 1993).

23. Ibid.

24. For details, see United States, *Foreign Broadcast Information Service Daily Report. Near East and South Asia (FBIS)* (October 8, 1993), pp. 40-41. For earlier criticisms of the free economy models of Turkey and South Korea, see *FBIS-NES* (February 2, 1993), p. 69. For the government defense on the plea that economic development should not be held up by ideological considerations, see *FBIS-NES* (February 2, 1993), p. 54.

25. *FBIS-NES* (October 28, 1993), p. 43.

26. *FBIS-NES* (November 19, 1993), p. 65.

27. *FBIS-NES* (November 9, 1993), p. 67.

28. *FBIS-NES* (October 18, 1993), p. 71.

29. *FBIS-NES* (November 4, 1993), p. 72.

Select Bibliography

Abrahamian, Ervand. *Iran Between Two Revolutions*. Princeton, N.J.: Princeton University Press, 1982.

AbuSulayman, AbdulHamid A. *Crisis in the Muslim Mind*. Herdon, Va.: International Institution of Islamic Thought, 1993.

Ajami, Fouad. *The Arab Predicament: Arab Political Thought and Practice Since 1967*. Cambridge: Cambridge University Press, 1981.

Alam, Asadollah. *The Shah and I: The Confidential Diary of Iran's Royal Court, 1969-1977*. London: I. B. Tauris, 1991.

Algar, Hamid, trans. *Islam and Revolution: Writings and Declarations of Imam Khomeini*. Berkeley, Calif.: Mizan Press, 1981.

Amin, Galal A. *Mihnat al-iqtisad wa'l-thaqafa fi Misr [The Plight of the Egyptian Economy and Culture]*. Cairo, 1982.

Arjomand, Said Amir. *The Turban for the Crown*. New York: Oxford University Press, 1988.

Asad, Muhammad. *The Principles of State and Government in Islam*. Gibraltar: Dar al-Andalus, 1980.

Baker, Raymond William. *Egypt's Uncertain Revolution Under Nasser and Sadat*. Cambridge, Mass.: Harvard University Press, 1978.

———. *Sadat and After: Struggle for Egypt's Political Soul*. Cambridge, Mass.: Harvard University Press, 1990.

Bromley, Simon. *American Hegemony and World Oil*. Cambridge: Polity Press, 1991.

Cragg, Kenneth. *The Pen and the Faith*. London: Allen and Unwin, 1985.

Duncan, Emma. *Breaking the Curfew*. London: Michael Joseph, 1989.

Enayat, Hamid. *Modern Islamic Political Thought*. Austin: University of Texas Press, 1982.

Esposito, John L., ed. *Voices of Resurgent Islam*. Oxford: Oxford University Press, 1983. (See Yvonne Y. Haddad, "Sayyid Qutb: Ideologue of Islamic Revival.")

Halliday, Fred. *Arabia Without Sultans.* Harmondsworth: Penguin, 1979.

Holden, David, and Johns, Richard. *The House of Saud.* New York: Holt, Rinehart and Winston, 1981.

Hourani, Albert. *Arabic Thought in the Liberal Age 1798-1939.* London: Oxford University Press, 1962.

——. *A History of the Arab Peoples.* Cambridge: Belknap Press, 1991.

Hussaini, Ishak Musa. *Moslem Brethren (Al-Muslimin).* Lahore: The Book House, n.d.

Iqbal, Dr. Sir Muhammad. *The Reconstruction of Religious Thought in Islam.* Lahore: Sh. Muhammad Ashraf, 1960.

Kamali, Mohammad Hashim. *Principles of Islamic Jurisprudence.* Cambridge: Islamic Texts Society, 1991.

Keddie, Nikki R. *Roots of Revolution.* New Haven, Conn.: Yale University Press, 1981.

Khomeini, Ayatollah. *Payamha wa Sokhanraniha-i-Imam [Messages and Speeches of Imam Khomeini],* 6 vols. Tehran: Intasharat Noor, 1980.

Kramer, Martin, ed. *Shi'ism, Resistance and Revolution.* Boulder, Colo.: Westview Press, 1987.

Lewis, Bernard. *Islam and the West.* New York: Oxford University Press, 1993.

Maudoodi, Sayyid Abul Ala. *Musalman aur Maujuda Siyasi Kashmakash [Musulman and Present Political Conflict].* Pathankot: Dar-ul-Islam, 1938.

Michalek, Laurence O., and Salacuse, Jeswald W., eds. *Social Legislation in the Contemporary Middle East.* Berkeley: University of California Press, 1986.

Mitchell, Richard P. *The Society of the Muslim Brothers.* London: Oxford University Press, 1969.

Muhsin, Mahdi. *Ibn Khaldun's Philosophy of History.* London: Allen and Unwin, 1957.

Nicholson, Reynold A. *A Literary History of the Arabs.* Cambridge: Cambridge University Press, 1988.

Nixon, Richard. *The Real War.* New York: Warner Books, 1980.

——. *Seize the Moment: America's Challenge in a One-Superpower World.* New York: Simon and Schuster, 1992.

Philby, H. St. John. *Sa'udi Arabia*. New York: Arno Press, 1972.

Pipes, Daniel, and Garfinkle, Adam, eds. *Friendly Tyrants: An American Dilemma*. New York: St. Martin's Press, 1991.

Piscatori, James P. *Islam in a World of Nation States*. Cambridge: Cambridge University Press, 1986.

Quandt, William B. *Saudi Arabia in the 1980s: Foreign Policy, Security, and Oil*. Washington, D.C.: The Brookings Institution, 1981.

Qutb, Sayyid. *Milestones*. Cedar Rapids, Iowa: Unity Publishing Press, n.d.

Rafsanjani, Akbar Hashemi. *Inqelab va Difa-e-Muqaddis [The Revolution and Sacred Defense]*. Tehran: Chapkhana-e-Kutbiya, 1989-1990.

Rahman, Fazlur. *Islam and Modernity*. Chicago: University of Chicago Press, 1982.

———. *Major Themes of the Qur'an*. Minneapolis: Bibliotheca Islamica, 1980.

Robinson, Jeffrey. *Yamani: The Inside Story*. London: Simon and Schuster, 1988.

Rodinson, Maxime. *Islam and Capitalism*. New York: Pantheon Books, 1973.

Ruthven, Malise. *Islam in the World*. Harmondsworth: Penguin Books, 1984.

as-Sadr, Muhammad Baqir. *Iqtisaduna [Our Economy]*. Tehran: World Organization for Islamic Services, n.d.

Said, Edward W. *Orientalism*. New York: Vintage Books, 1979.

Sayeed, Khalid Bin. *Politics in Pakistan: The Nature and Direction of Change*. New York: Praeger, 1980.

Shari'ati, Ali. *What Is to Be Done*. Houston: Institute for Research and Islamic Studies, 1986.

Shultz, George P. *Turmoil and Triumph: My Years As Secretary of State*. New York: Scribner's, 1993.

Simpson, John. *Inside Iran*. New York: St. Martin's Press, 1988.

Surush, Abd al-Karim. *Qabz va Bast-i Ti'urik-i-Shariat [Contraction and Expansion of the Theory of Sharia]*. Tehran, 1992.

Syed, Anwar. *Pakistan: Islam, Politics, and National Solidarity.* New York: Praeger, 1982.

Wolpert, Stanley, *Zulfi Bhutto of Pakistan: His Life and Times.* New York: Oxford University Press, 1993.

Woodward, Bob. *The Commanders.* New York: Simon and Schuster, 1991.

———. *Veil: The Secret Wars of the CIA 1981-1987.* New York: Simon and Schuster, 1987.

Yergin, Daniel. *The Prize: The Epic Quest for Oil, Money and Power.* New York: Simon and Schuster, 1991.

Index

Abd al-Aziz (King of Saudi Arabia), 7, 77
  British support of, 7
Abduh, Muhammad, 34-35, 139, 156
AbuSulayman, AbdulHamid A., 159-161
al-Afghani, Jamal al-Din, 6
Akins, James E., 15-16, 29
Algar, Hamid, 66
Algeria, 8-9
Amin, Galal, 47, 48, 148
Anglo-Iranian Oil Company (AIOC), 10-11
Arab nationalism, 11-14, 40, 42, 80
ARAMCO (Arabian American Oil Company), 78
Ashab-i-Bunuz, 167
Asad, Muhammad, 138

Ball, George W., 61
ibn Baz, Sheikh Abd-al-Aziz, 81-82
Bhutto, Zulfikar Ali, 63, 111, 126, 128
Bihishti, Ayatollah Muhammad Husayn, 66, 145
Binder, Leonard, 5
Bush, George, 28, 75, 98-99, 162

capitalism, 143-144

dar al-harb, 7
Deutsch, Karl, 60, 144

Egypt, 2, 9, 34-35, 37-49, 169-170

Fahd (King of Saudi Arabia)
  and Faisal, 15, 95
  petitions, 87-91
  reforms, 29-30
  wealth, 94
Faisal (King of Saudi Arabia), 11-14, 78
  Arab nationalism, 13
  Ikhwan al-Muslimun, 82-83
  and Nasser, 80, 82
  oil embargo, 14-18
  reforms, 79, 82

Gandhi, Mohandas Karamchand, 142-143

Halliday, Fred, 64
Haq, Zia-ul- (President of Pakistan), 120
  Hadood Ordinances and women, 120
hermeneutics, 159
historical process, 63-64, 133-134
Hourani, Albert, 34-35
human development, 132
Huntington, Samuel, 52, 144

ideological and political crises, 163
  Pakistan, 164
  Saudi Arabia, 163

Ikhwan al-Muslimun (Society of
    Muslim Brothers)
        founder, Hasan al-Banna, 35
        Nasser, 40, 42-43
        political support and orga-
            nization, 38-39, 169
        Qutb, Sayyid, 42-43
        role in Palestinian war, 39
Iqbal, Muhammad, 2, 132, 136-
    138, 140, 152, 156, 169
Iran, see also Islamic revolution
    and Rafsanjani
        Ashab-i-Bunuz, 167
        clerics, 58-60, 157-158
        conservatives, 146
        distribution of national
            income, 71
        election 1988, 67
        factions (ruhaniyat and
            ruhaniyoon groups), 67
        Five Year Plan 1990, 71-72
        Iran-Iraq war, 19-21, 162-
            163
        Khomeini. See Khomeini
        land reforms, 145
        military strength, 30
        poverty and unemployment,
            146, 165
        pragmatism, 30
        Rafsanjani. See Rafsanjani
        riots in Meshed, 145-146
        Shah, Muhammad Reza
            (Shah of Iran)
                American influence,
                    60-61
                policies, 51-55, 60-63
                Savak, 52, 62
        Shari'ati, Ali, 2, 55-57, 140-
            141, 157
        U.S. cultural penetration,
            167-168
        youth and Islam, 167
Islam
        "American Islam," 149
        and capitalism, 143-144,
            147

economic inequality, 148
government and adminis-
    tration, 66
human development, 140
ijma, 136-137, 156
ijtihad, 86-87, 138, 156
Islamic ideology, 42-43, 65,
    75-76, 132-136
Islamic political theory,
    131-132
and liberal democracy, 140
political Islam, 7-8, 136,
    152, 155
political theory, 131-132,
    152
and public sector, 148-149
Qur'anic interpretation, 81,
    157
schools of law, 136
secular tradition, 77
Sharia, 1, 31, 53, 86, 89,
    136, 149
shura, 140, 152
social justice, 141
socio-political Islam, 9, 152,
    155
sunna or hadith, 1, 148-
    149, 160-161, 168
threat of capitalism, 33
umma, 132, 135, 152, 156
values and regulations dis-
    tinguished, 33
women's rights, 119, 153
Islamic fundamentalism, 1, 22,
    29, 46-47, 89, 152-153, 157,
    168-169
Islamic ideology, 42-43, 65, 75-
    76, 132-136
Islamic political theory, 131-132,
    152
Islamic revolution in Iran, 18-19,
    164
        causes, 51-55
        Khomeini's role, 58-61
        Shah's defense expendi-
            tures, 61

Shah's repressive policies,
61-62
Shariati's role, 58, 61
U.S. support of Shah, 61-62
Islamicization and de-Islamiciza-
tion, 56, 164, 169
Islamization, 161, 169
Israel, 11-13, 16-18, 24, 155

Jinnah, Muhammad Ali (Governor-General of Pakistan), 37,
126

Keohane, Robert O., 10-11, 17
Keynes, John Maynard, 144
Khaldun, Ibn, 132-136
asabiya, 134-135
Khamene'i, Ali (spiritual leader of
Islamic Republic of Iran), 69,
166
Khan, Akhter Hameed, 142, 153
Khan, Sir Sayyid Ahmad, 139, 156
British education and Mus-
lims, 34
Khilafat movement, 7
Khomeini, Ayatollah Ruhollah, 8,
21, 33, 58-61, 63, 65-66, 135,
142, 144-145, 152
message to haj pilgrims, 67
parties, 66-67
U.S. domination, 67
Kissinger, Henry, 12, 15, 17, 61,
155

Lerner, Daniel, 144

Mao Tse-tung, 142-143
market economy, 147-148
Maudoodi, Sayyid Abul Ala, 33
capitalism and Islamic ideology, 36
influence on Ikhwan al-
Muslimun, 36

Jamaat-i-Islami, 36, 120
and Jinnah, 37
secular Muslims and Pak-
istan struggle, 36-37
Mohtashemi, Ali Akbar, 165-168
Myrdal, Gunnar, 32

Nasser, Gamal Abdul, 11-14, 40-
45
Arab nationaliam, 11-14,
40, 42
Ikhwan al-Muslimun, 42-43
Israel, 44-45
Soviet Union, 44
Nixon, Richard, 21-24, 61-62,
155

Oakeshott, Michael, 103, 125
Ottoman empire, 6

Pakistan
agricultural income tax, 164
army
chief of staff influence,
109
defense expenditure,
118
internal strains, 124
Bhutto, Benazir, 110-112
Bhutto, Zulfikar Ali, 63,
111, 126, 128
civil and military elites,
124-126, 129
living styles, 117-118
classes and interests, 164
constitution (1973), 108-
110
drug problem, 104
ethnic/provincial conflicts,
103
Haq, Zia-ul (President), 120,
126
Hadood Ordinances
and Women, 120

Pakistan *(continued)*
  and India, 104-105
  industrial concentration, 115
  Islamic state, 103, 107, 120
  Jamaat-i-Islami, 120
    socio-political pro-
      gram, 120-123
  Jinnah, Muhammad Ali
    (Governor-General), 37,
    126
  Kashmir problem, 106
  Khan, General Ayub (Presi-
    dent), 126
  Khan, Ghulam Ishaq (Presi-
    dent), 108, 110-112
  nuclear policy, 123-124
  political corruption, 112-113
  president and prime minis-
    ter, 108, 110-112
  privatization of industries,
    113-114
  sectarian riots, 120
  Sharif, Nawaz (Prime Minis-
    ter), 31, 103-108, 116
  soft state, 31-32
  Soviet-Afghan war, 123, 126
  Supreme Court, 110-111
  tax evasion, 115-116
  and United States, 25, 104,
    106-107, 126, 127
  welfare expenditures, 118-
    119
  women, 119, 120
political theory, 60, 131

Quandt, William B., 135
Qur'an, 1, 8, 26, 33, 58-59, 64,
  81, 131-133, 135, 138-141,
  148, 156-160
Qutb, Sayyid, 33, 42-43

Rafsanjani, Ali Akbar Hashemi
  (President of Iran)
    business connection, 68

  cabinet 1989, 70, 72
  clerics, 58-60
  conflicts between pragma-
    tists and militants, 65,
    70-76
  economic policies, 69-73
  elections, 165
  foreign loans, 73
  foreign policy conflicts, 74-
    75
  hostage issue, 74-75
  Islam and work ethic, 69
  Islamic ideology and devel-
    opmental change, 75-76
  Mohtashemi, Ali Akbar,
    165-168
  non-cleric economic minis-
    ters, 70, 72
  opposition, 165-166
  overtures to United States,
    166-167
  pragmatism, 68-70
  and Western modernization,
    68-69
  and umma, 21, 135
Rahman, Fazlur, 2, 119-120,
  138-140, 156-157, 161, 169
Reagan, Ronald, 96-97
Rodinson, Maxime, 146-147

Sadat, Anwar
  Ikhwan, 47-48
  infitah, 45-47
  Israel, 45-46
  United States, 45-46
as-Sadr, Muhammad Baqir, 149
Saudi Arabia
  Arab nationalism, 80
  conservative Islam, 149
  economic change, 84-85
  Gulf war, 87, 150
  al-Hawali, Safar, 85-86
  Islamic influence, 79
  middle class, 151
  news media, 100-101

petitions to King, 87-91,
    150
pressure for reforms, 29-
    30
radical intellectuals, 91-93
religious establishment, 81,
    96
royal family, 7
Sultan, Bandar bin, 97-99
social change, 93-94
state, 78
student opposition, 84
tax system, 163
and United States, 29, 96-
    100, 162-163
Utaibi, Juhaiman ibn
    Muhammad, 83-84
westernization, 86
Shah, Muhammad Reza (Shah of
    Iran), 51-55, 60-63
Sharia, 1, 31, 53, 86, 89, 136,
    149
Shari'ati, Ali, 2, 55-57, 140-141,
    157, 169
Shi'ism, 19, 57-58, 63, 66, 136,
    157
    jafari fiqh, 66, 145
    and Khomeini, 63
    Twelth Imam, 58
Shultz, George, 20-21
socio-political Islam, 9, 152-153
soft states, 31-32, 153
sunna, 1, 160-161, 168
Surush, Abd al-Karim, 2, 10,
    157-159, 161, 169

umma, 21, 132, 135, 152, 156,
    160-161
United States
    dominance, 5, 54, 60, 67,
        99, 123, 133, 168, 170
    "friendly tyrants," 22, 28,
        100, 169
    Gulf war, 87, 150
    hegemony, 5, 10-11
    and Iran, 20-23, 60-62, 67,
        75, 166-167
    and Pakistan, 25, 104, 106-
        107, 126-127
    and Saudi Arabia, 29, 96-
        100, 162-163

Wahhabis, 7
Wali Allah, Shah, 137
West
    and Arab nationalism, 40,
        43-44
    capitalism, 48-49
    dominance, 1, 25, 29-32,
        152-153, 155, 168, 170
    modernization theory, 84
    and Nasser, 40-45
    and oil, 21-22, 29
al-Wahhab Abd, Muhammad ibn,
    77
Wahhbism, 77-78
    Ikhwan, 78
women's rights, 119, 153

Yamani, Zaki, 14-15, 17-18